1758 - chase deco - Hoops + balls —

COLLECTOR'S ENCYCLOPEDIA OF
BOOKENDS

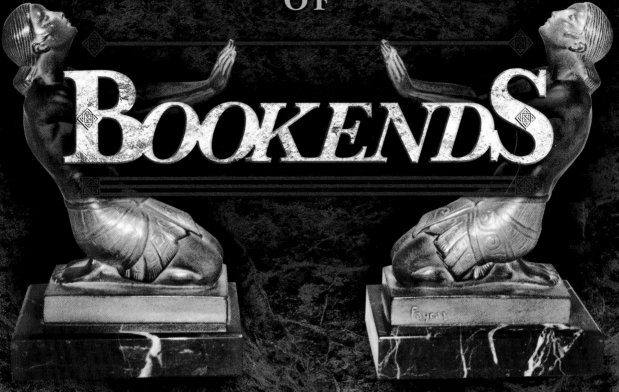

Identification & Values

Louis Kuritzky
and
Charles De Costa

COLLECTOR BOOKS

A Division of Schroeder Publishing Co., Inc.

Front cover: Plate 1062, Ecstasy, $1,200.00; Plate 1058, Drum Majorette, $195.00; Plate 408, Fox and Grapes, $495.00; Plate 2104, Angelus Call to Prayer, $50.00; Plate 741, Dante and Beatrice, $175.00.

Back cover: Plate 1170, Mournful Lady, $165.00; Plate 1640, Tilting at Windmills, $1,900.00.

Cover design by Beth Summers
Book design by Joyce A. Cherry

COLLECTOR BOOKS
P.O. Box 3009
Paducah, Kentucky 42002-3009
www.collectorbooks.com

Copyright © 2006 Louis Kuritzky & Charles De Costa

The current values in this book should be used only as a guide. They are not intended to set prices, which vary from one section of the country to another. Auction prices as well as dealer prices vary greatly and are affected by condition as well as demand. Neither the authors nor the publisher assumes responsibility for any losses that might be incurred as a result of consulting this guide.

Searching For A Publisher?

We are always looking for people knowledgeable within their fields. If you feel that there is a real need for a book on your collectible subject and have a large comprehensive collection, contact Collector Books.

Contents

Acknowledgements

Without the patience and endorsement of our spouses, who allowed not only ceaseless arrivals of bookends to our homes from assorted corners of the globe, but also countless research and photography hours, our happy task could not have been successfully completed. Numerous collectors and dealers have opened their collections to us, added information sources, and shared personal guidance. In particular we would like to thank: Sue Benoliel, Blythe Curry, George Houle, Agris Kelbrants, Vicki Nolten-Mair, Jim Phillips, Jim Rule, Lyndon Sheldon, David Surgan, Billie Trepanier, and Richard Weinstein. Finally, somebody had to do the less-than-glorious but essential part of sorting, sifting, stratifying, and error-checking all the thousands of bookend photographs and their citations; Lou's office assistant, Brenda J. Diaz, day after day started early, stayed late, and smiled through the whole thing....you're the greatest!!

About the Authors

Louis Kuritzky (Lou) has been an avid bookends enthusiast for over a decade. His profession as an academic physician often involves the opportunity for travel to diverse sites around the United States, and of course, at least a few minutes to spend foraging amongst local antiques dealers, thrift shops, flea markets, and the like. In addition to being coauthor of *Bookend Revue* and *Collectors Guide to Bookends*, he has published articles on bookends in sites such as *Martha Stewart Living* and serves as a consultant on bookends to several antiques resource guides. He has been editor of the Bookend Collectors Club Newsletter since its inception in 1997, and is an advocate for collectors of bookends at all levels of involvement, novice through expert. Lou lives in Florida with his wife, Virginia.

Charles (Chuck) DeCosta was born and raised in Boston, Massachusetts. He left Boston in 1962 and settled in California. He retired from the restaurant business in 1999 and moved to the San Bernadino Mountains where he built custom homes. Chuck has always had an interest in antiques. He has traveled in his motor home throughout the United States in search of special "treasures." In 1998, Chuck developed an interest in bookends and became an avid collector. He has searched hundreds of antique shows and stores in the pursuit of rare antique bookends. Chuck and his wife Louise, live in Palm Desert, California, during the winter months and also have a home in Washington state where they spend summers when not traveling in their motor home.

Louis Kuritzky (Lou)

Chuck DeCosta

Introduction

There have been several excellent books about bookends published in the last decade, and the number of folks who identify themselves as bookend collectors continues to grow. Collectors, dealers, and individuals who have but a passing interest in a particular set of bookends want better definition of the date of origin, maker, history, and value of their collectibles. To that end, this book contains the largest and most diversified database from which to identify bookends ever amassed.

Bookends are arranged alphabetically, as in a typical encyclopedia. Within any category, there may be sub-categories, so that under the larger heading of "Birds." there are subgroups of "Flamingos," "Pigeons." etc, rather than grouping them separately. Because neither Lou nor Chuck claims to have special knowledge in the fields of astronomy, astrology, veterinary medicine, horticulture, or other fields, we apologize in advance for any of the times when we mistakenly labeled an "African daisy" as a "Greek violet," or a "Canadian goose" as a "Mexican gander" and we invite interested or better informed individuals to write to us about any such misadventures. In order to be listed in a "category," we felt that at least four distinct examples were necessary. Some bookends have multiple areas of crossover potential. For instance, if the bookends depict an Egyptian woman playing a flute, is that best categorized as "Egyptian," "Female Figures," or "Musical?" Hence, we have employed a common-sense approach to group bookends by what appears to be their most salient characteristic. Because of such overlap, bookends are extensively cross-indexed.

You will find numerous examples where names of bookends have changed from one text to another. The names are assigned from one of several resources. The most definitive, we believe, is the name assigned by the manufacturer, as supplied in original company catalogs. Remarkably enough, even this is not fully consistent, as we have seen errors in spelling, punctuation, or even incorrect identification of subject matter. For instance, the very well-known sculpture "End of the Trail" has only one correct name; nonetheless, Connecticut Foundry elected to name this pair "The Last Trail" and imprint it upon the reverse of some of their bookends. In most circumstances, we have elected to continue with names indicated by makers, unless they obfuscate accuracy. Some manufacturers only include global names in their catalogs, such as "dog," or "boy"; in some circumstances, no name is given in catalogs, but only an identifying number. When names have been lacking, we have created names that we believe reflect the essence of the pair, or at least provide ready distinction from other bookends that address similar subject matter.

Some readers are tempted to conclude that a bookend pair they possess is extraordinarily rare because it does not appear in the book. Unfortunately, despite our intentions to provide the most broad possible coverage of the field, none of us possesses all of the entire field. In fact, oftentimes the most commonplace bookends are absent from advanced collectors' personal collections, as they are of less interest.

For questions or other communications, please feel free to contact us at

Louis Kuritzky
Bookend Collectors Club
4510 NW 17th Place
Gainesville, Florida 32605

Manufacturers

Armor Bronze

The company we know as Armor Bronze apparently began its marketing under the name National Metalizing Company, which is listed in the 1916 Thomas Register of American Manufacturers. At that time, the address was 333 4th Avenue, New York City. In 1917 and 1918 they were listed at 2236 5th Avenue, and by 1920 the name National Metalizing had disappeared. The name Armor Bronze is first listed in 1920, at the same address National Metalizing had previously done business. Although the New York facility apparently discontinued business in 1929, we again see Armor Bronze Company engaged in bookend production from Taunton, Massachusetts, in the 1934–1948 time period.

Art Craft

Only a single company paper tag from Art Craft Company has been seen, identifying the company as manufacturing in Chicago. Their shopmark appears as:"A – C." They produced a version of Bishop's Cathedral, marked "134; A—C." The only products we have seen manufactured by Art Craft Company were made of iron.

Bradley and Hubbard Manufacturing Company

The Bradley and Hubbard Manufacturing Company of Meriden, Connecticut, began as a partnership of Nathaniel L. Bradley and Walter Hubbard in 1854. Initially, they produced clocks, vases, mirror frames, tables, and other decorative metal articles. Later, oil lamps, and eventually, gas and electric light fixtures were manufactured by the company. Apparently well-known at the time, the Rayo Lamp was made for the Standard Oil Company by B & H. Elaborate chandeliers, candelabras, clocks, andirons, and even decorative clamp-on pincushions to be attached to a table-edge are depicted in their products produced in the 1854 to 1890 period. In 1940 B & H joined forces with the Charles Parker Company in Meriden, Connecticut. Parker had been developed in 1832, and was noted for lighting fixtures and architectural bronze and iron. What began as a popular market in Central and South America for its coffee mills spread later to the United States as it became fashionable to make freshly ground coffee in the home. Nathaniel Bradley was born in Cheshire, Connecticut, Dec. 27, 1829, the youngest son of Levi and Abigail Ann (Atwater) Bradley, and was educated at an academy in Meriden. His first position was as a clerk with EBM Hughes, a hardware merchant in New Haven, Connecticut.

After one year at that position, Nathaniel was called home to assist on his parents' farm. Shortly after his return, a small clock factory in nearby Southington employed Nathaniel and his good work eventually elevated him to director and primary salesman for the company.

In 1852, a joint stock company was formed, Bradley, Hatch & Co., with $5,000 capital, and his brother Walter was a member of the firm. The first factory was a small wooden building without power, employing six persons. In January 1875, the company became Bradley and Hubbard, Incorporated, with 150 employees (which expanded ultimately to employ 1,100), located at the corner of Hanover and Butler streets in Meriden. By 1892 offices and salesrooms were established in New York, Boston, Chicago, and Philadelphia.

Bradley was a very civic-minded individual. He was trustee of the Connecticut School for Boys for 14 years, after which he became president. He contributed building funds for and was president of the Meriden Hospital. He was a member of the Connecticut Society of the Sons of the American Revolution. His philanthropy was noteworthy to the local YMCA, and to the Curtis Memorial Public Library of Meriden, which houses a bronze plaque of acknowledgment.

Walter Hubbard, born Sept. 23, 1828, in Middletown, Connecticut, was the other principal of B & H. His father was one of the original settlers of Middletown in 1650 from England, and like Nathaniel Bradley, Walter was raised on a farm. Hubbard opened a dry goods and clothing store in Meriden in 1851. In 1852 he married Abby Ann Bradley, sister of Nathaniel Bradley. Several months after their marriage, Abby died, and Hubbard never remarried. Hubbard served as president of Bradley and Hubbard from its time of incorporation for more than 30 years. Hubbard's philanthropy resulted in the building of New England's Winthrop Hotel. His community involvement included being a member of the Union League Club of New York, The New England Society of New York, and the American Geographical Society. He was fondly memorialized by the Hubbard and Meriden Park, in Meriden, Connecticut.

The works of Bradley and Hubbard are consistently excellent, and command consistently higher prices than comparable pieces. The vast majority of bookends are iron, though a few examples of bronze have been seen, and it is reported that some pieces were manufactured of cast gray metal. In contrast to many pieces which were apparently destined for more decorative than functional careers, the majority of B & H bookends are of substantial weight and solidarity. The castings are often of much greater detail than is seen from other manufacturers, and the polychrome paints are more colorful and enduring than any other iron manufacturers. It is not at all uncommon to find B & H bookends with multicolored paint and shadings fully intact, even though they were produced in the 1920s. This is in stark contrast to many other iron pieces whose paint chips and corrodes much more readily. B & H pieces are sometimes marked with beige descriptive tags, on the underside, with titles or brief descriptors of the subject matter, and are clearly marked with the B & H logo, as well as (rarely) the B & H company tag, a triangular identifying marker which also locates them in Meriden.

Burwood

Pouter Pigeons (Burwood) was the initial source of information into the company called Burwood, and indeed the pair was purchased in Traverse City, Michigan, the home office of the business. The company has been located at this site since about 1890. Their product was called "burwood" because it was intended to resemble burled wood (burls are knotty projections off of tree trunks). Burwood went out of business in July 1997. All company artifacts were sold at public auction, and there has not been any formal conservation of their historical documents. Burwood is very similar to syrocowood. Products are produced by combining wood, glue, and plastic resins. Burwood is substantially heavier than syrocowood.

Carence Crafters

The Carence Crafters produced bookends in the Arts-and-Crafts style in the 1910 to 1925 period in Chicago. Their styling was similar to Roycroft (simple L-form bookends of brass, bronze, or copper). An example of their foundry mark is included in the shopmarks section.

Chase

Walter von Nessen is one of the most admired of designers for Chase Metal Works.

The Connecticut Foundry

Connecticut Foundry is believed to have manufactured solely in iron. A few examples of Connecticut Foundry items have been seen in bronze. However, the detail on these bronze examples is not pristine; there are substantial signs of wear on otherwise pristine sets like "The Aviator," suggesting that someone performed bronze castings from a worn iron original, but the exact timing of this endeavor is unclear. Also, Connecticut Foundry bookends were almost exclusively made in a simple paginated iron finish. Nonetheless, several examples of polychrome painted pairs have been discovered, including "The Last Trail," "Profanity," "The Storm," and "Yankee Clipper."

Crescent Metal Works

Crescent produced bookends of cast gray metal. The company incorporated in Newark, New Jersey, Nov. 19, 1924, and bonded their corporate status Jan. 13, 1937. Several of their pieces are especially elegant, and their female deco figures are characterized by lithe gracefulness. The registered agent of the company was Samuel S. Ferster, and the company was originally located at 800 Broad Street, Newark, at least in 1921. John Skiba obtained a copyright while the business was located at 313 Chestnut Street, Newark.

DAL (Decorative Arts League)

Little is known about DAL. The bookend pair "Lincoln and Tad" has been seen with a company paper tag affixed, which reads "Lincoln Book Ends. Patent Applied For. Decorative Arts League, 175 5th Avenue, New York, New York." In the 1900 to 1930 years, the convention was to write "book ends," rather than "bookends," which is currently the much more common usage.

Dodge, Inc.

Company tags identify Dodge offices existing in Newark, Los Angeles, and Miami. The U.S. Patent Office possesses a copy of the company brochure received Aug. 10, 1948, which depicts what the company calls "the master line of gifts. . . designed for the discriminating buyer." In 1948, one office was located at 126 South Street, Newark. Five primary finishes were used for their cast gray metal pieces: SunRay (gold colored), Silver Plate (silver, with an intended oxidized look), Diamond Black (ebony), Antique Bronze (traditional high gloss bronze finish with two-tone highlights), and Combination (muted bronze in combination with SunRay).

In addition to bookends, Dodge made pipe rests, holders for book matches, ashtrays, figurines, lamps, desk novelties, and other pieces. The 1948 catalog lists more than 20 different pairs of bookends, including numerous pieces by the designer McClelland Barclay. To date, all pieces identified as Dodge are made of cast gray metal. Pieces on onyx bases are distinctly less common. In the 1940s, bookends sold for $10 to $40 per pair.

Marshall Field

Marshall Field (September 18, 1834 – January 16, 1906) was the fourth born of eight children to Jack and Fidelia Field of Conway, Massachusetts. He began his history in sales as a shopkeeper for a dry good store in Pittsfield, Massachusetts, the Henry G. Davis Dry Goods and Crockery Store, at age 16. In less than five years time in this setting his sales skills were rewarded with advancement to the position of store manager. When Henry Davis learned of Field's wishes to migrate west to Chicago, he offered Field a position as partner in the business, but Field was convinced that the best profit opportunities were in Chicago. Davis' letter of recommendation at Field's departure reads "The bearer, Mr. Field, has been in my employ for nearly the past five years now and leaves me for the West. I can without qualification commend him as a young man of unusual business talent worthy of the confident of any who would employ him. His character and principles as well as his business qualifications are such I cannot doubt he will meet that success in life which usually accompanies industry, perseverance, and integrity when combined with strict energy and character."

In 1856, Field moved to Chicago and joined another dry goods firm called Cooley and Wadsworth, where in his position as sales clerk he was awarded a salary of $400 a year. One of the junior partners in the company, John Farwell, selected Field for on-the-road sales, which burgeoned into enhanced salary ($3,000 a year) and advancement in the company to the status of junior partnership. By 1864, Farwell, Field, and Company, with Levi Leiter (a former bookkeeper from Cooley and Wadsworth) emerged.

Several years earlier (1852), a man named Potter Palmer, a Quaker, had moved to Chicago with the intention of opening a shop specifically directed towards women. He had been a shopkeeper previously in upstate New York, and employed new ideas like using published prices, at a time when price haggling had been the standard of the day. By 1861 Palmer had been so successful that he moved into a five-story marble building at 112 Lake Street, and offered a previously unprecedented policy of a money-back satisfaction guarantee.

When Palmer got wind of a conflict between Farwell and Field, he solicited a newly formed alliance of Field, Palmer, and Lieter in 1865. Their business had difficulty sustaining itself through the Civil War, but quickly regained its footing such that by 1866 the company was highly profitable. One of the Field, Palmer, and Lieter sales person was a young man from Michigan named Montgomery Ward. Palmer became a passive interest in the company, whose name was changed to Field & Leiter. Philosophical differences led to a parting of the ways between Field and Leiter, who sold his part ownership to Field, in a company we all recognize as Marshall Field & Company in 1880. Throughout their successful history, the motto of the Marshall Field Company was always "Give the Lady What She Wants," which became the title of the 1952 history of the company by Wendt and Kogan. The 1896 catalog displays no bookends, despite 400 pages chock-full of atomizes, baking dishes, berry dishes, belts, buckles, buttons, broaches, cutlery, curling irons,.....well, you get the picture.

Fleuron, Inc.

Fleuron, Inc. was established in the 1920s in North Tonawanda, New York, housed at 73-79 Robinson Street. The earliest business listing for Fleuron Corporation in 1928 showed A.L. Hyde as president and Frank L. Moore as vice president. The company probably ceased business in 1933, since in 1934 a new company called Kobbe Pottery, named after its originator Alexander Kobos, took up residence at that address. Additionally, none of the principals whose names had been previously attached to Fleuron were listed in association with Kobbe. By 1935 both Fleuron and its successor Kobbe are absent from the business community. Fleuron is registered as a producer of synthetic marble and pottery. In 1995, former employees of the Fleuron Company conveyed that the product itself was made from sulfur and a special type of sand. The sulfur was heated to a liquid stag and then sand was added. If color was desired, dye was mixed in. Once cooled, the mixture hardened rapidly to a marble-like substance.

The full spectrum of products produced by Fleuron is unknown, but several sets of bookends have been seen, and a flowerpot and saucer made of Fleuron are part of the Historical Society of the Tonawandas collection. The bookends have a flat patina, a smooth-finished surface not unlike marble but much warmer, and have been seen in pale green (three examples) and beige (one example). The other examples have been busts of females. The material is of substantial weight, but chips easily like pottery, so pieces in good condition are difficult to find.

Forest Craft Guild

Forest Craft Guild bookends were fashioned in typical arts and crafts styling, with simple L-form bookends of brass. Their works were produced in Grand Rapids, Michigan, in the early 1900s. Their shopmark simply says "Forest Craft Guild." The leader of the Forest Craft Guild was Forest Emerson Mann. Popularity of their products led to studios outside of Grand Rapids. A 1913 catalog indicates a New York City office at 333 Fourth Avenue. The introductory page to their catalog "A Gift Folio" reads: "It is now eight years since the organization of the group of craft-workers known as the Forest Craft Guild. This endeavor toward a more rational expression in the lesser arts of goldsmithing, metalworking and kindred crafts has been most successful. The Guild has demonstrated that good design and practical constructive skill may be combined with efficient management to the extent of producing objects of real worth and artistic merit at a minimum cost; moreover, it has created a widespread demand for better things in pottery, metalwork and all objects for home decoration." A more discriminating public has been quick to respond to this appeal for better things in personal adornment and home furnishings. A frequent criticism often made relative to individual craftworkers is that they demand for this work a price which is prohibitive and altogether out of proportion with the value of the object. This has placed many desirable wares beyond the reach of many who would most desire to possess them. It has remained, however, for the Forest Craft Guild to solve the problem in a practical way. With its corps of designers and skilled craftsmen the Guild has been able to conceive and execute in its own shops a wonderful variety of artistic and practical article, the character of which is now well known and eagerly sought for by the more discriminating public. The Guild has built up a splendid following in 80 years which is now rapidly increasing in every state. The production of the Guild may be found in the better class of arts shops, book and stationery stores, and craft shops in every city…..Lovers of handcraft will be pleased to know that an exhibition of the Forest Craft Guild productions is maintained throughout the year at its showrooms, 333 Fourth Ave, New York

Frankart

To our knowledge, Frankart produced bookends only of cast gray metal. An exception to this was advertised on-line in 2003, in which a pair of Frankart nudes were advertised weighing over three pounds each, which is highly unusual for typical Frankart items, which usually weigh only a few ounces each. The very earliest Frankart pieces (in the early 1920s) were heavier than those of the late 1920s and 1930s, but this is the only piece to our knowledge produced in any material other than gray metal.

Frost Workshop

Frost Workshop made Arts-and-Crafts style bookends in copper. They produced wares in very simplistic designs typical of the Stickley era around 1910. The company was located in Dayton, Ohio.

The Gift House

Little is known about the origins of final disposition of The Gift House, Inc. (New York, September 29, 1928 – April 17, 1934). At one time there was an apparent liaison between them and Nuart of New York (see section on Nuart). Pieces have thus far been seen produced only in iron, and copyright records indicate product development as early as 1924, but the company's last copyright is recorded in 1926. Gift House bookends seen to date have the company name and date imprinted on the piece. Offices were located at 10 East 15th Street, New York, in 1924, but moved to 14 West 23rd Street in 1926. Most of the company's copyrights are issued to Salvatore Reina.

Gorham

The Gorham Company was founded in Providence, Rhode Island, in 1831 by Jabez Gorham. The business was initially developed as a small independent silversmithing shop, essentially designed to make spoons. After 1875, Jabez's son John expanded the company's scope to include art casting, and John brought European silversmiths skilled in aesthetic design to join the company. The company expanded to manufacture hollowware (legatee sets, pitchers, bowls, and vases). By 1887, Edward Holbrook had become president, and was famous for outstanding sterling silver productions. World acclaim was achieved by Gorham at international exhibitions of hand-hammered silver tables, silver cast statues, and hollowware. By 1915, Gorham was recognized as the greatest silversmithing company in the world. The world's largest selling sterling silver flatware pattern (Chantilly) is a Gorham product. The trophy for the Indianapolis 500, the Davis Cup (tennis trophy), and the America's Cup (yachting) are all designed and executed by Gorham. The Smithsonian Museum, as well as the White House, displays Gorham silver. Today, Gorham makes materials including sterling, silver-plate, stainless, pewter, china and lead crystal. Bronze casting began by Gorham in 1860. A separate ecclesiastical department was established in 1865. Small bronzes were made through the 1920s, some of which are not marked, though they maybe signed by one of the company's sculptors. Through the 1880s, bronze production expanded to include monumental bronzes (i.e., life-size or greater); by 1890 bronze sculpture had become sufficiently important to the company that a separate bronze division was begun.

Graham Bronzes

Graham Bronzes was established in 1861. The company was originally called James Graham & Company. A company catalog states: James Graham & Company, brass founders, at 292 Wooster Street, is one of the oldest concerns in their line in New Haven. The business was inaugurated in 1861 by Mr. James Graham, who has been the means of pushing the enterprise to a successful issue. The firm at present consists of Messrs James and Charles E Graham, and the house is favorably known throughout New England as one of the representative and leading brass-founding concerns in this section. A large group of furnaces are kept constantly in operation and the output of the concern is always of standard excellence, and in their special lines their work is unsurpassed. They give employment to a large force of skilled women and their plant is well equipped with all the modern appliances and improved machinery for their purposes. They manufacture all kinds of brass and composition castings and all grades of Babbitt metal. They make a specialty of the patent nickel bronze-center car-journal bearings which have become so popular in railway care work. The products of this concern are always reliable and possess the confidence and esteem of the trade. The senior member of the firm has had many offices of trust and is one of the most popular men in New Haven, politically, socially, and business-wise. City directories for New Haven list the company from 1920 through 1959, including citations to production of brass, weathervanes, bronze novelties, bronze aluminum, nickel silver, bronze tablets, gift wares, and sundials.

Griffoul

Auguste Griffoul was the founder of A. Griffoul Foundries of Newark, New Jersey. The only historical information we have is of a family member, Jean-Baptist Griffoul, who had been a principal of the firm Griffoul and Lorge, located at 6 Passage Dombasle, Paris, and had supplied bronzes to Rodin.

Heintz Art Metal

The Heintz Art Metal shop was established by Otto L. Heintz in Buffalo, New York. He was the son of Louis Heintz, half of the old Buffalo manufacturing jewelry firm of Heintz Brothers. By 1903, Otto had purchased and was proprietor of Art Crafts Shop, and had received the first of his patents. This was for enameled jewelry, utilizing silver webs to create the cavities to hold the different colored enamel powders. By 1906, he had changed the company name to the Heintz Art Metal Shop, and shifted his focus from enamels toward sterling silver as ornamentation, and from copper to bronze as the base material.

J. B Hirsch Foundry

J. B. Hirsch Foundry history begins with Joseph B. Hirsch's work with lead and tin in his homeland, Romania. In the early 1900s Hirsch immigrated to the United States, and after brief employment with Con-Edison as a tinsmith, began his own company, originally called The New York Art Bronze Works which soon became one of the country's largest manufactures of bookends. The company was originally located on East 17th Street, in Manhattan. At the time, it was not uncommon for distributors and gift jobbers to import French statuary used as newel post lamps at the bottom of banisters. Often, these pieces arrived in need of repair, which was also a part of Hirsch's metalsmithing ability. Soon after this business demonstrated its potential for success, he began to import his own pieces directly from French foundries, and after World War I when French occupation closed one of his primary suppliers, he went to Paris and purchased that company's molds to begin his own casting foundry.

Subsequent acquisition of French, German and Italian bronze molds resulted in what has been regarded as the largest, finest and rarest collection of these items in the world, reported valued at over two million dollars.

World War II produced some surprising changes for the foundry, as French foundries hid their Beaux Arts molds in cellars to avoid plunder from invading armies, and subsequent utilization of the metals for conversion into war materials. Part of the evasion process included breaking the molds into many small fragments, scrambling them, and hiding them underground.

It was not until 1948 that Abe Hirsch, son of Joseph, who by that time was managing the family business, went to Paris to try to resurrect these works of art. Abe personally spent days digging, pulling up floorboards, or moving heavy bins, searching for hidden caches of old bronze works. Abe's son Stanley, a recent college graduate, was was placed in charge of re-assembling exhumed molds that arrived in various pieces. Over the next 15 years, multiple trips abroad resulted in the acquisition of complete molds for over 100 subjects, as well as numerous unidentified pieces, or incomplete molds.

Serendipity propelled the step of company development. Stanley Hirsch attended a symposium on the Beaux Arts presented at the New York Metropolitan Museum of Art. Stanley was surprised to note that he had in his possession the original molds from which the pieces on display were cast. When Hirsch consulted the curator of the Western European section of the museum, he was linked up with Harold Berman, author.

Berman was so impressed with the Hirsch pieces, he obtained permission from the company to include 40 examples of their pieces in his next volume of the *Bronze Encyclopedia*, and planted the suggestion that in addition to their focus on lamps, they might consider producing limited editions of their remarkable French pieces, which has subsequently been a major interest of the company and continues today.

Many Hirsch pieces are marked with their logo, and some are dated, but oftentimes the only clue to the maker is the style of the piece. As you will note from the photographs, Hirsch pieces are often romantic, elaborate, and elegantly designed. To date, only figural pieces have been seen. Most of the pieces are cast in pure spelter, and often they reflect the chryselephantine movement, displaying ivorine (celluloid) faces, hands or other parts. Sometimes the figures are entirely metal (spelter) with parts painted to resemble ivorine.

"Beethoven" and "The Cellists" are two of the most popular Hirsch pieces. Some of their figural pieces are also seen in plaster; these pieces were made from the same molds as the original metal pieces, but when metal shortages and wartime demand diverted metals to other uses, plaster was substituted.

Hubley

The Hubley Manufacturing Company began in Lancaster, Pennsylvania, in 1894, and is most well-known for its production of iron toys. In 1965 the company became part of Gabriel Industries, which continued to use the Hubley name until 1978. In addition to numerous interesting bookends, Hubley produced ashtrays, banks, clocks, cage hooks, curtain hold-backs, button plates, door knockers, doorstops, place card holders, pet feeding dishes, desk novelties, and art novelties. Many of their bookends reflected popular artwork or sculpture ("Washington at Valley Forge," "End of the Trail," "Angel's Call to Prayer," "St. George and the Dragon"). Representative artists or sculptors associated with their pieces include G. G. Drayton and Fred Evett. Flowers were the single subject portrayed with the greatest frequency in doorsteps. When considering bookends, dogs were their most widely utilized subject matter. Many pieces came in more than one finish, but unfortunately, many of the pieces suffer great loss of painted finish over time. One of the most colorful is "Serenade Tonight," which comes in a delightful polychrome, or a very attractive bronze finish. Most pieces were completed in iron, but some in bronze also. Hubley bookends are generally imprinted with a two or three digit number on the back, but no specific company logo. A single example of a Hubley company tag, a one centimeter diameter circular green paper tag with the company name, has been found on their wirehaired terrier bookends.

Hummel

Hummel figures were originally created by Berta Hummel, a Franciscan nun also known as Sister M. Innocentia. She was born in Massing, Bavaria, on May 21, 1909. Her family included two brothers and three sisters. Even in early school years (1916 – 1921) she had painted little cards for family birthdays and holidays, most often choosing subjects which remain principal in her adult art: flowers, birds, animals, and little children. From 1921 – 1927 she attended a girls' finishing school at Simbach, during which her artistic talents produced sufficient acclaim that upon graduation she moved to Munich to attend the Academy of Fine Arts there. During her tenure at the academy, she met two Franciscan nuns who were attending the School for Industrial Arts. Her relationship with these sisters led her into her own religious commitment with subsequent taking of her vows in the Convent of Siessen on August 30, 1934. This convent was the site of her drawings which led to Hummel Cards and Hummel figures, derived dominantly, we are told, from her memories of childhood friends. Berta Hummel died on November 6, 1946.

The W. Goebel Porzellanfabrik, of Rodental, West Germany, is a factory which produces china and porcelain, established by Franz Detlev Goebel in 1871. The first Hummel figures were produced about 1935, thanks to the inventiveness of Franz Goebel, who secured permission from Berta Hummel and her convent to make figurines of Berta's drawings. During Nazi reign, the factory progressively diminished and ceased, until during the U. S. military occupation, support from the American government allowed renewal of factory production. U.S. servicemen in Germany found the pieces quite attractive, and brought many back home with them. Pieces produced in the 1946 to 1948 occupation are marked with usual company trademarks, as well as "US Zone, Germany" or "US Zone." In the time period during which the Goebel factory was not functioning, Herbert Dubler, of New York, produced figures which look much like Hummels, but were not designed from Berta Hummel drawings. These figures are marked "Authentic Hummel Figure Produced by Ars Sacra, made in USA."

In 1971, commemorating their 100th anniversary, the W. Goebel firm issued its first annual Hummel plate. In 1975, the first anniversary plate was issued, intended to be reissued every five years.

Authentic Hummel figures are marked. Since 1940, a bee, or baby bee, has been placed on figures along with factory trademarks. This choice was pertinent since the English translation of the word Hummel is "bumblebee" and since "bee" was reportedly a nickname of Berta Hummel. Hummel bookends on a wooden base should display the factory marks as wall as the signature MI Hummel (for Mary Innocentia Hummel). The pieces should be marked with a "V," containing within it a bee, or for pieces prior to 1940, should be marked with a crown and the signature of the company, either a "WG" or "Goebel." From 1960 to the current day, pieces are produced with a "V" containing a bee in a variety of configurations. Beginning in the late 1960s, some pieces have also been marked with a copyright insignia and "W Germany." The porcelain figures are marked on the bottom with a number assigned at the factory. Thus far 450 different motifs have been numbered by the factory, but not all have been put into production. Since some figures were produced in multiple sizes, pieces may be marked with both an item number and a size number. The W. Goebel factory continues today in active production.

Jennings Brothers

Jennings Brothers, usually known as "JB" among bookend enthusiasts, was begun about 1891 in Bridgeport, Connecticut, by Edward Austin Jennings. The Jennings Brothers Manufacturing Company evolved into a multi-generational business which provided some of the most finely crafted art metal pieces existing today. Their typical methods of production required meticulous techniques which did not lend themselves well to machine-directed mass production, but rather depended upon the direct handiwork of expert artists, sculptors, and metal craftsmen. By the late 1940s, procuring such artists and utilizing their techniques were of such economic burden to art metal crafters that monetary survival became a precarious situation.

E.A. Jennings (Jan. 8, 1963 – Sept. 13, 1952) was born in Greens Farms, Connecticut. He was educated at Greens Farms Academy and Park Avenue Institute. His first employment was with G.W. Barker (Bridgeport), followed by 10 years employment with the National Bank of Bridgeport and the Consolidated Rolling Stock Company. In 1888, the American Jewelry Company was founded by Edward and his brother Erwin, which was re-organized and renamed Jennings Brothers Manufacturing Company several years later. The first formal listing of JB as a business appears in the 1892 Bridgeport City Directory, and the last listing was in the 1953 directory. The Bridgeport Directory of 1929 states that the company was incorporated in 1896 with a capital of $400,000; according to one grandson, this sum was put up by Edward's first wife and the wife of Henry Jennings, one of Edward's brothers. The business was located at 219 Elm Street from 1905 when the Bridgeport Gun Implement Company building was purchased. At that time the company was known also as a major silver manufacturer. In 1953 the site was purchased by James J. Sullivan, with the intention of razing the edifice to provide a parking lot, which was subsequently accomplished in 1954.

The company prospered under the leadership of successive family members, including E.A. Jennings' son, Henry Ashton Jennings. When H.A. Jennings died in 1937, he was succeeded by his son Erwin Strickland Jennings. H.A. Jennings had substantial community involvement, evidenced by being a member of the Pequot Yacht club, and his achievement of 32nd degree Mason at the Pyramid Temple of the Mystic Shrine. In 1941 the company was threatened by fire that caused $100,000 damage, overcame 13 firemen, and gutted the building, but they were able to resume business.

All Jennings Brothers pieces are marked somewhere with the letters JB. On the other hand, since the molds of the company were purchased by the Philadelphia Manufacturing Company (also known as PM Craftsman, or simply PMC) in the 1960s, recently manufactured examples of Jennings Brothers designs do exist. For instance, New Bedford Whaler has been seen as the original JB piece, as well as a recent reissue by PMC. Usually, the patina of the more recent pieces is easily discerned from the much earlier original JB creations. Sometimes the JB markings are not easily visible, but are instead placed in very out-of-the-way locations. JB pieces were made only of cast gray metal, but JB was also known for a silver-plating process they developed, so some silverplate pieces are likely to be seen. Their finishing processes made pieces of such quality that bronze finishes on cast gray metal pieces are easily mistaken for solid bronze. Indeed, there is no other major manufacturer with pieces whose finish remains as durable as that of JB, allowing one to often find pieces in pristine condition, though more than 50 years old. One catalog of JB pieces is reported to have more than 3,000 different offerings, to include such items as ashtrays, jewelry boxes, bookends, desk sets, figurines, paperweights, tea sets, candlesticks, table flatware, etc. At one time, the company had a showroom at the Gifts and Arts Center, 225 Fifth Avenue, New York.

Though obviously a drastic oversimplification, the basic process of metal casting went as follows: Once a mold of a figurine or statue was made, a bronze mold was then created, often in two pieces if simple, but perhaps with several separate pieces for legs or other parts as necessary. A spelter or similar type metal was poured into the bronze mold and when cold, the mold was taken apart and a finish applied by a specially developed electroplating process. The actual origin of a substantial portion of the subject matter is unknown; that is, none of the pieces are directly artist signed. On the other hand, many of the works are done by famous artists that are internationally recognized (e.g. the "Lion of Lucerne" on page 155, the "Seated Lincoln" on page 214 by Daniel Chester, "Pioneer Woman" on page 187 by Baker). Even so, we are uncertain as to how miniature versions of these famous pieces were obtained or constructed. Edward Austin Jennings is reported to have made jaunts to New York City to meet immigrants, Polish, Latvian, and Slavic peoples, whose entire families he successfully encouraged to become Jennings Brothers employees. At that time, Edward himself worked six days a week, and his factory workers (numbering about 125 during his leadership) worked five full days and half-day Saturday. Pieces were marketed at dog shows, horse shows, hunt clubs, and yachting events, as well as by various private stores. Business was at its peak in the 1920s and 1930s. During World War II, metal shortages redirected JB efforts away from their usual lines into production of hubcaps for military trucks. Post war imports of ceramic and plastic items drastically reduced demand and economic viability of the metal crafted items, leading to the eventual demise of the company. At the close of JB, molds were sold to a concrete block entrepreneur, who was unable to make an economic success of their use, but since their PMC has successfully obtained and used the original molds.

Judd Company

Morton Judd began a small machine shop and foundry in New Britain, Connecticut, in 1817, developed the M. Judd and Sons Company in 1830, and was eventually joined by all three of his sons in 1855. In the 1850s there was also a factory in New Haven, Connecticut. In 1870, H.L. Judd (one of Morton's sons) took over the company and the name was changed to H.L. Judd. Growth of the company resulted in a larger, more modern factory located in Brooklyn, New York, in 1875. Unfortunately, in 1884 a fire destroyed the factory. A new home was established in 1885 in Wallingford, Connecticut, as the permanent home of the new factory, administrative and sales offices remaining in New York City. H.L. Judd Company was acquired by Stanley Works in 1954, and became the Stanley-Judd Division, still located in Wallingford, Connecticut.

Judd pieces are some of the highest quality iron pieces seen, with great attention to detail, enduring and interesting paint techniques, and durable two-piece construction in many cases. In addition to bookends, the company also made brass beds, inkwells, and fishing lures.

LaFrance Bronze Arts

Little is known about this company. They produced bronze-clad bookends, with the only confirmed item of this company similar to the Knights bookends appearing in the Marion Bronze catalog, item 682. The location of LaFrance Bronze Arts was listed as Frankford, Philadelphia, Pennsylvania.

Littlestown Hardware and Foundry Co. Inc. (Littco)

Littco is still in operation at P.O. Box 69, Charles Street, Littlestown, Pennsylvania, 17340 (717-359-4141). It was founded by Emory H. and Luther D. Snyder, two brothers who were engaged in 1915 in a hardware supply company. At that time they also operated a garage in Wrightsville, Pennsylvania. The Snyders moved to Littlestown, and in 1916 began a general hardware buying and selling business. Later that year an iron foundry developed and played a key role in the company's growth as a hardware manufacturer and supplier. The brothers remained active in the business until shortly before their deaths, one at age 97, the other at age 98.

In the 1920s and 1930s, Littco brought out their bookends and doorstops. All pieces were manufactured in the Littlestown foundry, and marketing was handled by a sales agency at 225th Avenue, New York. Company executives report that designs for the bookends were sculpted by a local artist residing in Wrightsville. In 1941, the price of the most expensive bookend pair issued by Littco was 80 cents per pair (plus freight). World War II called up some of the employees, and raw materials were utilized for essentials only, so production of bookends and doorstops ceased. Of the more than 40 different kinds of bookends pictured in a Littco catalog, all but one have been seen and identified, as well as numerous pieces that are not in the catalog. Littco pieces are generally very heavy, solid iron. Painted pieces are distinctly less common among bookends, but quite routine among doorstops.

Marion Bronze

The history available about Marion Bronze Company is very sketchy. Despite contacting the chambers of commerce from cities in which Marion Bronze was known to have done business, and the local historical societies, definitive information about the company is not forthcoming. From a business tag seen on one of their products, we know they began producing metalware in 1922. A catalog of Marion Bronze pieces is detailed in the book on bookends by Gerald McBride, and this catalog apparently dates from the 1960s. Marion Bronze reportedly manufactured through 1971. Although "recent" (1958 – 1971) products routinely bear the Marion Bronze logo (MB), numerous older bookends were unmarked. Globe is an excellent example of the potential for bright, enduring colors using their electroformed methodology. Older examples were very often in bronze-tone only, several examples of which you will find in this book. Early Marion Bronze pieces are quite uncommon, and their more colorful mid-century work has more universal appeal for collectors. Marion Bronze appears to have been the last commercial entity to produce bookends by the electroform method in the United States. In this book, numerous pieces have been identified as Marion Bronze because they were bought as a collection from a New York City landlord who had retrieved them from the abandoned apartment of a tenant. This tenant had apparently been an employee of Marion Bronze and had brought home over 50 examples of their products.

Miller Brass Foundry

The Miller Company is one of the oldest industrial plants in Meriden, beginning in 1844 as a producer of candlesticks and oil-burning lamps. In 1858, the process for distilling kerosene from bituminous coal was developed, and Miller was the first to design, produce, and market a kerosene-burning lamp. The company's progress paralleled the development in the lighting industry, as they initially made gas fixtures, then lamps using the Wellsbach mantle, then Edison's carbon filament incandescent lamp, the mercury-vapor lamp, and in 1938 fluorescent lamp.

In order to produce brass parts used in making lamps, Miller began a brass rolling mill in 1868, but soon expanded it to become a national supplier of phosphor bronze and brass. The Miller Company still exists today in Meriden. Only a single example of bookend work by Miller has been seen (see plate 750) which you will note is produced using the same design as the polychrome piece by K&O Company (see plate 749).

Nuart Metal Creations

Nuart was apparently a subsidiary of The Gift House, Inc., which was located at 1107 Broadway in its 1931 catalog. In addition to bookends, the company made lamps, ashtrays, candlesticks, and paperweights. The 1931 catalog lists four different finishes for their products: bronze, ebony black, green, and oriental red.

The 1931 catalog lists 28 different pairs of bookends, but there were many more on the market. Nuart's most inventive pieces were Art Deco females, especially those designed for lamps. Unfortunately, the paint process was of a poorly enduring quality, and it is routine to find either flaked or unusually chipped off paint areas for pieces that have been, for the most part, well protected. Nuart used at least two shopmarks, one with the name spelled out in a linear fashion, the other with the name along the periphery of a circular imprint.

Paul Mori and Sons

Also known as Galavano Bronze, Paul Mori produced pieces in the bronze-clad style, the earliest of which is pictured as "Dante & Beatrice," and dated 1915. The company was located in New York City, and continued production through the 1920s.

Pompeian Bronze Company

Little is known about the Pompeian Bronze Company. They have over 30 copyrights for bookends and other art metal goods, the first of which is dated 1921, the last 1930. During this period, their offices were at 603 Dean Street, Brooklyn, New York. No traditional cast bronze pieces are known by Pompeian Bronze, rather, they produced bronze-clad, or heavy gray metal pieces. Often the bronze-clad pieces are imprinted with the company name. Sometimes, the gray metal pieces merely have "PB, Inc.," but fortunately the gray metal pieces are often dated and named on the back. All copyrights are registered to Peter Maneredi, who may have been one of their designers.

Roman Bronze Works

Ricardo Bertelli immigrated to the U. S. from Genoa, Italy, in 1895. He had a degree in chemical engineering and training in art as well. Within two years, he had begun a small foundry in New York City with Giuseppe Moretti (sculptor and founder) and John Zappolla, a 17-year-old craftsman who was familiar with the lost-wax method of bronze casting. The firm was titled Roman Bronze Works, and initially was located at 152 West 38th Street, but the next year was moved to Forsyth Street into a building that had previously housed other bronze foundries. The trade name "Roman Bronze Works" was registered in 1900, soon after which the company moved from Lower Manhattan to Greene Street in the Greenpoint section of Brooklyn, where business was active through 1928. The most publicly visible of RBW pieces are those done in New York City. RBW was commissioned to do the sculptural work at Rockefeller Center, including "Atlas" (Lee Lawrie, sculptor), and "Prometheus" (Paul Manship, sculptor). Other sculptors associated with RBW include Charles Russel,

James Earl Fraser (designer of the Buffalo nickel), Bryant Baker (sculptor of "Pioneer Woman," Ponca, Oklahoma), Gutzon Borglum (sculptor of Mount Rushmore), Cyrus Dallin ("Appeal to the Great Spirit"), Victor D. Brenner (designer of the Lincoln penny), and Daniel Chester French (Lincoln memorial), to name but a few.

Ronson

Ronson, variously labeled as LVA, LV Aronson, Louis V. Aronson, or Art Metal Works, is generally regarded as one of the most prolific, as well as most creative of all art metal bookend producers. The first art metal piece recorded in the U.S. copyright office is dated November 8, 1915, though we know that Mr. Aronson obtained a patent for one of his works in 1909. At the time of the initial 1915 work, the company was located at 9 Mulberry Street in Newark, New Jersey. Over 150 copyrights are registered to Aronson or Art Metal Works. It is usually not clear who is the artist/sculptor of the pieces. Many of those registered to Art Metal Works (1931 – 1937) are credited to Frederick Kaufmann, at the office location 46 Center St., Newark, New Jersey, and a few are credited to John Skiba.

A 1936 catalog of Art Metal Works, Inc. has more than 150 examples of Ronson bookends. At that time, the central office of AMW is listed as Aronson Square, Newark, New Jersey, but letterhead details include permanent display rooms for AMW products in New York (347 Fifth Avenue), Chicago (136 South State Street), Los Angeles (728 South Flower Street), Canada (Dominion Art Metal Works, Toronto), England (Ronson Products, London), and Australia (W.G. Watson & Co., Sydney). Ronson bookends were complemented with at least 16 different finishes, descriptions of some of which are:

Imperial Bronze: two-tone antique copper-bronze effect
Venetian Bronze: two-tone dull green-gold effect, hand relieved in verdi-green
Tyrrhian Bronze: two-tone dusty bronze effect with copper highlights
Royal Bronze: black-bronze effect, hand relieved in verdi-green
Polished Brass: traditional brass
Colonial Bronze: medium bronze effect combined with copper-colored highlights
Georgian Bronze: deep bronze effect combined with brass-colored highlights
Lincoln Bronze: two-toned green-gold effect, hand relieved in brown
Chromium Plate: high-gloss chrome finish
Copper: brilliant red-hued copper finish
Ebony: matte finish black
Decorated polished-gold effect: gold-colored metal with polychrome enameling

Depression green: creamy light green matte finish
Gun Metal: silver-gray glossy finish

Seymour Products

Seymour Manufacturing Company was organized in May 1880, and incorporated in January 1887 in Seymour, Connecticut, a small town in New Haven County. The scanty details that we currently know come primarily from a book published in 1902 by W.C. Sharpe Publisher, in Seymour, authored by Reverend Hollis A. Campbell and William C. Sharpe, in which they report that by 1920 the company had amassed a capital of $500,000. The company was known to manufacture sheet brass, wires, rods, tubing, and wire for telephone, telegraph, and "electric roads." One of the company's specialties was German silver, used for tableware. In 1902 the company employed 250 persons. Seymour Manufacturing displayed special generosity in contributing $1,000 of the $6,000 necessary to purchase the town's first fire engine. The original Seymour Products plant was built by architect H.B. Wooster, who was born in Naugatuck in 1827 where he lived until an 1860 move to Waterbury, Connecticut. in 1879 he moved to Seymour to become a stockholder, superintendent of construction, and primary architect of Seymour Manufacturing.

About 1925, Seymour Manufacturing split off into Seymour Products Company, and moved into the plant of H.A. Matthews, which had been organized in 1890 for manufacturing of stove trimmings, hardware, and bicycle parts. H.A. Matthews was equipped to turn out brass, steel, and composition metal. Several years later, the Seymour Products Company closed, but details of its demise are unavailable.

Snead Iron Works

Snead Iron Works was founded in Louisville, Kentucky, in 1849. From that date until 1890 it fashioned ornamental iron work. In 1890 it was awarded a contract from the government to replace the wood shelving in the Library of Congress, with metal. The company also produced shelving for the Vatican Library in Rome, the Sterling Library at Yale University, the National Archives Building in Washington, D.C., and other internationally known libraries. Countless individuals have tread the stairway in the Washington Monument, produced by Snead & Co. From 1897 until 1940, they were located in Jersey City, New Jersey, at which time they moved to Orange, Virginia.

Copyrights in the company name for bookends were issued as early as 1924(see page 301, here, copyright #73078, December 1, 1924, by Olga Popoff Muller). All together, 10 cpoyrights are issued to this company for bookends, although they produced other art metal goods ("Wild Rose Candlesticks" copyright 1925, to Angus MacDonald of Snead and Company).

Susse Freres

Susse Freres (literally "Susse brothers") is a Paris-based foundry founded in 1839 by Michael and Amedee Susse. Around 1900 the firm opened at 13 Boulevard de Madelaine (Paris) a retail shop, including desk items, candelabra, clocks, sculpture, and (through the 1920s), car mascots.

Syroco, Inc.

The Syracuse Ornamental Corporation currently is housed at 7528 State Fair Boulevard, Baldwinsville, New York 13027 (315-635-9911 ext. 2242). The company had its origins in 1890. A group of European craftsmen soon were in great demand as a result of the hand-carved fashion pieces they provided for fine homes and institutions, including the governor's mansion in Albany. In an effort to make such styles available on a wider scale, a technique was developed of molding reproductions by compressing a mixture of waxes, woodflour, and resin. This type of product was used primarily to provide carving details to furniture. After World War II, Syroco developed a line of home decorative accessories, including many bookends. Syroco bookends most often have a support plate attached to the resin figure, with natural wood hue the most common finish, although pieces are also available in a variety of colors. The company's historical records were lost in a recent fire, preventing greater insight into the company's history.

Tiffin Glass

The Tiffin Glass Company was not a prolific producer of bookends. Of the approximately 2,000 interesting glass items that appear in the book *Tiffin Glassmasters, Book II*, only two pairs of bookends are depicted (page 133). Tiffin Glass Company, of Tiffin, Ohio, also known as A.J. Beatty and Sons, was established in the 1800s. They joined the U.S. Glass Company in 1916, and were known as Factory R of the U.S. Glass Co. from that point on, though Tiffin insignia markings were kept on paper tags through 1978. Tiffin glass products were not marked in the glass itself, the glassmakers' preference being not to alter the artistic lines of the glass with a signature. On the other hand, numerous different style paper labels were used, each clearly displaying the Tiffin name and an insignia of a large "T" with serifs.

Up until the time that Tiffin Glass joined U.S. Glass, the latter had produced primarily pressed glass tumblers and bar-ware. The lighter glassware made by Tiffin was not immediately embraced by U.S. Glass, but eventually embarked upon production of high-quality light glassware. By 1927, when numerous other glass companies were going out of business, Tiffin flourished. By comparison, two other well-known glass manufacturers, A.H. Heisey & Co, and Cambridge Glass Company were producing less than half the amount that Tiffin achieved. Tiffin Glass was sold throughout the U.S., Canada, Australia, Cuba, England, Mexico, and South Africa. The only other bookends known to be made by Tiffin are ships.

Tiffany

In 1900, Louis Comfort Tiffany established Tiffany Studios in New York City. Tiffany Studios was an outgrowth of the Tiffany Glass & Decorating Company that started producing and selling lamps in 1895. Tiffany Studios made not only the bronze bases for Tiffany lamps, but also candlesticks, figurines, enameled bronze pieces, tableware, desk sets, and many other useful and decorative objects. It was Tiffany's intent to mass-produce beautiful gift items and accessories that could be afforded by middle-class families. His prime consideration was always craftsmanship and durability.

Tiffany Studios produced and sold matched desk sets in more than 15 patterns during the first two decades of the twentieth century. Each item of the set was sold and priced individually, so there was never really a "basic" set. Bookends were added to the sets in 1916. Prior to 1916, the price list for the sets included book racks, which we refer to as "expandable." Tiffany Trade catalogs listed bookends in the Abalone, Bookmark, Chinese, Etched Metal and Glass, Graduate, and Zodiac patterns, but there are many many others.

All Tiffany bookends were carefully handworked by either chasing or etching and then plated or paginated. An advertisement for a Zodiac Desk Set reads:

"Finished in Green, Brown, or Gold, and ornamental with a primitive design rudely modeled, these pieces are very dignified and simple in character. The Zodiac Signs are carved in low relief on the Medallions formed by the interlacing band ornament." In the original catalog, Zodiac bookends are priced at $1,800. Individual pieces were handstamped "Tiffany Studios, New York" with an accompanying stock number.

There is very little information available specifically on Tiffany bookends. Robert Koch, in his book Louis C Tiffany Glass-Bronzes-Lamps (Crown Publisher, Inc., new York, 1971) states "no desk sets, candlesticks, cast bronzes for lamp bases, or accessories were manufactured and stamped Tiffany Studios after 1918. Metal production was diverted during World War I, and the business was reorganized with the retirement of L.C. Tiffany (1919). The company was liquidated in 1938. (Thanks to Sue Benoliel for Tiffany information)."

Virginia Metal Crafters

VMC was founded in 1890 by WJ Loth, having purchased the Waynesboro (Virginia) Stove Works assets to form W.J. Loth Stove Company. In 1922 Fred Cuffe left Canadian General Electric to join Mr. Loth and designed the electric cooking range, eventually marketed as the Hot

Point Range. In 1930, Edison General Electric purchased Loth Company, including the Hot Point Range patent, subsequently closing (1932) the Virginian plant and moving the Hot Point Range manufacturing site to Chicago.

The Rife-Loth Company was established in 1934, when R.H. Clemmer purchased the remaining Loth company materials, incorporating the Rife Ram Pump Factory. The ram pump was used to draw energy from falling water, quite useful prior to rural electrification. Art metal crafting was begun in earnest in 1936, with miniature souvenir cast iron reproductions, the first of which was a miniature iron frying pan. In 1938, equipment was added to include brass and other non-ferrous metal. These miniatures were sold under the name Virginia Metalcrafters. After a hiatus for World War II, brass production resumed. R.H. Clemmer commissioned a carving of the great race horse Citation (artist Calvin Roy Kinstler) which is used as the model for a number of VMC pieces. In 1951 Rife-Loth entered into an agreement with Colonial Williamsburg to produce brass and iron reproductions. Since that time the company has continued to make alliances with such agencies as Harvin Company of Baltimore, E.T. Caldwell Company of New York, and others to produce fine cast brass items, including (since 1987) a license as manufacturer for the Smithsonian Institution. VMC utilizes the sand-casting process for brass making, a process employed by colonial craftsmen. In this process, each product is made in an individual sand mold. Molten brass (temperature 2000 degrees Fahrenheit) is then poured into the mold. After cooling and hardening, the mold is broken apart and the casting removed. Each piece is then buffed and polished. The entire process involves from 20 to 400 hand-finishing steps, depending upon the size and complexity of the piece.

Most VMC bookends are marked with the shopmark "VM," between which is the arm of what has been termed a "Betty Lamp"—reportedly an oil lamp used on whaling vessels. Bookends are made of either solid cast iron or solid cast bronze. The oldest available catalog of VMC wares is dated in the 1960s. Products of VMC have also been issued bearing labels "Historic Newport Reproductions." "Old Sturbridge Village," and "Colonial Williamsburg Restoration."

Weidlich Brothers

The shopmark "WB" in a shield is usually a sign of a quality design. Weidlich Brothers Manufacturing Company was founded in 1901 in Bridgeport, Connecticut and specialized in sterling and plated trophies. The company closed in 1950. They used several markings for their pieces, including WB, "W" inside a pentagon, the "Warner Silver Co," and others. There was another Weidlich, Incorporated, also in Bridgeport, unrelated to this producer of bookends.

Comments on Individual Bookends

Classical Men (see Plate 1500)

The story of Classical Men begins in 1972, when an Italian amateur scuba diver, diving for fish, found two half-buried statues close to the shore of Riace Marina, near Port Foricchio, Italy. In ancient times, this area along the southern coast of Italy was on the shipping lanes between Roman ports and Greek harbors. Archaeologists responded quickly with a search, recovering two statues each 6'7" tall (2.06 meters), which were ultimately confirmed to be classical mid-fifth century BC sculptures. During the recovery operation, searchers sought the ship that had carried the sculpture, but only found some rings from the ship's sails and fragments of amphora (Greek two-handled vases). Finding the rings by the statues indicates the likely scenario: the ship may have lost a mast at about the time the statues went overboard, suggesting a violent storm-induced breakage of the mast, following which eight of the statues broke loose from their moorings, or the foundering vessel loosed them to lighten its load. Archeological experts suspect that they were used in a common public monument, but state that they were sculpted by different artists.

Wealthy Romans are reported to have been avid collectors of Greek sculpture, and soldiers returning from conquests in Greek lands sported stolen statues as prizes. Although the bookends just contain the "bust" of the figures, originally they were full-sized total-body compositions. The statues are primarily bronze, but also have copper lips, silver teeth, and eyes made of ivory and colored stone. Both statues are currently housed in the National Museum, Reggio Di ACalbria, Italy, and they are titled "Warrior A" and "Warrior B." Warrior A originally possessed a shield on the left arm. There are no inscriptions on either warrior.

Dickens Characters

Job Trotter is the figure in the red outfit with the yellow vest, cuffs, and epaulets, holding a blue book with his right hand, and handkerchiefs in his left. Job Trotter is a character from Pickwick Papers. Job Trotter was "the manservant and friend of Jingle, and a worthy confederate in his rascalties. With his lachrymose contrition, Job was cunning enough to deceive Sam Well twice, but after their meeting in the fleet prison, Sam forgave him, and Job turned into a trusty messenger for Mr. Pickwick. Faithful to Jingle to the last, Job accompanied him to the West Indies."

The figure in the umber-colored suit and vest, with hands in pockets, is Artful Dodger, the nickname of the young pickpocket, Jack Dawkins. "Also known as the Artful Dodger, Dawkins was one of Fagin's most promising young thieves. He was a snub-nosed, flat-browed, common-faced boy enough, and as dirty a juvenile as one would wish to see; but he had about him all the airs and manners of a man. He found Oliver Twist at Barnet, and took him to Fagin's Den, where he was, in his own way, a friend to the child. A deft pickpocket, the Dodger was cut off in his prime, for having been arrested with a stolen snuff-box on him, was tried and sentenced to transportation for life."

Plate 1. Dicken's Characters, ca. 1928, gray metal, 8", rarity 5, $350.00.

Don Quixote's Respite (see Plate 1513)

Our cover is graced with a favorite of mine since I first saw the pair at the Miami Beach Convention Center Show in January 2001 "Don Quixote's Respite." Which depicts Don Quixote and Sancho Panza resting up against tree stumps. This pair is made by Le Verrier Foundry, and I have seen it in two formats, a marble base, and a bronze base which is "L"-shaped that rises up behind the trees. The sculptor is Janle. I don't know why they don't appear in the Le Verrier catalog; they are products of this foundry. The bronze lance tip screws into place on the hub of the lance, but the juncture is not. The book Don Quixote, by Cervantes, is a very entertaining one, but very long. I checked out two translations, and chose to read the shorter one, but it is not an easy read. The basic story, for those of you who haven't read it, is that Don Quixote is a demented senior citizen who has spent the greater portion of his adult life digesting tales of great knights and their intrigues. In his partially demented state, he feels called upon to become a great knight himself. So he selects a woman to whom he dedicates his efforts, and sets about to accomplish great and chivalrous deeds. Along the way, he adopts Sancho Panza, a somewhat slow-witted but well intended farmer who, with the promise of a kingdom of his own for appropriate service to the Gallant Knight Quixote, provides companionship, assistance, and sometimes protection for his usually wayward boss. The phrase that we commonly hear which alludes to Don Quixote is "…tilting at windmills," which comes from the episode in the novel when Quixote, who sees windmills in the distance, becomes convinced that they are actually giants who have disguised themselves as windmills. Insistent upon uncovering the plots of these giants, he engages them in a joust, ultimately piercing one of the windmill blades with his lance. Through most of the adventures of Quixote, Sancho Panza tries to provide a temperate voice, though he is usually unsuccessful, and often suffers the brunt of Quixote's misadventures himself, sometimes at substantial physical and mental suffering. You will see that Don Quixote is usually depicted with a hat possessing a defect along the brim. There are numerous battles in which Don Quixote is outnumbered and outpowered, but his unanticipatable bravado, misperception of reality, and consistent willingness to pay a physical price (lost teeth, broken lances, damaged armor, various and sundry blows) for vociferous assaults upon alleged doers of misdeeds somehow allows him to pass through maelstrom after maelstrom still able to (eventually) remount his trusty steed.

Fox and Grapes (see Plate 408)

There are several versions of tales involving a fox and grapes, which might be synthesized as follows:

Once upon a time a very hungry fox was walking through the forest. Not having had anything to drink or eat for several days, he was eagerly seeking sustenance. The fox entered an area of the forest which was lined with grapevines, but dismayed to note that almost all of the grapes had been eaten by other animals. The only available bunch of grapes left was high above the ground, hanging from the limb of a tree.

The grapes were most enticing to the fox, looking juicy and delicious, but jump though he did, he could not reach the grapes. His attempts at clambering up the tree were thwarted by slippery bark and inefficient paws for climbing. Jump after jump failed to attain the grapes. The more he tried the more it became clear that the luscious grapes were beyond his leaps. After a last mighty heave resulted in a still-distant miss, the fox landed with a thud against a nearby tree stump haughtily shaking himself off,

he walked away, the while sneering "Those crummy grapes were doubtless sour, anyway." Moral: It is sometimes easier to disparage what we cannot attain than admit our inability to achieve it.

Grand Old Man (see Plate 2253)

Amos Alonzo Stagg graduated in 1863 from Orange High School (NJ) and attended Phillips Exeter Academy prior to matriculating at Yale, where he had enrolled in the divinity school. At college, he participated on the Yale baseball team and what was then a brand new game, basketball. Stagg considered his involvement in athletics a way to influence young men towards Christian ideals, and to that end he left Yale and joined the International YMCA College where he coached football and baseball.

Stagg went on to become athletic director at the University of Chicago. He is credited with numerous innovations in football, including the direct snap to the ball carrier, tackles, back and standing quarterback (today called "shotgun"), wing backs, the first football helmet, and a diversity of other fundamental evolutionary steps in the sport. Stag created the Rose Bowl, the first football bowl game, and in addition to his seven Western Conference Championships, led five undefeated seasons. His skills were not limited to football. He coached track and baseball as well, and became a member of the American Olympic Committee on more than one occasion. Stagg field at University of Chicago is named after him, and the Football Coaches Association named him "Coach of the Year" at age 81.

Indochina Beauty (see Plate 1107)

The pair "Indochina Beauty" is marked "Made in French IndoChina." French colonization of the Asian mainland between China and India began in the seventeenth century. Prior to advent of European influence, the Khmer Empire (area now called Cambodia) rose and fell. A Thai kingdom called Ayutthaya was in control over the area we now know as Thailand, which had been called Siam until 1939. Domination of the area by European nations began in the 1500s. Burma was completely controlled by Britain by the late 1800s, and in 1947 achieved independence. The French established Cochin China (southern Vietnam) as a colony in the 1800s. What is now known as central Vietnam and northern Vietnam were French protectorates Annam and Tonkin, respectively. Cambodia was a third French protectorate. In 1887 the French joined Cambodia, Annam, Tonkin, and Cochin China into French Indochina (also called the Indochinese Union). In 1893 Laos was added to this union. The existence of French Indochina ended with Japanese occupation of the region, following which, in March 1945, the area was proclaimed to be the autonomous state of Vietnam. The stability of this area quickly tumbled, as Ho Chi Minh assumed power over what he proclaimed as a Democratic Republic of Vietnam. The French then re-occupied Laos and Cambodia, designated as the Indochinese Federation, soon followed by the Indochina wars, whereupon Laos, Cambodia, and Vietnam were recognized as independent self-governing states. The markings "French Indochina" define this pair as pre-1945. During the years of World War I, it is unlikely that metals would be used for art castings, suggesting that this pair was most likely made in the 1930s.

Kiss, The (see Plate 707)

The Kiss depicts a woman with her face upturned, being kissed by a man in a cape from above. Reportedly, this scene was first created by the Edvard Munch in Norway as a woodcut titled "The Kiss" (1902). Subsequently, Austrian artist Gustav Kindt painted a scene titled "The Kiss" in 1908. Although the artistic depictions are not always identical, various artists or foundries have recreated this scene with similar likeness, including Pompeian Bronze and Armor Bronze.

Kleek-O (see Plate 631)

No matter how you slice it, there aren't a lot of Eskimo bookends. Clicquot (pronounced "Kleek-o") ginger ale was invented by Lansing Millis, a retired railroad man who decided to go into the business of soft drinks. The town of Millis, Massachusetts, home of Clicquot beverage plants, was named for Mr. Millis. Mr. Millis incorporated Jamaican ginger and Cuban cane sugar in his high quality product, which soon found great favor with the public palate, despite the absence of the advertising media we have today, so that his products were quickly in demand in Boston and Rhode Island. Success with ginger ale prompted the addition of a diversity of other beverages, including sarsaparilla, rootbeer, cola, and orange. The name "Clicquot" was chosen because the ginger ale beverage was reminiscent of French champagne, and the Clicquot family name was already associated with fine French wine. There were two different branches of the Clicquot family, spelled "Clicquot" and "Cliquot." Clicquot club ginger ale was named after the "Veuve Clicquot" French champagne. In an advertising blurb titled "Who put the "C" in Clicquot," the authors add "...I suppose it's fair to point out that the extra 'c' stands for such things as Cleanliness, Clarity, Class, Carbonation, and best of all the Confidence we all have in Clicquot Club quality." Another report ascribes the name of the company to a tribute to the Widow Clicquot of Reims, who reportedly was well known in the American market for blends of champagne wine. The first-ever soda can as a packaging device for soda is

attributed to Clicquot Club, in 1938. Kleek-O, the Eskimo, became the trademark of Clicquot club beverages sometime between 1907 and 1912.

Mark Twain and Tom Sawyer (see also Plate 1462)

The first version of the Mark Twain and Tom Sawyer, set I had ever seen appeared on eBay some six or seven years ago, and as I recall, was purchased by one of our club members. I had not personally seen a set until May 2004 at Brimfield (May's market show), which is the one pictured in our newsletter. As I sought information about the statue depicted, certain that it must be a popular public park, national museum, etc, that housed the "original" I set about "Googling" and looking through books to find more information. Every avenue turned up blank. There was no picture I could find that just contained Mark Twain and Tom Sawyer in anything close to the relationship shown in Mark Twain and Tom Sawyer.

Ultimately, we contacted Henry Sweets of the Mark Twain Home Foundation, and promptly received a copy of "The Fence Painter," the Bulletin of The Mark Twain Boyhood Home Associates, Volume 5, Number 2, Summer 1985. This newsletter contains a photograph titled "Mark Twain Memorial Sketch Model by Walter Russell," along with the following information:

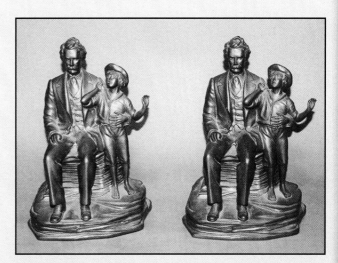

Plate 2. Mark Twain and Tom Sawyer, ca. 1936, Jennings Brothers, grey metal, 7¾", marked "© JB 707" paper tag on bottom reads "Mark Twain and Tom Sawyer," Reproduction of the central figure of Mark Twain Memorial, Hannibal Missouri, Designed and copyrighted by Walter Russell. Manufactured exclusively by the Jennings Bros Mfg Co, Bridgeport, Conn.," rarity 5, $275.00.

Plate 3. Mark Twain Memorial is the photograph contained in the bulletin of The Mark Twain Boyhood Home Associates, Volume 5, Number 2, Summer 1985; as we now know, the monument never happened! Nonetheless, you can clearly identify Mark Twain and Tom Sawyer as the central figures in the intended monument depicted in this photo.

"Walter Russell began his career as a portrait painter. In the late 1920s he began to concentrate on sculpture. He was appointed by the Mark Twain Centennial Commission of Hannibal to do a sculpture related to Mark Twain for the centennial year. Russell was a member of the Authors' Club of New York and had met Mark Twain several times. In speaking of his work while in Hannibal for the Mark Twain Museum dedication, Russell noted:

"I am especially pleased that the decision has been arrived at to erect this monument in the delightful town of Hannibal where I believe it will be of greater sentimental value than though placed in any other portion of the country. In a metropolis such as New York and Washington, it could be seen by a great number of people but Mark Twain did not write of great cities, he wrote of the middlewest, and I believe it most appropriate that the monument should be placed in Hannibal." Russell is referring to his vision of a huge grouping of statues and bas-reliefs to be placed along the walls of a hexagonal garden measuring 300 feet in diameter. He envisioned a foundation raising the funds for construction of this memorial garden and very optimistically forecast it would be ready by November 30 of the same year.

But, since the centennial occurred during the years of the Depression, the money could not be secured for the project.

The artist's design model for one of the six statue groupings is on display at the museum. This design features Mark Twain in the center flanked to the left by characters from Joan of Arc and the Prince and the Pauper, Mark Twain with his hand around Tom Sawyer, and to the right characters from Tom Sawyer and Huckleberry Finn.

Two more of these models exist, one at the Mark Twain Memorial, Hartford, Connecticut, and one at Russell's home, Swannanoa in Virginia.

Mr. Winkle's First Shot (see Plate 1559)

The Posthumous Papers of the Pickwick Club - a summary from *The Charles Dickens Encyclopedia.*

The Pickwick Club as a body makes an early and brief appearance, at one of its London meetings. Thereafter the central figures of the book are its president, the middle-aged, stout, jovial, and naïve Samuel Pickwick, a retired gentleman who sets out on a tour of investigation of scientific and cultural matters, and the three friends who accompany him: Nathaniel Winkle, who fancies himself as a sportsman but fails dismally to justify his pretensions; Augustus Snodgrass, melancholy and romantic in the fashionable Byronic manner (the period of the story is 1827-1831); and the somewhat older Tracy Tupman, a plump bachelor amorist. Their first adventure occurs at Rochester, where the cowardly Winkle is mistakenly challenged to a duel, the real offending party being Alfred Jingle, a strolling player. Jingle joins the party; it is the first of his mischievous appearances in Mr. Pickwick's life. At a military review in Chatham the Pickwickians meet Mr. Wardle, a country squire, his daughters Bella and Emily, his spinster sister Rachael, and their servant Joe, an immensely fat and greedy youth with a tendency to sleep on his feet. An invitation from Wardle takes the party down to his Kentish manor at Dingley Dell, where the unfortunate Winkle, taken out shooting, misses his bird and shoots Tupman in the arm. The story goes on from there.

Napoleon (see Plate 1716)

Most adults in the USA are familiar with the pose of Napoleon shown in these bookends, hand in jacket-pocket. We share with you the commentary of Tom Holmberg,

"Many theories have been presented as to why Napoleon is traditionally depicted with his hand in his waistcoat. Some of these theories include: that he had a stomach ulcer, he was winding his watch, he had an itchy skin disease, that in his era it was impolite to put your hands in your pockets, he had breast cancer, he had a deformed hand, he kept a perfumed sachet in his vest that he'd sniff surreptitiously, and that painters don't like to paint hands."

A simpler and more elegant theory is contained in an article titled, "Re-Dressing Classical Statuary: The Eighteenth-Century hand-in Waistcoat portrait" by Arline Miller, Art Bulletin (College Art Association of America, vol 77, no 2, March 1995, p 45-64. Miller points out that the hand-in portrait type appeared with "relentless frequency" during the eighteenth century and became almost a clichéd pose in portrait painting. The pose was used so often by portraitists that one was even accused of not knowing how to paint hands. In real life, Miller observes, "the hand-held-in was a common stance for men of breeding." Miller goes on to give many examples of this posture in painted portraits dating from the early and middle 1700s, well before Napoleon's birth. In 1738 Francois Niveton published a book of genteel behavior describing the hand-in-waistcoat posture as signifying "manly boldness tempered with modesty." Miller says that the hidden hand was a feature of some statues of the ancient Greeks and Romans, and that later painters based their poses on classical models.

NCR Schoolhouse (see Plate 313)

National Cash Register (NCR) has been a major economic force in Dayton, Ohio, for many decades. NCR was formed in 1884, with the company producing only one product: cash registers. Today the name is just as often associated with computers, data processing, telecommunications, semiconductors, software, and business forms. John Henry Patterson was instrumental in the early development of NCR. He had been in the dry goods business in Ohio in the early 1800s, but had run into economic difficulty because business clerks were not recording sales and were taking the money! James and John Ritty, of Dayton, Ohio, had recently started a company (NCR) that made a machine called a cash register, which Patterson correctly saw could change his employee theft problems handily, and he immediately purchased two of the innovative devices. In 1882 the company was renamed National Manufacturing Company.

Prior to 1884, NCR had sold less than 500 machines per year. Within two years of Patterson's leadership, the company was selling more than 1,000 machines per year, and employees had increased from only a dozen to over 100. A company newspaper, *Output*, was published beginning in the late 1880s and included sales, details of cash register advantages, and testimonials from satisfied customers.

The 1890s were difficult economic times in the U.S., requiring a scaling-down of the company, but thanks to skillful management which included intense advertising and heavy patent defenses, competitors had been reduced from more than 80 in 1887 to less than three. By the early 1900s, NCR had more than 1,000 employees, occupying foreign sites including Norway, New Zealand, and China.

Up until 1906, all NCR cash registers were manually operated. Charles F. Kettering developed the very first electric cash register, which dramatically spurred sales.

By 1912, the NCR company so dominated the cash register marketplace that an antitrust suit, initiated by the complaint of the American Cash Register Company, was filed, and multiple officers of the company were initially found guilty of trade restraint and monopoly, a decision which was reversed 2 years later by a higher court.

By 1913, the city of Dayton suffered a flood, and NCR found a fond place in the hearts of citizens when production was suspended to provide relief and shelter for local citizens in NCR buildings. Through World War I, the company was active in production, but as with most other manufacturing concerns, focus was diverted to materials pertinent to the war.

Post-war production found NCR controlling more than 90% of the cash register market, but as competitors eroded their control, they diversified into other accounting machines. In 1921 John Henry Patterson (who died in 1922) passed the company presidency on to his son Frederick.

Progressive right moves for the next few years were eventually counteracted by the Depression, during which NCR nearly went bankrupt. Edward Deeds was solicited to take the helm of the flagging company. He had joined NCR around 1900, was in charge of engineering and construction of one of the new factories, and by 1910 had been vice president of NCR. In 1915 he left NCR for Delco (batteries) and later founded the Wright Airplane Company with Orville Wright (he was joined in this endeavor by Charles Kettering). After the on-set of the Depression in 1934 the company had made a turn-around. This is the time period during which the American version of NCR Schoolhouse bookends was awarded.

NCR Schoolhouse was made or distributed over at least a four-year period, since pieces from foreign contest recipients dating as early as 1927, and US recipients as late as 1931 have been seen. The material is heavy cast brass, with a plate that removes with four inset screws. Communication with the NCR company historian indicates that the "smokestack" contest for which these bookends were awarded was so titled because the employees were exhorted to get the factory smokestacks puffing away through their sales of machinery. The NCR schoolhouse was a building in which many of the company's training sessions were held. The original structure was on Main Street, Dayton, Ohio, but was torn down in the 1970s. According to Mr. West (NCR historian), the number of sets of bookends issued is not recorded, but it is his estimate that it would likely have been several hundred sets, and certainly no more than 1,000.

Pan (see Plate 1866)

The story of Pan, who in mythology is known as the great god of nature, goes something like this: Pan's father was Hermes, who was actually quite pleased with the unusual appearance of his child, despite the fact that Pan's mother, a nymph, is reported to have run away screaming at first sight of her new child. Hermes brought young Pan to Olympus, where other gods found the young god charming and amusing, rewarding him with a position in the hills of Greece as the great god of nature. Pan's assigned duties included protection of hunters, shepherds, and curly-fleeced sheep.

Apparently, Pan had a somewhat volatile disposition. When in a gloomy mood, he would habit a cool cave, and if an unfortunate traveler unwittingly crossed his path, would emit a horrifying scream of such impact that the listener would invariably flee in terror. It is from this mythological scenario that the "panic" evolved.

On the other hand, Pan had a bright side, which typically was displayed on moonlit nights at which time he was noted to play sweet and mystic tunes which enraptured nymphs and satyrs who danced and followed him through glades and forests.

The physical appearance of satyrs (defined as "one of the category of anthropomorphic woodlands gods or demons often having the pointed ears, legs, and short horns of a goat" [*American Heritage Dictionary of the English Language*, 1979, Houghton Mifflin Company, Boston]) is quite close to that of Pan, their master. Pan was very fond of nymphs, who maintained their youthful appearance for thousands of years. Echo was one of the nymphs with whom Pan fell in love, but his success with her was somewhat limited because she had the habit of constant gay chatterings, leaving little room for Pan to woo her with his music or poetry. When a curse was placed upon Echo by Hera—the ability to only repeat words of other—Pan finally had his chance. Alas, it was too late. Echo had already fallen in love with the handsome Narcissus. Pan and Echo never became a couple because she pined away for the self-

distracted Narcissus until nothing was left but her voice, which of course manifests itself today when words are shouted into mountain canyons. Pan's grief at the loss of Echo was assuaged when he met another pretty nymph called Syrinx. Syrinx was not nearly so taken with Pan as he was with her: she fled. In order to hide from him, she changed herself into a reed, which amongst the many reeds at the riverbank, made her invisible.

Hearing the whistling sound made by wind passing through the reeds, Pan cut ten reeds into unequal lengths, and made the first panpipe by tying them together. He would play the pipe and recall the voice of his intended beloved. Syrinx is the other common name applied to the panpipe. Appearances of Pan, and of satyrs, go through some evolution throughout Greek mythology. The typical satyr has a low forehead, snub nose, pointed ears, and a hairy body ending in a goat's tail with cloven hooves. Over time, the features became more smoothed into simple pointed ears with small horns, and a gentle, rather than frightening appearance

Pegasus (see Plate 1873)

The figure Pegasus is probably recognized by almost all adults, doubtless due to the popularity of the romantic notion of a flying horse, coupled with the universal familiarity of the Pegasus figure chosen by Mobil Oil Company as its official mascot, hence seen by all of us on gas stations, television advertising, or any products upon which Mobil Oil Chose to display the figure. The story of Pegasus from Greek Mythology is much less well known. It begins with Perseus, the son of Zeus, who rescued Andromeda, chained as she was to a rock by the sea. Even before saving Andromeda, Perseus was on a pilgrimage to slay Medusa (the one with snakes growing out of her head). Medusa was an ominous beast, but thanks to some pleasing gifts Perseus had given to the Nymphs of the North, he received in return three very useful tools for individuals bent upon slaying Medusas: winged sandals (enabling him to fly), a cap to make him invisible, and a magic bag that would hold whatever was put into it. Remembering that to look at the head of Medusa cost a dreadful consequence (one would be instantly turned to stone), Perseus wisely looked instead into the mirrored surface of his polished shield, and with a single stroke, cut off the head of Medusa. Once the head was severed, out of the body of the slain Medusa sprang the beautiful winged horse, Pegasus.

As one might imagine, a winged horse is quite the rarity, and became the dream of the great tamer of horses, Bellerophon, to ride such a horse. Bellerophon was the grandson of Sisyphus In a dream, the Goddess Athena provided Bellerophon a golden bridle that would make the wild and swift horse docile. Bellerophon was successful in riding Pegasus, thanks to the magic bridle, so the pair set off to fight the Chimera, a fire-breathing beast that was ravaging the kingdom of Lycia. Thanks to his clever and talented horse, Bellerophon was able to kill the Chimera, whereupon the king offered the hand of his daughter in gratitude. At the king's death, Bellerophon became king. Unfortunately, his newfound position of power went to his head, and he began to think of himself as a god. Trying to join the other gods in Olympus, he flew ever higher in the sky on Pegasus. When Bellerophon actually tried to enter Olympus, his pridefulness caused him to fall from the horse, landing in a distant country, where he wandered aimlessly as a beggar until he died. On the other hand, Pegasus did enter Olympus, and Zeus made him the official carrier of his thunderbolts, a position that Pegasus may well maintain to this day. Pegasus is typically currently most often depicted as a white horse (though the Mobil Oil symbol was often seen in red), and the pair designed by Wheeler Williams was also white. Collectors often ask about pros and cons of repainting. There is a dealer who is a "regular" at Brimfield, who routinely repaints his bookends and lamps; they are usually Frankart or Bronzart. He readily sells them, with no reduced premium compared to typically seen prices. On the other hand, just last week I purchased a pair online that I have returned because they are repainted. My own habit is NOT to repaint pairs I think I might potentially sell, but for those I intend to keep for my own enjoyment, if the quality of the finish is too poor to really enjoy them, I don't mind repainting them. I have seen the set three times, each in a mottled brown color, with gold highlights only along the bottom of the base. The brown finish has not held up well in the three sets I have seen, so this set was repainted.

Pony Express (see Plate 2328)

The original Pony Express statue is located in St Joseph, Missouri, and was dedicated April 21, 1940. It is located in St. Joseph because that is the starting point of the Pony Express. The sculpture stands 12 feet tall on its two-piece pedestal made of Vermont granite. The statue itself weights 7,200 pounds. The Jennings Brothers bookends are an exact likeness of the statue

Remington Rye (see Plate 2331)

Remington described this sculpture as "four cowboys on running horses…men shooting pistols and shouting." The artistry and sculpture is considered remarkable in that only six of the horses' 16 hooves touch the ground. The story being told in this sculpture was reflective of two prior published illustrations by the artist, in which he depicted cavorting cowboys running wild on Saturday night with pistols blazing. The title "Comin Through the Rye" refers to the disinhibition induced by whisky made from Rye, and borrows loosely from poetry by Robert

Burns. When the sculpture was purchased by the Corcoran Gallery in 1900, quite a bit of political turmoil ensued, because some patrons didn't think the title, which implied whiskey-soused cowboys, was politically correct. They asked Remington if he had any other name they might call the piece, and he said he had also called it "Off the Range". Reportedly, the gallery was appreciative of this more PC name, but as you see, the original name is the one that has withstood the test of time. Some of Remington's own words about cowboy energy go: "When he turns loose in town, he does it in a thorough way. His animation vents itself in shrieks and yells, the firing of a revolver, and the mad gallop. Every wild and lawless instinct of the cowboy seems to have their fullest development. The air is supercharged with electricity….it is imparted to his horse." Remington died December 26, 1909 of peritonitis following an emergency appendectomy.

Santa Barbara Mission (see Plate 316)

There are 21 missions along the coast of California, each one about a day's march from the next, if one is an enthusiastic marcher. Their history begins late in 1769, when Ferdinand and Isabella of Spain, having emerged successfully after decades of war, sent experienced armies to far away lands seeking riches. Hundreds of years prior, Pope Alexander VI had divided the world into two parts, half to be owned by Spain, and the other half by Portugal. Spanish territory was characterized by colonization, and included Mexico, Central America, the Caribbean, half of South America, and much of the US. The Spanish king directed the course of events in the colonies through delegates known as viceroys (= vice kings). Colonized lands were subdued by the sword, the cross, or the combination, and the clergy-military alliance was fundamental to further development. In areas where natives were docile or "receptive" to new religious beliefs or new governing authority, clergy were the pre-eminent force, accompanied by a military escort: this was the case in California.

Father Junipero Serra, a Franciscan friar, was chosen by the Spanish government to begin some settlements in southern California, which at the time was known as Alta California, to distinguish it from the Mexican peninsula Baja California just to the south. The first mission was inaugurated by Father Serra in San Diego, July 16, 1769. In 1770, the Mission at Monterey, dedicated to St. Charles of Borromeo was established, and the presiding officer-clergy of both was Father Junipero Serra. The great distance between these two missions (500 miles), and the need for many more personnel to develop religious interest in the native populations prompted development of a whole chain of missions, radiating out from the two original ones in San Diego and Monterey.

The Santa Barbara Mission was the 10th California

mission, founded December 4, 1786. The third church at the site had been destroyed by and earthquake in 1812, necessitating that a new church be built from 1815 to 1820. The second tower was added in 1831, and this is the only California mission distinguished with two similar towers.

Spirit of Ecstasy (see Plate 1255)

The first Rolls-Royce mascot (also called "hood ornament") appeared in 1911. The origination of the mascot followed a craze for applying such ornamentation to cars, both as adornment on the hood and the gas-cap. The sculptor Charles Sykes was commissioned by Rolls-Royce founder/creator Claude Johnson to create a fitting mascot, and was taken for a ride in the vehicle, whereupon "....inspired by its power, silence, and grace [he] quickly knocked out the famous statue." The Spirit of Ecstasy, in one form or another, has been on the Rolls-Royce ever since. There have been a diversity of business enterprises that have pirated the figure for their own uses, but Rolls-Royce maintains a department specifically to deal with such improprieties amounting to as many as 700 cases per year. The model for Spirit of Ecstasy is believed to be Eleanor Velasco Thornton, who was one of Sykes' favorite models. Ms. Thornton was also the mother of a child born to Sir John Scott Montagu, one of the co-founders of Rolls-Royce, who had introduced Charles Sykes to Claude Johnson in the original discussion that lead to the Spirit of Ecstasy sculpture.

All Spirits of Ecstasy mascots were signed by Charles Sykes through 1951, but no longer bear his signature. Through 1948, all the sculptures were actually produced by Charles Sykes and a team of his craftsmen, but after that time Rolls-Royce produced them themselves in their division known as the Precision Components division. The first mascot was 7" tall. In the 1930s, Mr. Royce felt that it was too conspicuous at that height, so a kneeling version was developed which appeared in 1934, but the standing Spirit of Ecstasy has been the most commonly seen ornament in all years. From 1911 to 1914, the mascot was silver plated, but rumor had it that they were solid silver, prompting a rash of thievery which stimulated engineering developments like hood ornaments which disappeared beneath the surface of the hood.

The hood ornaments are made of copper-zinc-nickel alloys, and most recently, stainless steel. The description of the manufacturing method in Rolls-Royce/The Complete Works is as follows: "Every mascot is made by the ancient lost wax casting method: a wax model is made by pouring molten wax into a jelly mold of the original sculpture. This wax model is then banished by hand—this is why no two mascots are exactly the same—and then set in a plaster cast. Molten metal is then poured into the cast, flowing into the space left by the wax as it melts out." The final

polishing of the mascot is done with powdered cherry stones. For the first 17 years of production, Mr. Sykes himself checked each mascot personally, with ultimate discretion about which pieces were rejected or accepted.

My favorite apocryphal story about Rolls Royce also comes from *Rolls-Royce/The Complete Works:*

"The classic, and most often repeated, piece of Rolls—Royce apocrypha dates from the 1930s, but is born anew with each model. An owner is driving a Corniche in the South of France, and incredibly, his rear axle breaks. After a phone call to the nearest distributor, two men fly in from England, and in less than twenty-four hours the offending part is replaced and the astonished owner is on is way. He is even more astonished not to receive a bill. Being, like all Rolls-Royce owners, an honest man, he writes asking for one. The reply: 'We have no record of the incident to which you refer. Rolls-Royce axles do not break'."

Statue of Liberty (see Plate 2096)

Frederic Auguste Bartholdi (b. August 2, 1834), the sculptor of SOL, was raised in Alsace, France, though his family was originally of Italian origin. His career as a sculptor was catapulted to prominence when he received a commission at age 18 to produce a monument in honor of General Jean Rapp, one of Napoleon's marshals, for the city of Colmar, France.

In 1871 Bartholdi made a visit to the U.S. aided by letters of introduction which led to meetings with such influential individuals as President Ulysses S. Grant and Henry Wadsworth Longfellow, with whom he shared his idea that a monument should be created of a harbor lighthouse in the U.S. shedding light on liberty to enlighten the Old World. His monument was to be titled "Liberty Enlightening the World."

To raise money for the project, lottery ticket sales were added to a six-year campaign of fund raising which ultimately achieved the $400,000 needed to cover the construction costs.

The model for Liberty was none other than the sculptor's mother. Originally, with plaster statues only four feet high as prototypes, SOL was depicted as a draped women holding a torch in her left hand, and lacked the spiked crown. He was assisted in structural planning for SOL by Alexandre Gustave A. Eiffel, who would later achieve fame for designing the Eiffel tower. Eiffel had proposed that the statue be composed of iron, with sheets of bronze attached. Because the size of the statue precluded the too-weighty bronze plates originally intended, copper was ultimately substituted. French supporters watched Bartholdi create a 36-foothigh version of SOL, from which the final 150-foot statue was transferred. Once dismantled, Liberty was carried by the French warship Isere to New York, in May 1885. The Isere arrived to transfer the statue parts to

Bedloe's island on May 17, 1885.

President Grover Cleveland presided over the inauguration ceremony of Liberty which occurred on October 28, 1886. Bedloe's island had originally been devised (1806 – 1811) as a defense post against naval attack upon New York. It had been abandoned in 1877, leaving a ready home for Liberty. It was not until the 1950s that a museum to commemorate immigrant contributions to American life was developed and housed in the base of the Statue of Liberty.

In 1903 a plaque was added to the statue with poetry by Emma Lazarus of which most of us only recall the popular lines "…give me your tired, your poor, your huddled masses…." The poem titled "The New Colossus," which reflected upon the increasingly important flow of immigrants who disembarked at nearby Ellis Island, is printed in entirety below:

> Not like the brazen giant of Greek fame,
> With conquering limbs astride from land to land;
> Here at our sea-washed, sunset gates shall stand
> A mighty woman with a torch, whose flame
> Is the imprisoned lightning, and her name
> Mother of Exiles. From her beacon-hand
> Glows world-wide welcome; her mild eyes command
> The air-bridged harbor that twin cities frame.
> "Keep, ancient lands, your storied pomp!" cries she
> With silent lips. " Give me your tired, your poor,
> Your huddled masses yearning to breathe free,
> The wretched refuse of your teeming shore.
> Send these, the homeless, tempest-tost to me,
> I lift my lamp beside the golden door!
> [Reference: Handlin O. *Statue of Liberty,* Newsweek
> Book Division, New York 1971

USS Vulcan (see Plate 2080)

Vulcan was the Roman god of fire and metalworking (also known to Greeks as Hephaestus). Venus and he were an item at one time. The story of the USS Vulcan is as follows.

"Shipbuilding begun on 16 December 1939 at Camden, NJ. By the New York Shipbuilding Copr; launched on 11 December 1940, sponsored by Mrs. James Forrestal, wife of the Under Secretary of the Navy, and commissioned at the Philadelphia Navy Yard on 14 June 1941, Comdr. Leon S. Fiske in command…In July 1941, at the request of Icelandic government, the United States had occupied Iceland—the strategic island which, as the German geopolitician Karl Haushofer wrote, lay pointed 'like a pistol…at the United States'–and had established bases at the barren ports of Reykjavik and Hvalfjordur. Marine wags soon nicknamed these places 'Rinky Dink' and 'Valley Forge,' respectively. During the midwatch on 17 October 1941, U-68 torpedoed the USS Kearney while the latter was screening Convoy SC-48. With 11 bluejackets dead, Kearny limped into Reykjavik, a gaping hole and buckled plating disfiguring her starboard side below and aft of the bridge. Vulcan provided timely and effective assistance to the stricken warship. Since permanent repair facilities were nonexistent, Kearny pulled up alongside the repair vessel, and her port side was flooded to raise the torpedo hole above the water level. Soon, Vulcan's repair force had cut away the damaged plating and had fixed a patch. By Christmas 1941, Kearny could sail for the east coast and permanent repairs at Boston…., [in Algiers on June 27] , Vulcan sent a fire and rescue party to the burning British ammunition ship Arrow. Three Vulcan sailors brought a boat alongside the flaming vessel and cut through her side plating to rescue British sailors trapped below decks. For their bravery and resourcefulness, the trio from the repair ship received decorations from the British government and Navy and Marine Corps medals. Vulcan remained based on the North African coast into the summer of 1944. In August and September, the repair ship supported the invasion of southern France and received her sole battle star for providing repair services to the ships and craft involved in the operation. "When American intelligence pinpointed the presence of Russian missiles in Cuba in the fall of 1962, the United States and the Soviet Union stood 'eyeball to eyeball' in the Caribbean. Vulcan sailed to San Juan, where she provided essential repair services to the ships operating on the 'quarantine' line off Cuban shores to prevent the arrival of any further Russian military equipment."

In 1978, she became the first U.S. Navy ship to have women permanently stationed aboard. Vulcan was decommissioned in 1991. [also see www.lib.odu.edu/aboutlib/spccol/Vulcan.shtml]. Our bookends in addition to being inscribed "USS Vulcan" and "AR-5," are imprinted on the base "Presented to CWO4 Russell W. Golding From R-2 Division" CWO stands for Chief Warrant Officer.

Sculptors, Artists, and Designers

Just Andersen

Just Andersen was born in Greenland in 1884 and died in 1943, and was a well-known sculptor in Scandinavia. In Denmark he was particularly prominent. From my conversation with an antiques dealer in Copenhagen, Just's works are highly recognized. And were quite popular in the 1930s. He is reported have been a prominent designer of bronze and silver jewelry, distributed through showrooms in New York, Los Angeles, and London. In addition to the pair of bookends, St George and the Dragon, he is credited with figural elephant bookends. His signature is simply "JUST."

Leo Hendrik Baekeland

The inventor of Bakelite, Leo Hendrik Baekeland, was a Belgian chemist who was seeking a new kind of shellac or varnish to be used in bowling alleys, whose popularity was rapidly expanding at the turn of the century. In 1907, his mixture of phenol and formaldehyde was an attempt to develop a resin that, after hardening wouldn't melt, which he called "phenolic." Since this chemical is very resistant to electrical current as well as heat and harsh chemicals, the product was appealing to industry in uses like electrical wiring sheaths. Baekeland himself dubbed his product "the material of a thousand uses."

At its introduction in the Art Deco period as a component of jewelry, the product was highly valued, as opposed to the plebian status of plastics that followed in the 1940s. Initially, the product was manufactured only in amber, the color of unadulterated phenolic. Subsequently, addition of dyes developed a variety of colors and even tortoiseshell patterns. When the patent expired on Bakelite in 1927, several other companies (Englishtown, Sta-Brite, Freehold, A & J Kitchen Tool Co, and others) were ready to produce less expensive versions of the now wildly popular product. The America Catalin Corporation modified the manufacturing process to cast the plastic rather than mold it, by pouring it into lead molds and allowing hardening. Their casting techniques greatly reined the appearance of the product. When World War II diverted utilization of many chemicals to military use, production of the Catalin plastics became prohibitively expensive and manufacture dwindled.

Bakelite collectors can often distinguish this product from other plastics simply inspection characteristics, but less experienced individuals may consider specific testing techniques. Probably the easiest identification method is to use pink Simichrome metal polish in a thin layer on the surface of the plastic, which will turn mustard yellow when its ammonia reacts with the bakelite. Scrubbing Bubbles (Dow Chemicals) will also produce this reaction, but is reported to be more destructive to the surface of the bakelite. Local application of heat to the surface of Bakelite produces a characteristic odor due to release of carbolic acid. Hot tap water or even friction from fingers can release this scent, which dissipates quickly as soon as the local heat diminishes. For Bakelite products in general, blue is the most prized color.

Antoine-Louis Barye

Barye was born in Paris in 1796. His upbringing appears to have been in modest surroundings, as it is reported he did not learn to red until the age of 12. Barye did not receive any formal schooling. His first exposure to metal working began with his apprenticeship to a die maker named Fourrier who produced such items as uniform buttons and military decorations. Barye was employed here until he was almost 17, and during this time developed his interest in the art of medal engraving and subsequently, sculpture. He was drafted in 1812, and as fortune would have it, was attached to a corps of engineers which involved him in topographical modeling.

After leaving the military, Barye entered the studio of an art academician named Bosio, and it is said that Barye's aversion for the artificiality of academic art drove him in the totally opposite direction of traditional advice. By 1819, Barye had undertaken a very serious study of nature, stimulated by an interest in animals as art objects. He repeatedly, and often unsuccessfully, entered his animal sculptures into local art competitions. It was not until the 1830s, when the son of the French monarch became a patron of Barye, that public recognition and commissions of his work began to flow. By the 1850s, his works had become diversely known and he assumed posts such as Professor of Zoological Drawing at the Jardin des Plantes of the Museum of Natural History in Paris. Barye produced hundreds of noteworthy pieces, mostly through the lost wax or sand casting method. Barye remained artistically productive through his seventies, continuing to produce museum-quality sculptures only a few years before his death in 1875. In 1873, 120 of his bronzes were purchased by WT Walters for the Corcoran Gallery in Washington, DC.

Clio Hinton Honecker Bracken

Clio Bracken (1870 – 1925) studied art under Chapu, Carpeaux, and Saint-Gaudens. She is the sculptor of other well-known works, including statues of Generals Fremont and Pershing.

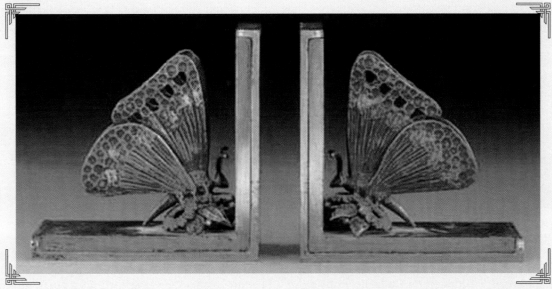

Plate 4. Brandt's Butterflies, ca. 1929, Edgar Brandt, iron, size not stated, marked "E Brandt," rarity: 5*, $24,000.00. *Photo Courtesy © 2004 Artists Rights Society (ARS) New York/ADAGP Paris.*

Edgar Brandt

Edgar Brandt's name is not well known amongst bookend collectors, yet the charming pair shown on our cover, Brandt's Butterflies provides ample reason to reconsider why works by this artist should find widespread acclaim! I first saw this pair in an article with a commentary in *Maine Antique Digest* (June 2004, 1-E), where I learned that they had been auctioned by Christie's South Kensington, at the quite remarkable price of $24,055!! The description of the pair describes "…the pair of ferrous and lepidopterous bookends…" I am uncertain just what 'lepidopterous' includes, but somehow, Brandt has provided memorable elegance in iron with this pair. Our thanks to Maine Antique Digest, Artists Rights Society, and Christie's South Kensington for allowing us to share this photograph with you.

Edgar Brandt was born in Paris on Christmas Eve, 1880. He entered a technical high school at age 14, where he learned the art of ironwork, including industrial design and decorative ornament as well as general blacksmithing.Both Edgar and his brother graduated from the Vierzon technical school in 1898. For their graduation projects, each brother forged a wrought-iron rose, which is reportedly a possible tribute to their father, for whom roses were a particular gardening interest.

Brandt fulfilled his army obligation for two years after graduation. Then in 1901 he began his first studio, where he produced small items, primarily jewelry. Within a few years, his scope of work expanded to include mirrors, signs, fireplace equipment, and more. At this time he began exhibiting both his iron work and ability to create furniture at French Art Salons. Brandt worked in numerous metals, including bronze, silver, copper, and gold. In 1912, Brandt was commissioned to provide a grand staircase for the Pavilion Mollien in the Louvre, and numerous public and private structures continued to seek his artistic ironwork over succeeding years.

During World War I, Brandt was instrumental in the design and development of a new form of mortar, which was employed subsequently in the Battle of Verdun and in Champagne. After the war, in 1918 he returned to peace-time artistic productions, opening a new studio in 1920. By this time, Brandt's works were well established in France. He was commissioned to provide ironwork for the newly designed "Unknown Soldier" monument near the Arc de Triomphe, inaugurated in 1927.

The Exposition des Arts Decoratifs et Industrials Modernes is often recognized as a sentinel event in the development of what we now call Art Deco. Works by Edgar Brandt at this exposition gained him an international reputation, and his craftsmanship was displayed at multiple different pavilions. His popular studio ultimately was closed in 1933, at the recommendation of his son-in-law, because of the Depression. He continued to display his works at the Salon des Artistes until 1932. Wrought iron products were losing fashion by the 1930s. Brandt continued working in iron as late as the 1950's when he participated in restoration of wrought-iron grilles at the Chateau de Versailles. He died in Geneva, Switzerland, in 1960.

The book *Edgar Brandt. Master of Art Deco Ironwork*, although lavishly completed with literally hundreds of photographs of diverse works by Brandt, contains only two sets of bookends, dated in the 1927 – 1931 time period.

Demetre Chiparus

Demetre Chiparus was born in Dorohoi, Romania, on September 16, 1886 to Haralamb and Saveta Chiparus. A brother, his only sibling, was reported to have been assassinated as part of political conflict. The family was quite well-to-do and was regarded as amongst the aristocracy of wealthy land owners. The young Demetre was fluent in French, the language used at the dinner table in his home, as was dictated by the fashion at the time for families of his status. His first departure from his native land, which was also his final one, occurred at the age of 22 when he left for Italy to study sculpture. His passport indicated a four month travel allowance, but he never returned home. Chiparus supported himself with a fund from his mother's inheritance until he was 38, enabling him to be free to study and develop skills in sculpture, drawing, painting, and ceramics.

Chiparus studied in Florence with Raffaello Romanelli, a sculptor whose commissions included works sent to the United States, England, Austria, Cuba, and Romania. In 1912 Chiparus left Italy for France to study at the most renowned fine arts school in Europe, the Ecole Nationale Superieure de Beaux-Arts, joining another Romanian artist destined to have widespread influence as a sculptor, Constantin Brancuse. Chiparus met his wife, Julienne, in 1924 while she was working as a clerk in a perfume shop. He was sixteen years older than she. Julienne had been raised in an orphanage due to the untimely death of her father.

Chiparus sculpted a wide variety of exotic poses of women, often directly selecting his models from Paris music hall theatrical productions in particular. Popular magazines of the times depicted lavish photographs of music hall dancers, direct sources of subject matter for Chiparus' work. He sculpted in bronze, marble, plaster, and of course, the format for which he became most noteworthy, chryselephantine (bronze and ivory). His style was prototypic of Art Deco, which we often date to the 1925 pairs International Exposition. Oriental and Egyptian influences are often reflected in his works.

Chiparus was able to live throughout much of his life in a very lavish fashion, but with the approach of World War II, most of the Parisian founders who produced his works were Jewish, and they were forced out of business. This progressively more narrow market for production of his pieces forced an economic revision of his circumstances, so that he moved from his plush three-story home to a more modest apartment in 1936. A protracted war further depleted Chiparus' opportunities for sale of his works, forcing the couple to sell much of their personal possessions and move to a one room apartment. It was during this relatively impoverished period that Chiparus began to sculpt animals at the local Vicennes zoo. Even

though there was little market for his works, and economic prosperity was a thing of the past, his widow reports that he was generally of good spirits and continued to sculpt for his own pleasure on a consistent basis. Chiparus suffered a stroke on January 19, 1947, to which he succumbed three days later.

Leopold Dreifuss

Leopold Dreifuss' studios were located in San Francisco, California. They produced bronze bookends, marked with "L.D." and a copyright symbol.

Abastenia St. Leger Eberle

Ms. Eberle was born in Webster City, Iowa, in 1878 and died in 1942. She lived most of her life in the northeast predominantly New York City, and Southport, Connecticut. In New York, she studied at the Art Students League, producing works including portrait sculpture and fountains. In 1915 she exhibited at the Panama-Pacific Exposition. Some of her work is on display at the Metropolitan Museum of Art, the Newark Museum, the Peabody Art Collection, the Worcester A. Museum, the Chicago Art Institute, the Carnegie Institute, and the Toledo Art Museum, among others.

Laura Gardin Fraser

Laura Gardin Fraser (1889 – 1966) was born in the Chicago area and raised in New York. Even as a young adult, her mother encouraged her artistic talents, and she produced portraits and sculptures. In her first and last years of enrollment in the Art Students League she won the Saint-Gaudens Medal. She joined the faculty of the Art Students league in 1920, where she worked with James Earl Fraser, who she subsequently married (1913). Ms. Fraser is the first woman to design a coin for the U.S. Treasury. She designed the statue of Robert E. Lee and Stonewall Jackson that stands in Wyman Park, Baltimore, Maryland, the relief panels at the entrance to the West Point Library, and the Pegasus.

Hagenauer

Authors' lives would be simpler if there were just one Hagenauer, but Carl, Karl, Franz, and Grette Hagenauer all had some hand in the metal crafting business. The Hagenauer workshop was begun by Carl, who lived from 1872 to 1928, in Vienna, Austria. Many of his works are marked "Wien" (means "Vienna"). Hagenauer's initial products were tablewares, lamps, mirrors, and vases, but in the 1920 to 1930 period their stylized streamlined figurines became very popular throughout Europe. Karl is the eldest son of the founding father. Karl joined his father in the company in 1919 , and was later accompanied by his brother Franz (1906 – 1986) and sister Grette,

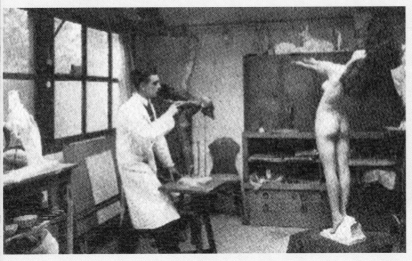

Plate 5. Max Le Verrier in his studio sculpting from one of the three live models which he used to develop "Clarte," one of his most famous sculptures, also shared by his great-grandson, Damien. Photo courtesy of Damien Blanchet–Le Verrier.

who helped manage the company upon their father's death in 1928. By this time, the company was known as Hagenauer Werkstatte. The firm produced bronzes and small sculptures designed by Carl and other designers including Josef Hoffman, Otto Prutscher, and E.J. Meckel. Son Karl (1898 – 1956) began in the firm designing silver, bronze, copper, enamel, ivory, stone, and wood domestic wares. Franz began as a belt-buckle maker, and progressed to copper and bronze sculpture. He is the designer of the Austrian parliament building state coat-of-arms. Hagenauer pieces are usually marked with a "wHw" insignia, which stands for Weiner Hagenauer Werkstatte (Viennese Hagenauer Workshop).

Max Le Verrier

Max Le Verrier was the primary figure in an art design studio in Paris. The term "Art Deco" evolved from the 1925 Paris Exposition Internationale des Arts Decoratifs et Industriels Modernes, where the new style was widely displayed.

Gracing the cover of this book is "The Fruit Gatherer" by Max Le Verrier. The French title of this pair is "Cuillette," which means fruit picker or gatherer. Through the generosity of Damien Blanchet-Le Verrier (grandson of Max Le Verrier), we have recently obtained a substantially greater insight into Max Le Verrier and his works. Damien shares the following information:

"My great-grandfather Max Le Verrier, was born in Neuilly-sur-Seine on January 29, 1891. He was really attracted for drawing and sculpture, nonetheless he had a very strong fascination for aviation. That's why he decided to go to England where he passed his pilot

license in 1911. In 1914, during the First World War he was called up and held a rank. Then he went to the 'Beaux Arts' in Geneva with the famous sculptors Pierre le Faguays, and Bouraine who will be his friends during all his life. In 1919, he came back to France where he opened his own studio and realized his first sculpture: the famous 'Pelican.' It was the start of a large collection. In 1926, he opened his company holding a gold medal from the decorative artists exhibition dated back to 1925. It is his 'animal' period: panthers, lions, monkeys, horses…"

"In 1928, he sculptured his famous 'Clarte' ("the woman with a ball") from a live model. For that he needed three models: one to sit for the head, the other for the bust, and the last one for the legs (an American black woman who danced in Josephine Baker's ballets). Then he settled down in 1933 at 32 Rue Depardeux in the 14th arrondissement in Paris. Not only did Max le Verrier realize and edit his own work, but he also dealt with other sculptors' work. In 1944, he was arrested by Petain's militiamen as he was a great resistant. When France was liberated he reopened his studio and carved new models drawing his inspiration from the Greek, and Egyptian antique period. In 1955 the tireless sculptor realized a new range of animals edited in a small size. Until his last breath, he sculptured and realized a small panther before he died on June 6, 1973. His second son, Jean Paul Le Verrier kept leading the company and carving many humoristic sculptures until 1995. After my grandfathers death in 1996, I decided to keep taking care of this familial work."

The Fruit Gatherer is very consistent with other works of Le Verrier in styling. The strong greens visible in patination are typical of bronzes by the Le Verrier foundry,

Plate 6. Fruit Gatherer, ca. 1930, Le Verrier, bronze, 6½", M. Le Verrier, rarity 5, 1930, $1,100.00; current production, $500.00.

Plate 7. Pegasus (Le Verrier), ca. 1925, Le Verrier, bronze, 7", marked Le Verrier Paris, rarity 5, 1925, $1,100.00.

though there have been other pieces seen with a diffusely green finish, and no bronze undertones penetrating through. The Le Verrier Factory is currently producing bookends, using the same molds that were utilized in the 1920s and 1930s. There are no markings to distinguish the older from the newer pieces, so buyers should seek the provenance of the piece from the seller. Signs of metal deterioration in the screws affixing the figure to the base would suggest an older pair, as would a "paper" base cover: many 1920 – 1930 French bookends have a wallpaper-like covering over the bottom of the bookend marble. I have seen this in all sorts of solid covers, patterns, etc. Since the bronze figure screwed to the marble base of bookends would not uncommonly become loose, you may see holes in the bottom paper that the owner punctured in order to access the screws and tighten the figure.

Pegasus (Le Verrier), is another treat from the Le Verrier Foundry. We may have to rely upon folks who really know their horses to tell us if the posture depicted in Le Verrier's Pegasus is a real life one…I don't recall seeing horses sitting back on their hind feet like that….but perhaps more is to be expected of winged horses. A detailed explanation of the origins of Pegasus in Greek Mythology is found in Bookend Collector Club newsletter April/May/June 2002.

Joseph Lorenzl

Lorenzl (1892 – 1950) was an Austrian sculptor who was most prolific in producing sculptures of lithe women in the Art Deco style. Numerous chryselephantine (bronze and ivory) compositions of his are known. Recognized signatures of Lorenzl include "Lorenzl," "Lor," and "Renzl."

Hermon Atkins MacNeil

McNeil (1866 – 1947) pursued training in sculpture with Henri Chapu and Alexandre Falguiere in Paris in 1888. The Columbian Exposition at the World's Fair in 1904 employed his sculptural skills. Noteworthy public sculptures of his include "Ezra Fornell" at the Cornell University, and sculptures of George Washington on the Washington Arch in New York City. Other public commissions include the President McKinley Memorial Arch (Columbus, Ohio), the frieze for the Missouri state capitol, the Flushing war memorial (Long Island, New York), and the Soldiers and Sailors Monument (Albany, New York). A public park in New York City has been named after him. The Pony Express monumental sculpture (St. Josephs, Missouri), is also sculpted by him.

Jean-Francois Millet (1814 – 1875)

The artwork of Millet is a popular source for bookends, including "The Angelus Call to Prayer" and "The Gleaners." Millet was born into a peasant family in Normandy. Because of his artistic talents identified even when he was a child, he was sent to apprentice as an artist in Cherbourg and then to Paris where he studied under the artist Paul Delaroche, who did not believe the artistic ability of Millet was significant. Although his earliest artworks were of little acclaim, he moved to the village of Barbizon with his wife sometime between 1848 and 1849. While living there in the Fountainbleu Forest he began painting rural scenes with peasants that ultimately he is best remembered for. Millet is credited with bringing a grace and dignity previously not attained to simple lifestyles and peasant scenes. Though his paintings were not universally admired during his lifetime, luminaries like Vincent van Gogh recognized and praised his remarkable talents. "The Angelus Call to Prayer" painting, painted 1857 – 1859, is housed in the Louvre, Paris.

Roland Paris

Roland Paris was born in Vienna, Austria, in 1894, and worked in Berlin. He was a student of Henry van de Velde at the Academie in Weimar, Germany. Many of his sculptures are whimsical or even parodies. Probably his most famous is a bronze titled "Mephisto," a bronze and ivory sculpture.

Frederic Remington

Remington was born October 4, 1861, to Seth Pierre and Clara Sacrider Remington in Canton, New York. At the age of 12 he moved to Ogdensburg, New York, where his father received an appointment as collector of the Port. In 1875 he enrolled at the Vermont Episcopal Institute, in Burlington, Vermont, and the following year at Highland Military Academy in Worcester, Massachusetts.

At age 27 Remington enrolled at the Yale College School of Art, but only attended three semesters there. A little over a year after the death of his father, in February 1880, Remington made his first trip to the west during a Montana Territory vacation. Within six months of that visit, his first illustrations were published in *Harper's Weekly.* In 1883 Remington purchased a sheep ranch near Peabody, Kansas, but a year later moved into Kansas City, where he first invested in a hardware store, then in a saloon. In October of 1884, he married Eva Caten of Gloversville, New York, and returned with his bride to Kansas City, but only briefly. A year later he moved to Brooklyn, New York. Remington's first art exhibitions were subsequent to travels through North Dakota, Montana, Wyoming, and western Canada, at the American Watercolor Society and National Academy of Design (1887). By 1888 Remington was becoming internationally known, and he won a silver medal at the 1889 Paris International Exposition. Surprisingly, his first sculpture (Broncho Buster) was not copyrighted until 1895. By 1900 he had established a relationship with Roman Bronze Works, of New York to do his castings, and he continued this relationship through 1989, for the last of his important sculptures, "The Stampede." All castings done with Roman Bronze Works were done by the lost wax method.

Robert Garret Thew

The following information comes from the newspaper obituary, March 3, 1964, about Mr. Thew: "Robert Garret Thew, 71, of 45 Roseville Road, Westport, prominent artist, died Monday morning in Norwalk Hospital.

Throughout his career, which ran from advertising to design of industrial plants and bric-a-brac and returned to painting only a year ago, he sought 'to discover new and contemporary beauty.'

His goal was also 'color and spontaneity rather than traditional tonal perfections.'

Born in Sharon, he was educated at Syracuse University and the Art students League of New York City.

He studied with John Carlson and discussed art and exhibited locally with George Bellows, Eugene Spelcher and Alexander Brooks.

He then became associated with J. Walter Thompson Co, New York City advertising firm as a commercial artist.

During World War I, he was a camouflage expert with the U.S. Army. He moved to Westport in 1923 and worked with the design of various New England manufacturing plants. In 1927 he formed Garret Studios, creating and selling lamp bases, custom signs, weather vanes, and sundials."

Dirk Van Erp

Dirk Van Erp was born January 1, 1860 in Frieland, Netherlands. Dirk was one of seven children, who learned from his father the craft of chopper working. His father made cans, pots, and milk cans for dairy farmers and women's home use. He immigrated to the United States in 1886, choosing a community with established Dutch population in which to settle: Merced, California. Several years later he moved to San Francisco, employed as a coppersmith at Union Iron Works. There he met and married Mary Richardson Marino, a divorced woman with children.

The couple soon moved to Benicia, California, where Dirk transiently worked in a plumbing and hardware business, but soon sought a return to San Francisco (1896), where Dirk rejoined Union Iron Works.

Soon afterwards, Dirk was attracted to the Alaska gold rush, and left his young wife and children behind to seek fortune. In the first few weeks of his escapade, 75 men died, and then an avalanche killed another 175 men. His search for gold was not successful, and after about a year in the Klondike, he returned once more to Union Iron Works.

In 1900, Van Erp was working at Mare Island Naval Shipyards, and was forming attractive brass and copper vessels made from shell casings hammered into handsome useful products. Local gift shops and art dealers sought his work, so that by 1908 Van Erp moved to Berkeley, and opened his own Copper Shop at 1760 12th Street, in Oakland. From that time forward, he spent his life designing works of copper and brass. In 1910, he began collaborating with Elizabeth D'Arcy Gaw, a Canadian with experience in crafting arts. They established a partnership. Works produced in their partnership are marked with a windmill and the names "D'Arcy Gaw, Dirk Van Erp."

Two of Van Era's children, Agatha and Harry, pursued advanced training in art. The Van Erp studios had a going out-of-business sale in 1942, but reopened after World War II, continuing in business until the death of his son William in 1977.

Walter Von Nessen

Walter Von Nessen is one of the most admired designers for Chase Metal Works. Von Nessen came to the U.S. from Germany in 1923, with artistic design accomplishments including the redesign of the Berlin subway station interiors. One of his first creations, at his own Nessen Studio in New York, was the swing-arm lamp, but he also made mirrors, tables, lamps, and bookends. His ingenuity is described by a fellow designer at Chase, Lurelle Guild: "He took some brass plumbing elbow joints, designed some amusing heads and tails to attach in the prescribed places, planted them on firm bases, and Chase added to their line some of the doggiest, cattiest, and horsiest bookends you ever saw….and they're selling." No one has ever discovered the "doggiest" bookend to which Mr. Guild alludes.

Wheeler Williams

Wheeler Williams is recognized as a sculptor, painter and lithographer. He was born in Chicago and pursued art study at Yale University and Ecole des Beaux Arts, Paris. His works of public note include sculpture at the entrance to the Holland Tunnel and the tablet to the French Explorers and Pioneers, Michigan Avenue, Chicago. One of his most popular sculpture endeavors was titled "The Children of the Gods" in which he presented small children, perhaps age 2-3, as they might appear to the artist's eye. Eight separate sculptures depicting the most famous Greek deities were produced in monumental size as garden sculpture. Wheeler Williams was born in 1897 and died in 1972. The Pegasus Skyward bookends with which we are familiar was originally a monumental sculpture, at least 7 feet tall!

Descriptions about Bookends

For each set of bookends, information is presented in a similar fashion: name, date, maker, material, size, markings, rarity, and value. We have already discussed names and classification of names.

Date is established from catalogs as well as our experience in establishing dates from the thousands of bookends both of us have examined. Because most bookends are not dated, readers can expect some divergence of dates, and the notation "ca" in front of a date indicates "circa," meaning within a period of a few years from that date. The most difficult pieces to date are jade, ivory, wares manufactured in Asia, and glass. Readers are cautioned to deal with experts or reputable established dealers before embarking upon significant investments in difficult-to-date pairs.

Maker is established through catalogs, paper company tags, and sometimes even the design of the piece. For example, Ronson produced a burgundy bronze-tone finish that no one else employed, so that experienced bookend collectors can identify Ronson pairs by this finish alone! Similarly, Ronson made metal bases for their bookends that have a "marbleized" finish (made to appear like marble), which again distinguishes their works immediately. Several companies have never been confirmed by name, but are instead identified simply by "X." For instance, Butterfly Girl, Loie, and Read to Me were all clearly created by the same manufacturer. Each is characterized by similar casting styles, identical color combinations, and typical ornate book rest (the rear of the bookend) markings, including an item number embossed on the bookend. Hence, this company, though we do not know its name, is represented as "X-1," so that you will be able to identify all the bookends made by this same maker.

Material: To be effectively involved in collecting bookends, you must become familiar with detecting the four primary categories of bookend material: iron, gray metal, bronze, and bronze-clad. Iron is the simplest: any material that attracts a typical refrigerator magnet *must* be iron, no matter what appearance it has. Some bookends do indeed have a coat of bronze, silver, or copper added to the finish above iron, but the bookend is nonetheless regarded as iron. Gray metal is known by several names, including spelter, white metal, pot metal, type metal, and others.

Because gray metal has a lower melting point than other commonly used metals, it was easy to rapidly manufacture goods that had the same visual appeal as bronze or iron, but were much less expensive and required less intricate machinery for manufacture. Since bronze (and bronze-clad) bookends do not attract a magnet, collectors (and sometimes, unfortunately, even dealers) mistake gray metal with a bronze finish for bronze. When the surface of gray metal is scratched with a hard object, a silvery-gray material is seen. Bronze will scratch yellow-gold. Gray metal is most commonly hollow, and the surface inside will be silver colored. There are rare exceptions of "white bronze," but such differentiation should be left to experts if there is any question, since bronze items consistently are much more highly valued than gray metal objects of the same configuration. Bronze-clad items (also called weighted-bronze, plaster-filled bronze, bronze-coated, bronze-armored, Galvano bronze, electroformed bronze) were very popular in the world of bookends from about 1905 to 1935, and only a single manufacturer, Marion Bronze, continued their manufacture after World War II, because it is an expensive and time-intensive method of production. bronze-clad items can be recognized by lightly tapping the side of the material, whence it will be noted that there is a layer of metal upon a solid plaster base. Bronze-clad, like bronze, will scratch yellow-gold.

Markings are listed as they appear on the bookend, with the occasional omission of a prominent title on a bookend. For instance, if a bust of George Washington says "WASHINGTON" in prominent letters on the front, that may be omitted from our description, since it is self-evident. Other inscriptions such as date, copyright symbol, sculptor's signature, or other marks are generally included. Because not all manufacturers placed the same mark on both members of a pair, the fact that markings are not present on your pair is not proof-positive that your bookends are not by that particular manufacturer. For instance, Connecticut Foundry bookends were first identified as such when one of the pair said "Connecticut Foundry," and the other was simply marked with their shopmark (a "C" inside a triangle, in a circle, which is commonly mistaken for a copyright symbol). Also, since sometimes manufacturers only marked one member of a pair, it is quite commonplace to find sets where both members are marked, or both members are unmarked. The only time such minutia makes much difference is when "high-end" bookends are being marketed. Most serious collectors of items like Tiffany or Hagenauer will only accept as authentic those pieces with company signatures or shopmarks. You will often hear dealers mention that the pair is "signed." This should most often indicate that the sculptor's signature is inscribed; sometimes the rubric of "signed" is extended a bit to include the foundry mark or company, so that some dealers will describe pairs marked "Tiffany" as "signed." As with signatures in any other venue, there have been some unscrupulous individuals who try to take advantage of the greater value attached to signed pairs by inscribing a signature in the base, for instance, of a pair. In the last five years, there has been frank misuse of signatures in pairs particularly from England, where incorrect (but well-known) designers' names are affixed to bookends, in an attempt to lure the unwary. It is wise to become familiar not only with the markings inscribed in metal, but also company paper tags. There have been numerous bookends identified as to source simply by the presence of part of a company paper tag. Our section on shopmarks includes many of the companies represented from 1910 – 1960.

Size is measured as greatest vertical height, in inches. Sometimes bookends are of two markedly different heights. In that circumstance, the height of the taller bookend is given. No horizontal or depth measurements are given. Even for the most exotic bronzes from France and Austria in the peak of Art Deco period (1920 – 1935), multiple sizes of the exact same figure were manufactured. There is much less existence of multiple sizes for bookends, although Ronson commonly made some of their most popular sets in at least two different sizes. Hence, sometimes you will see examples such as "Borglum's Lincoln" and "Borglum's Lincoln" (petite). Occasionally collectors have requested information on bookends to include weight. Some bronze bookends are indeed more majestic due to the combination of their artistic beauty and weightiness. However, weight should not be a primary consideration for valuation, and is not included in our descriptions.

Rarity of bookends is described on a 1-5 scale, with one being the most common, and 5 the most rare. Items which have been seen only once are designated with "5*." The concept of rarity has become completely reshaped by the existence of prominent Internet marketing. As recently as 10 years ago, the enthusiastic bookends collector, in a day-long antiquing journey might be able to visit a dozen or more shops in one locale, perhaps encountering a few dozen bookends, with a greater selection allowed by visiting antique malls. Now, on any given day one can see over 3,000 sets of bookends for sale offered by the most prominent on-line sales sites. In the past, we described rarity based upon the experience gleaned from visiting shops and shows. Since the experience gained on-line is so much more dramatically voluminous, we must defer to the marketplace forces at hand and re-define rarity based upon this much more expansive window of observation.

The rarity scale would be best described as:

1 – 2 : VERY COMMON
: Consistently available online or at antique malls at all times.

3: COMMON
: Available with regularity, typically seen several times each week on-line, found with ease in malls or shows.

4: UNCOMMON
: In online sales, may be seen as often as several times per month. Sporadically found at shows or shops

5: RARE
: In online sales, seen only a few times per year. Seen at shows and antiques shops rarely.

5*: SINGULAR
: The pair has only been seen once by the authors.

Uncategorized: some items have only been noted in company catalogs, hence they are unrated as to rarity, though obviously they fall into the categorization of 5 or more rare.

Although there are exceptions, bookends are mass-produced items. Even though an item is very rare, it is not likely to be the only existing example, as opposed to paintings and furniture.

Value is linked to a variety of indicators. The high-end items, such as Tiffany and Gorham, always seem to find an audience of appreciative and well-heeled buyers that maintain their value over many decades of experience. In the last 20 years, Art Deco items have become progressively more popular, and the price has risen accordingly. Some areas of collecting wane as their notoriety flags due to the aging of the collector market. Hence, Shirley Temple, Bing Crosby, Howdy-Doody, and other names of the first half of the twentieth century may have lost some of their following simply due to age-attrition of the interested population. My own children have heard of the Beatles, and do enjoy some of their music, but clearly don't assign any special sentimentality to them or their music. Classical art and sculpture consistently show durable appeal, so that time-honored sculpture maintains its allure when presented as bookends.

When discussing value, several generalizations apply to bookends as in any other antique market area. First and foremost, if you come upon a truly rare set that is in excellent condition, do not pass it up. You will long remember the great set you let slip by for a few dollars, while commonplace pairs cross your path again and again, and the price of the truly unusual will likely only increase over time. This implies, however, that you know what is really a premium pair. Early in collecting, most of us get caught up in simply encountering pairs we have not seen before, and their novelty attracts our attention and our wallet. It is wise to consult a reference before purchasing expensive items to ascertain whether the item is truly rare, or rely upon the advice of an experienced antiques dealer or other expert in the field.

Rarity and value are not always concordant. Some highly rare pieces, perhaps only a handful having been manufactured, are of little appeal to collectors. For instance, numerous businesses created bookends to give to sales persons as "premiums." Although such items were made in small number, they may hold little value. Surprisingly, some relatively more common bookends still command a premium, usually because of collecting convention. That is, Tiffany bookends are all valuable. Although bookends such as the Tiffany Zodiac and Tiffany Buddha are not very rare, they continue to be highly priced, it appears, simply because they fall under the large umbrella of Tiffany, which continues to have a special notoriety with collectors. As novice collectors, many of us have made the error of finding several pairs by a maker that were rare or highly valued, and falsely assuming that therefore all pairs by this maker must be valuable. As with real-estate, although there is some value-added enhancement by associating your modest house in an upscale neighborhood, a few famous makers help sustain the value of their bookends by name alone (Bradley and Hubbard, Griffoul, Gorham, Tiffany, Roycroft, Rookwood, Roseville). Most of the time, however, it is the artistry and subject matter of the pair that drives valuation.

Overall, all things being equal, bronze bookends are the most highly valued. Polychrome finishes (more than one color) are generally more valued than monochrome (one color). Figural pairs (three dimensional) are most often more valued than flat (also called "L-form"). The most expensive pair of bookends of which the authors are aware sold in 2004 for $24,000 (see photo of Brandt Butterflies). One of the very nice things about bookends is that a highly diverse collection can be built with a very modest budget. Additionally, since the number of bookend collectors is relatively small compared to most other fields of collecting, there is still ample opportunity to obtain even the choicest of bookends, with a little footwork and making your local shops aware that you are interested in bookends.

Reproductions

As recently as 1998, the issue of bookends reproductions was not a problem. That situation has changed. Numerous companies make reproductions of bookends, the most problematic of which appear to be issued in England. Unfortunately, some recent productions are not clearly advertised as such. Before investing in goods of uncertain vintage, it may be worth consulting an expert. Most of the time, the age of bookends can be discerned by an experienced eye, but it is sometimes quite challenging, and all of us have seen the newspaper headlines about world-class experts who learn that their appraisal of a work of art was foiled by a very fine job of reproduction. At the time of publication of this book, the most commonly seen reproductions are deco girls and dogs. In photographs, these items look quite similar to the originals, but on personal inspection they are usually easy to distinguish from old items.

Bookend Configurations

There are numerous "right" ways for bookends to be configured. Some items that have been clearly designated as bookends in manufacturers catalogs hardly seem to fit that description. Most commonly, bookends will have a clearly identified plane of contact with books that will allow for at least two points of vertically linear contact. However, that is not always the case, and one might wonder what manufacturers had in mind when they created pairs with oddly shaped figures, overhanging protuberances, or fragile contact points.

The three basic forms for bookends are flat, L-form, and figural. Flat bookends are simple, usually rectangular polygons, which typically have a base that is at least slightly more prominent or flared than the rest of the bookend, to ensure stability. L-forms are often better suited for functionality, with their wider base. Bookend collecting became attractive, however, not because of functionality but because of beauty, hence figural pieces (fully three dimensional) usually become the most highly sought after. Between L-form and figural is semi-figural, in which an L-form is adapted to include at least a partial figural item. Often, L-form is combined with figural, such that a fully figural item is placed on an "L." This format is very commonly employed in French Art Deco pairs from the 1920 to 1930 periods.

Bookends are "right" whether they are identical, mirror image (as in right and left glove), or complementary. Complementary pairs are those in which the bookends are intended to go together, but they are different in some regard. For instance, "Tilting at Windmills" depicts Sancho Panza on one bookend, and Don Quixote on the other, in markedly different depictions. At the same time as complementary bookends are quite charming, it is tempting for sellers with two "orphan" bookends to combine them in an attempt to resemble a pair. Ultimately, it is up to the judgment of the buyer whether two separate bookends comprise an appropriate pair. For instance, Dante and Beatrice are widely represented in bookend art. They may be seen as Dante and Beatrice, two Dantes, or two Beatrices, any of which combinations is appropriate. On the other hand, I have seen "pairs" sold of a bust of George Washington and a bust of Abraham Lincoln with substantially different structure, suggesting that perhaps they were not originally intended as a pair.

It is not at all uncommon to find single bookends sold as doorstops. Common sense dictates that a doorstop must be of sufficient height and weight to function in that role, so it is sensible to dismiss light-weight gray metal from any potential role as a doorstop. Similarly, since bronze-clad pieces do not fare well with even modest trauma, they would be unsuitable for a doorstop. Iron and bronze are the only metals consistently suitable for doorstops. There may be some degree of crossover, however, in that some catalogs have been seen where items are grouped together under the heading "Doorstops and Bookends," without any distinction as to which is which. Bradley and Hubbard, and Hubley issued catalogs in which you can see the same item produced as bookends, and then in a substantially larger format, also as a doorstop. Again, your personal judgment may be the ultimate arbiter, since some pairs of items originally designated as doorstops may function handsomely as bookends. Beware of well-intended offerings by dealers who offer to sell you, in the absence of any bookends in the shop, some item which "surely could be used to hold up books." Most collectors of bookends shun items which could function in the role of bookends, but are clearly not made with that intent.

References

Griffoul—Pierre Kjellberg, *Bronzes of the 19th Century,* Schiffer Publishers, Atglen, PA, 1994 Auguste Griffoul was the founder of A. Griffoul Foundries of Newark New Jersey. The only historical information we have is of a family member, Jean-Baptiste Griffoul, who had been a principal of the firm Griffoul and Lorge, located at 6 Passage Dombasle, Paris, and had supplied bronzes to Rodin.

Tiffin Glass—Bickenheuser Fred, *Tiffin Glassmasters, Book II.* 1981, Glassmaster Publications Grove City, Ohio.

Dickens Characters—Arthur L Hayward. *The Dickens Encyclopedia.*

Mark Twain and Tom Sawyer—This commentary is referenced to the Hannibal Courier-Post newspaper, April 25, 1935.

NCR Schoolhouse—Rouland RW, McNulty. *M NCR Corporation.* Information Technology 199?: 264-268. The journal from which this information was obtained does not have a date on any page. A notation at the end of the article quotes newspaper commentaries as recent as 1992, hence the date of publication must be some time subsequent to that.

Pan—Ingri and Edgar Parin D'Aulaire. *Book of Greek Myths,* 1962, Doubleday Publishers, New York. *New Larousse Encyclopedia of Mythology.* 1978 Hamlyn Publishers London.

Pegasus—Ingri and Edgar Parin D'Aulaire. *Book of Greek Myths,* 1962, Doubleday Publishers, New York.

Spirit of Ecstasy—Mike Fox and Steve Smith. *Rolls-Royce/The Complete Works.* 1984, Faber and Faber. London, Boston.

Statue of Liberty—Handlin O. *Statue of Liberty Newsweek Book Division,* New York 1971.

Antoine-Louis Barye—Stuart Pilar. *The Barye Bronzes,* Antique Collectors Club Books, Woodbridge, Suffolk.

Edgar Brandt—Joan Kahr. *Edgar Brandt .Master of Art Deco Ironwork.* Harry Abrams, Publishers, New York, 1999.

Demetre Chiparus—Alberto Shay Chiparus. *Master of Art Deco,* Abbeville Press Publishers, New York, 1999.

Abastenia St Leger Eberle—*Famous Small Bronzes,* 1928, the Gorham Company, New York City.

Dirk Van Erp— "The Arts and Crafts Studio of Dirk Van Erp," an Essay by Dorothy Lamoureux, © 1989 ISBN #1-877742-01-5, Library of Congress Catalog Card #89-61391.

Photo Gallery

Agricultural

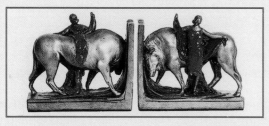

Plate 8. Agriculture, ca. 1930, bronze-clad, 5¾", marked P. Mori & Son, rarity 4, $250.00 – $350.00.

Plate 9. Digger and Sower, ca. 1925, Judd, bronze, 5", rarity 5, $100.00.
Photo courtesy of Agris Kelbrants.

Plate 10. Farmer, ca. 1930, BFM, iron, 4", marked BFM, rarity 4, $50.00. Photo courtesy of Agris Kelbrants.

Plate 11. Farmer and Sower (Griffoul), ca. 1918, Griffoul, bronze, 5¾", marked Theodore B Starr, Inc, Cast by Griffoul Newark, NJ, rarity 5*, $350.00.

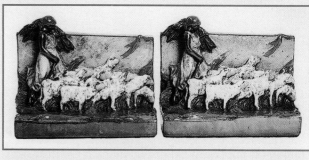

Plate 12. Girl and Flock, ca. 1922, attr Armor Bronze, bronze-clad, 5", rarity 5, $175.00.

Plate 13. Gleaners (K & O), ca. 1925, K & O Company, gray metal, 4¼", shopmark, rarity 4, $125.00.

Plate 14. Goose Shepherdess, ca. 1925, Judd, gray metal, 6", rarity 5, polychrome, $195.00; monochrome, $125.00.
Photo courtesy of Joyce Derian.

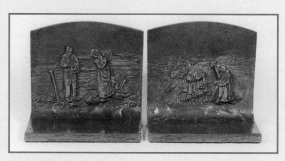

Plate 15. Millet Scenes, ca. 1920, Solid Bronze, bronze, 5", marked J L Lambert, rarity 5, $125.00.

Plate 16. Millet Scenes (Griffoul), ca. 1916, bronze, 5", marked J L Lambert (sculptor), Griffoul Foundry, 1916, rarity 5, $225.00.

Plate 17. Pioneers, 1925, Pompeian Bronze, gray metal, 4¾", marked The Pioneers © 1925, rarity 4, $95.00.

Plate 18. Variation: Pioneers, gray metal, 4¾", marked The Pioneers © 1925 Pompeian Bronze Co., rarity 4, $150.00.

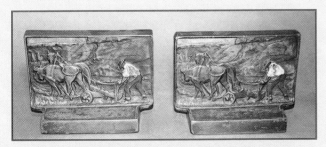

Plate 19. "Ploughman, The," ca. 1925, Pompeian Bronze, bronze-clad, 5¼", marked with artist signature on front: A Maneredi, rarity 5*, polychrome, $150.00; monochrome, $100.00. Photo courtesy of Josephine Amon.

Plate 20. Shepherdess, 1925, Pompeian Bronze, gray metal, 5", shopmark, rarity 4, $100.00.

Plate 21. Sower, 1925, Decorative Arts League, iron, 4¾", marked DAL 1925, rarity 3, $50.00.

Plate 22. Sower (BFM), ca. 1925, BFM, iron, 4¾", marked BFM, rarity 3, $50.00.

Plate 23. Sowing Farmer, ca. 1920, HMH (Austria), bronze, 4¼", marked HMH Austria, rarity 5*, $850.00.

37

Plate 24. Viewing the Land, ca. 1925, Solid Bronze, bronze, 4½", marked Solid Bronze, rarity 5, $175.00.

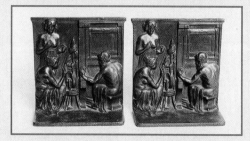

Plate 25. Weavers, ca. 1925, gray metal, 5", rarity 3, $75.00.

Arabian

Plate 26. Arab, ca. 1925, Hubley, iron, 6½", marked Hubley #314, rarity 4, $100.00.

Plate 27. Arab Defender, ca. 1925, attr Pompeian Bronze, bronze-clad, 8¾", rarity 5*, $525.00.

Plate 28. Arab Scenes, ca. 1920, gray metal, 6", marked Austria, rarity 5, $325.00.

Plate 29. Arab Scholar, ca. 1920, bronze on marble base, 6", marked Made in Austria, rarity 5*, $795.00.

Plate 30. Arab Sheik, ca. 1920, Armor Bronze, bronze-clad, 9", P Beneduce (sculptor), shopmark, rarity 5*, $295.00. Photo courtesy of Billie Trepanier.

Plate 31. Arabian Bazaar, ca. 1920, bronze, 6¼", marked Austria, rarity 5*, $1,900.00.

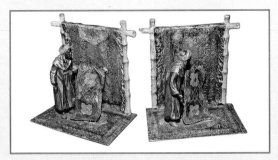

Plate 32. Arabian Bazaar (Coronet), ca. 1920, Coronet (Austria), gray metal, 5", marked Trademark Coronet, Registered Austria, rarity 5, $325.00. Photo courtesy of Dave Udstuen.

Plate 33. Bedouin, ca. 1920, Hubley, iron, 5¾", marked 418, polychrome, rarity 4; other finishes, rarity 3; polychrome, $125.00; other finishes, $95.00.

Plate 34. Bazaar Scene, ca. 1920, gray metal, 6¼", marked Austria, rarity 5, $325.00.

Plate 35. By the Oasis, ca. 1920, bronze on marble base, 7", marked KAR (sculptor), Austria, rarity 5*, $1,500.00.

Plate 36. Camel Driver, ca. 1926, iron, 6", rarity 5, $150.00.

Plate 37. Charging Arab, ca. 1920, Bradley and Hubbard, iron, 4½", shopmark, rarity 5, $95.00. Photo courtesy of Bette Russell.

Plate 38. Imam, ca. 1920, (attr Austria), 8", bronze, rarity 5*, $2,400.00.

Plate 39. Leading His Camel, ca. 1920, iron, 4½", rarity 4, $65.00.

Plate 40. North African Warrior, ca. 1920, Pompeian Bronze, bronze-clad, 11", marked Paul Herzel (sculptor), rarity 5, $450.00.

Plate 41. Rug Dealer, ca. 1920, bronze on marble base, 10", rarity 5*, $1,750.00. *Made in Austria.*

Plate 42. Sheik, ca. 1925, Hubley, iron, 4½", polychrome, rarity 5; monochrome, rarity 4; polychrome, $175.00; monochrome, $100.00.

Plate 43. Turbaned Scholar, 1923, Ronson, gray metal, 3¼", marked LV Aronson 1923, polychrome, rarity 5; monochrome, rarity 3; polychrome, $125.00; other finishes, $65.00.

Asian

Plate 44. Asian Home, ca. 1950, brass, 4", rarity 4, $95.00.

Plate 45. Asian Scholar, ca. 1930, bronze, 5", Japanese inscription, rarity 5, $195.00.

Plate 46. Buddha, ca. 1960, resin, 6", rarity 5, $35.00.
Photo courtesy of Agris Kelbrants.

Plate 47. Buddha (Armor Bronze), ca. 1922, Armor Bronze, bronze-clad, 7", rarity 5*, polychrome, $275.00; monochrome, $175.00.

Plate 48. Buddha (Ronson Petite), 1922, Ronson, gray metal, 4", marked LVA 1922, rarity 5, $95.00.

Plate 52. Variation: Chinese Couple, painted gray metal, 8¼", rarity 5, $150.00.

Plate 49. Buddha (Ronson), 1922, Ronson, gray metal, 6¼", marked LV Aronson 1922, company tag #8505, rarity 5, $135.00.

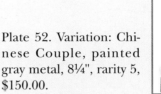

Plate 53. Chinese Man, ca. 1933, attr JB Hirsch, gray metal on marble or polished stone base, 8¼", rarity 5, $150.00.

Plate 50. Buddha (Tiffany), ca. 1920, Tiffany, bronze, 5¾", shopmark, rarity 4, polychrome, $650.00; monochrome, $450.00.

Plate 54. Chinese Students (base variety 1), ca. 1930, Ronson, gray metal, 5¼", company tag #16138, rarity 3, $95.00.

Plate 51. Chinese Couple, ca. 1933, attr JB Hirsch, gray metal on marble or polished stone base, 8¼", rarity 5, $150.00. *It is curious that of the many figures made by JB Hirsch, we have not seen this with a celluloid face.*

Plate 55. Chinese Students (base variety 2), ca. 1930, Ronson, gray metal, 5¼", rarity 5, $135.00. *Note "quilted fabric" styling to base.*

Plate 56. Chinese Students (base variety 3), ca. 1930, Ronson, gray metal, 5¼", rarity 4, polychrome, $125.00; monochrome, $75.00.

Plate 57. Chinese Turtle, ca. 1960, brass, 5", none, rarity 3, $35.00. *It is very difficult to establish the age of un-dated Chinese brass or bronze. Much older examples exist. Consult an expert for clarification. Made in China.*

plate 58. Fantasie, ca. 1930, Pompeian Bronze, gray metal, 4", marked PB Fantasie, rarity 4, $75.00.

Plate 59. Foo Dogs, ca. 1920, iron, 5", rarity 5, $250.00.

Plate 60. Geisha, ca. 1925, Pompeian Bronze, gray metal, 4¾", marked Geisha PB Inc, rarity 3, $90.00.

Plate 61. Geisha Bust, ca. 1920, bronze on marble base, 7", marked Made in Austria, rarity 5, $350.00.

Plate 62. Japanese Woman, ca. 1929, Jennings Brothers, gray metal, 8½", marked JB 1808, rarity 5, $175.00.

Plate 63. Kimono Couple (Armor Bronze), ca. 1926, Armor Bronze, bronze-clad, 7½", rarity 5, polychrome, $275.00; monochrome, $175.00.

Plate 64. Kimono Couple, ca. 1926, bronze-clad, 7", marked with Japanese inscription, rarity 5, $175.00.

Plate 65. Kimono Couple (Pompeian Bronze), ca. 1926, Pompeian Bronze, bronze-clad, 7½", rarity 5, polychrome, $275.00; monochrome, $175.00.

Plate 66. Madrigal, 1925, Pompeian Bronze, 4½", marked PB Inc Madrigale 1925, rarity 4, $75.00.

Plate 67. One of Us Was Studying, ca. 1930, Ronson, gray metal, 9", company paper tag #12552, rarity 4, polychrome, $195.00; monochrome, $135.00.

Plate 68. Oriental Meditation, ca. 1925, Solid Bronze, bronze, 6", shopmark, rarity 5, $275.00.

Plate 69. Oriental Meditation (K & O), ca. 1927, K & O, gray metal, 6", shopmark, rarity 5, $325.00.

Plate 70. Siam Couple (Solid Bronze), ca. 1926, Solid Bronze, bronze, 4¾", shopmark, rarity 4, $150.00.

Plate 71. Sumo Wrestlers, ca. 1925, bronze, 7½", marked with Japanese inscription, rarity 5, $2,500.00.

Plate 72. Tutor, ca. 1925, Pompeian Bronze, gray metal, 4¼", marked PB Inc., The Tutor, rarity 5, $175.00.

Plate 73. Two Mandarins, ca. 1930, Ronson, gray metal, 9½", rarity 5, $195.00.

Aviation

Plate 74. Airman Lindbergh, ca. 1928, iron, 6", rarity 5, $125.00. Photo courtesy of Lyndon Sheldon.

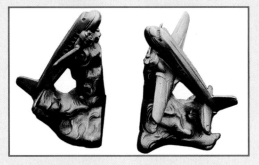

Plate 75. Airplane, ca. 1930, gray metal, 6", rarity 5, $125.00.

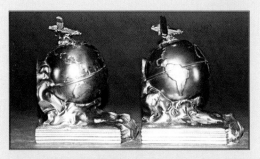

Plate 76. Around the World, ca. 1930, K & O, gray metal, 5¾", shopmark, rarity 4, $175.00.

Plate 77. Aviator, 1928, Connecticut Foundry, bronze or iron, 6", shopmark The Aviator , bronze, rarity 5*; iron, rarity 4, bronze, $225.00; iron, $125.00. *This piece is cast generally in iron as are all Connecticut Foundry pieces. The lack of detail and wear on the lettering would suggest that this particular example has been produced from an iron original.*

Plate 78. Colonel Lindbergh, ca. 1928, iron, 8", none, rarity 5, $295.00. Photo courtesy of Lyndon Sheldon.

Plate 79. Famous Flyer, ca. 1930, iron, 8", rarity 5, $300.00. Photo courtesy of Lyndon Sheldon.

Plate 80. First Nonstop Flight, ca. 1928, iron, 6", marked "First nonstop flight New York to Paris May 21st-22nd Piloted by Charles Lindbergh," rarity 5, $125.00.

Plate 81. Flight, ca. 1930, gray metal, 6", rarity 5, $120.00.

Plate 82. Flyboy, ca. 1928, iron, 6", rarity 5, $175.00. Photo courtesy of Lyndon Sheldon.

Plate 83. In the Clouds, ca. 1928, iron, 5½", rarity 5, $150.00.

Plate 84. Lindbergh, ca. 1928, iron, 5½", rarity 4, $95.00.

Plate 85. Lindbergh Profile, ca. 1920, WE, iron, 6¾", marked WE, rarity 5, $200.00.

Plate 86. Lindbergh Propeller, ca. 1928, iron, 6½", marked NS 650, rarity 5, $175.00. *This exact same figure has been seen with markings "Amelia Earhart," 5¼".*

Plate 87. Lindy, ca. 1928, Verona, iron, 6", shopmark, rarity 4, $100.00.

45

Plate 88. Lone Eagle, ca. 1928, bronze, 6", rarity 5, $195.00.

Plate 89. Premiere Travelersee, ca. 1928, bronze, 8", marked La Ville de Paris, Charles Lindbergh, rarity 5, $325.00. *Made in France.* Photo courtesy of Lyndon Sheldon.

Plate 90. Spirit of St Louis, ca. 1928, bronze, 6½", marked Spirit of St Louis, rarity 5, $195.00. Photo courtesy of Lyndon Sheldon.

Plate 91. Spirit of USA, 1927, Armor Bronze, bronze-clad, 5½", marked "Nonstop Flight New York to Paris 3626 miles, 33½ hours, May 20-21," Armor Bronze, rarity 5, $195.00.

Plate 92. Viking Spirit, ca. 1928, iron, 5¼", rarity 5, $110.00.

Plate 93. Wings, ca. 1928, iron, 4", none, rarity 4, $65.00. Photo courtesy of Lyndon Sheldon.

Bears

Plate 94. Bear at the Door, ca. 1925, attr Hubley, bronze, 5¼", rarity 5*, $175.00.

Plate 95. Bear Couple, ca. 1930, Syracuse Ornamental, Syrocowood, 6", rarity 4, $75.00.

Plate 96. Bear Frolic, ca. 1928, iron, 4½", rarity 4, $90.00.

Plate 97. Bear on Log, 1934, 5½", rarity 5, $125.00. *This bookend appears in the original US Patent office as Design Patent #65.035, filed February 23, 1924, assigned to John Scalabrino of New York, NY.*

Plate 98. Bear on Pedestal, ca. 1920, bronze figure on gray metal base, 3½", rarity 5, $250.00. Photo courtesy of Agris Kelbrants

Plate 99. Bear on the Prowl, ca. 1930, Jennings Brothers, gray metal, 4½", marked JB 2212, rarity 5*, $175.00.

Plate 100. Bull and Bear, ca. 1920, Gorham, bronze, 5¼", marked Gorham Co., rarity 5, $2,000.00.

Plate 101. Classic Polar Bear, ca. 1930, Ronson, gray metal, 6½", rarity 5*, $325.00. Photo courtesy of Dealers Choice Antiques.

Plate 102. Mountain Bear Cub, ca. 1920, Reed & Barton, silver-plate, 7", marked Reed & Barton #103, rarity 5*, $175.00. Photo courtesy of David Poston.

Plate 103. Polar Bear (Hubley), ca. 1925, Hubley, iron, 3½", rarity 5, $150.00. Photo courtesy of Billie Trepanier.

Plate 104. Polar Bear (JF), ca. 1925, JF Company, gray metal, 4½", shopmark, rarity 5, $250.00.

Plate 105. Sitting on Guard, ca. 1920, bronze with red glass eyes, 8¾", marked VolVol, rarity 5, $800.00.

Birds-Ducks, Geese, Swans

Plate 106. Duck (Bruce Fox), ca. 1950, Bruce Fox, aluminum, 6¾", marked Bruce Fox Hand Finished Wrought Metals, rarity 4, $110.00.

Plate 107. Duck (Littco), ca. 1928, Littco, iron, 5", company paper tag, rarity 4, $150.00.

Plate 108. Duck (PMC), ca. 1965, PM Craftsman, gray metal, 4", marked PMC, rarity 3, $50.00.

Plate 109. Flying Duck, ca. 1925, attr Pompeian Bronze, bronze-clad, 9¼", marked ©, rarity 5, $250.00.

Plate 110. Flying Geese, ca. 1928, Judd, iron, 5½", marked 9688, rarity 5, $165.00.

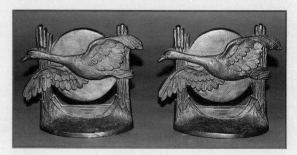

Plate 111. Hunter's Moon, ca. 1930, Acorn, iron, 5¾", Hunter's Moon #603 shopmark, rarity 4, $165.00.

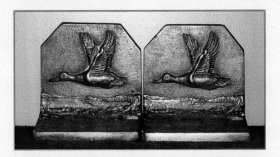

Plate 112. Mallard, ca. 1925, iron, 4½", rarity 5, $110.00. Photo courtesy of Agris Kelbrants.

Plate 116. Swan Design, ca. 1930, Ronson, gray metal, 4¾", company paper tag #10817, rarity 3, $65.00. Photo courtesy of Richard Weinstein.

Plate 113. Searching Goose, ca. 1930, Jennings Brothers, gray metal, 4¾", marked JB 879, rarity 5, $150.00.

Plate 117. Swan on the Lake, ca. 1929, Nuart, gray metal, 5", shopmark, rarity 5, $95.00.

Plate 114. Swan, ca. 1930, Acorn, iron, 6", #602 shopmark, rarity 4, $135.00.

Plate 118. Swan Reflections, ca. 1925, Bradley and Hubbard, gray metal figures, iron base, 6", shopmark, rarity 5, $175.00.

Plate 115. Swan (JB Hirsch), ca. 1928, attr JB Hirsch, gray metal figure on polished stone base, 7", rarity 5, $175.00.

Plate 119. Take Off, ca. 1925, Littco, iron, 7", rarity 4, $110.00.

Birds-Eagles

Plate 120. American Eagle, ca. 1925, bronze-clad, 6", rarity 5, $250.00.

Plate 121. American Eagle (CF), 1930, Connecticut Foundry, iron, 6", American Eagle copr 1930 shopmark, rarity 5, $165.00.

Plate 122. American Eagle (B & H), ca. 1925, Bradley and Hubbard, iron, 5¾", shopmark, rarity 4, $80.00.

Plate 123. American Eagle (Ronson), ca. 1930, Ronson, gray metal, 5½", company paper tag, rarity 4, $85.00.

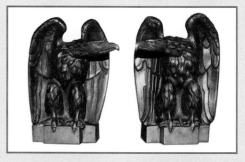

Plate 124. Angry Eagle, ca. 1925, Wm H Jackson Co, bronze, 8", marked Wm H Jackson Co, NY, rarity 5*, $395.00.

Plate 125. Brass Eagle, ca. 1986, Virginia Metal Crafters, brass, 6", marked VM, rarity 3, $95.00. Photo courtesy of Sue Benoliel.

Plate 126. Eagle (B & H), ca. 1925, Bradley and Hubbard, gray metal figure on iron base, 5¾", shopmark, rarity 5, $175.00.

Plate 127. Eagle (Banthrico), ca. 1930, Banthrico, 6¼", marked DS Banthrico, Inc, Chicago, USA, rarity 5, $75.00. Photo courtesy of Agris Kelbrants.

Plate 128. Eagle, ca. 1950 (England), bronze, 6½", marked England R 710378, rarity 5*, $150.00.

Plate 132. Eagle and Shield, ca. 1930, gray metal, 8", rarity 5, $95.00. Photo courtesy of Agris Kelbrants.

Plate 129. Eagle (Frankart), ca. 1930, Frankart, gray metal, 6¾", marked Frankart Inc, Patent Appld For, rarity 3, $85.00. *This figure is occasionally seen on a marble base, but to our knowledge, Frankart produced no marble products.*

Plate 133. Eagle Head, LaLique, glass, 5", rarity 5, $1,200.00.

Plate 130. Eagle (Griffoul), ca. 1916, Griffoul, bronze, 4⅝", marked Barye (sculptor), Cast by Griffoul, NJ, rarity 5, $325.00. *The design for this pair comes from bronze tablets that were sculpted by Louis-Antoine Barye. The original bronze tablets were similar in size to the bookends: 10 C 14 centimeters. For detailed information on Barye, see page 26.*

Plate 134. Eagle in Flight, ca. 1920 (Austria), bronze, 7", marked Made in Austria, rarity 5*, $1,200.00.

Plate 131. Eagle (Snead), ca. 1925, Snead, iron, 3½", marked Snead NJ Patent Pending, rarity 2, $35.00. Photo courtesy of Agris Kelbrants.

Plate 135. Eagle Landing, ca. 1920, bronze, 4½", rarity 4, $175.00.

Plate 136. Eagle Waiting, ca. 1920, bronze on marble base, 5", marked Made in Austria, rarity 5, $300.00.

Plate 140. Heraldic Eagle, ca. 1935, Syracuse Ornamental, Syrocowood, 6", rarity 3, $30.00.

Plate 137. Eagle Wave, ca. 1925, bronze-clad, 9", rarity 5, $400.00.

Plate 141. Nesting Eagle, ca. 1925, bronze, 6¾", rarity 5*, $275.00.

Plate 138. Emblem Eagle, ca. 1925, Judd, iron, 5¾", 4 digit number, rarity 5, $145.00.

Plate 142. Patriotic Eagle, ca. 1970, coated chalk, 5", rarity 3, $20.00.

Plate 139. God Bless America, ca. 1930, Ronson, gray metal, 5½", company tag #16607, rarity 5, $125.00. Photo courtesy of Richard Weinstein.

Plate 143. Perched Eagle, ca. 1934, gray metal, 7½", rarity 4, $115.00.

Plate 144. Side-Glancing Eagle, ca. 1925, Littco, iron, 6", company paper tag, rarity 4, $75.00. Photo courtesy of Agris Kelbrants.

Plate 145. Spread Eagle, ca. 1920, bronze, 7", marked Made in Austria, B Altman & Co, rarity 5, $800.00.

Plate 146. Wings Astride, ca. 1942, Fostoria, glass, rarity 5, $190.00.

Birds-Flamingos

Plate 147. Beak to Neck, ca. 1925, iron, 7½", rarity 5, $175.00.

Plate 148. Bird Takes a Bow, ca. 1925, bronze, 7½", rarity 5, $350.00. Photo courtesy of Sue Benoliel.

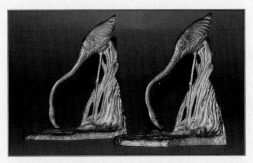

Plate 149. Drinking Flamingo, ca. 1920, bronze, 7", marked Made in Austria, rarity 5*, $650.00.

Plate 150. Flamingo, 1948, Everstyle, iron, 5¼", piece shown is unmarked but identical piece with company markings has been seen, rarity 4, $95.00. *Design Patent #149282 for this piece was issued April 13, 1948 to Alexander Leva, New York, NY.*

Plate 151. Flamingo (Crescent), ca. 1932, Crescent Art Novelties, gray metal, 8", TK, shopmark, rarity 5, $165.00.

Plate 152. Flamingos (PB), ca. 1925, attr Pompeian Bronze, bronze-clad, 7½", marked Paul Herzel (sculptor) ©, rarity 5, $325.00.

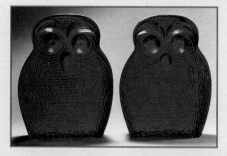

Plate 156. Amber Owl, ca. 1950, Viking, glass, 5", rarity 3, $25.00.

Plate 153. Flamingos, ca. 1920 (Austria), bronze on marble base, 7", rarity 5*, $550.00.

Plate 157. Glassy-eyed Owl, ca. 1975, ceramic with glass eyes, marked 1879A, 1975, rarity 5*, $25.00.

Plate 154. Flapping Flamingo, ca. 1930, Jennings Brothers, gray metal, 6½", shopmark #3024, rarity 4, $125.00.

Plate 158. Lamp of Knowledge, ca. 1926, Judd, iron, 4¾" rarity 4, marked #9886, rarity 4, $80.00.

Birds-Owls

Plate 155. Aesculapian Owl, ca. 1930, iron, 5½", marked Germany, rarity 3, $50.00.

Plate 159. Majestic Owl, ca. 1922, Marion Bronze, bronze-clad, 11½", rarity 5*, $375.00.

54

Plate 160. Musical Owl, ca. 1940, Zimbalist (Switzerland), chrome and brass, 8½", rarity 5*, $500.00. Photo courtesy of Susan Koch (Memory Lane Antiques).

Plate 161. Back view of Musical Owl.

Plate 162. Night Watchman, 1943, Fostoria, glass, 7½", rarity 5, $350.00. Photo courtesy of Michael Horseman.

Plate 163. Owl, ca. 1925, bronze-clad, 6", rarity 5, $125.00.

Plate 164. Owl (B & H), ca. 1925, Bradley and Hubbard, iron, 6", shopmark, rarity 4, $150.00.

Plate 165. Owl (Judd), ca. 1925, Judd, iron, 5¾", 4-digit shopmark, rarity 5, $175.00. Photo courtesy of Agris Kelbrants.

Plate 166. Owl (PB), ca. 1925, Pompeian Bronze, bronze-clad, 4½", marked PB, rarity 4, $125.00.

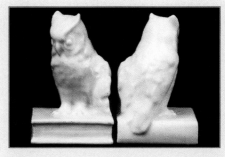

Plate 167. Owl (Rookwood), 1942, Rookwood, pottery, 5½", marked 1942 XLII, #2655, designed by McDonald, rarity 4, $250.00.

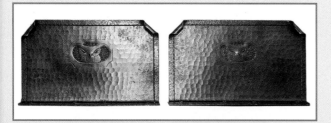

Plate 168. Owl (Roycroft), ca. 1920, Roycroft, copper, 4¼", shopmark, rarity 3, $110.00. Photo courtesy of Jay Mendlovitz.

Plate 169. Owl Family, ca. 1929, Weidlich Brothers, gray metal, 6¼", marked WB #645, rarity 3, $65.00. Photo courtesy of Agris Kelbrants.

Plate 170. Owl in Archway (Fleuron), ca. 1920, fleuron, synthetic marble, 4½", paper tag Fleuron, Durez, North Tonawanda, NY, rarity 5*, $125.00.

Plate 171. Owl in Archway (X-1), ca. 1925, X-1, gray metal, 4¼", marked #506, rarity 5, $175.00.

Plate 172. Owl on Books (MB), ca. 1960, Marion Bronze, bronze-clad, 8", shopmark, rarity 5, $125.00.

Plate 173. Owl on Books (PB), ca. 1925, Pompeian Bronze, bronze-clad, 7", marked Pompeian Bronze, rarity 5, $150.00. Photo courtesy of Billie Trepanier.

Plate 174. Perched on Book, ca. 1920, gray metal, 5¼", rarity 5, $150.00. Photo courtesy of Agris Kelbrants.

Plate 175. Says Who, ca. 1930, Ronson, gray metal, 7½", paper label #12554, rarity 5*, $195.00. Photo courtesy of Richard Weinstein.

Plate 176. Sleepy Owl, ca. 1925, bronze-clad, 7", rarity 5, $195.00. Photo courtesy of Agris Kelbrants.

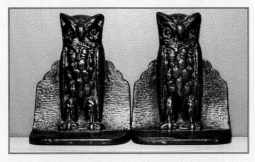

Plate 177. Standing Owl, ca. 1925, iron, 4", rarity 4, $65.00. Photo courtesy of Agris Kelbrants.

Plate 178. Student Owls, ca. 1928, Jennings Brothers, gray metal, 5¼", marked JB 1460, rarity 4, $90.00.

Plate 179. Winsome Owl, 1978, Shopping International, marbelloid, 6", marked Shopping International, Norwich, VT, rarity 1, $15.00.

Plate 180. Well-Read Bird, ca. 1922, attr Pompeian Bronze, bronze-clad, 8½", rarity 5, $275.00.

Plate 181. Wise Eyes, ca. 1925, Bradley and Hubbard, iron, 4", shopmark, rarity 5, $175.00.

Plate 182. Wise Face, ca. 1924, Judd, gray metal figure, iron base, 6¼", marked #3773, rarity 5, $195.00.

Birds-Parrots

Plate 183. Parrot, ca. 1930, iron, 6⅜", rarity 4, $95.00.

Plate 184. Parrot (AMW), 1927, Art Metal Works, gray metal, 5½", marked AMW 1927; paper tag: Ronson #12405, rarity 5, $375.00.

Plate 185. Parrot on Book, ca. 1928, K&O, gray metal, 6", shopmark, rarity 4, $125.00.

Plate 186. Parrot on Perch, ca. 1934, Frankart, gray metal, 6¾", shopmark, rarity 5, $250.00.

Plate 187. Perched Parrot, ca. 1924, iron, 5⅛", rarity 4, $85.00.

Plate 188. Perched Parrot (Heintz), ca. 1914, Heintz Art Metal, bronze with French gray bronze patina, 5½", shopmark, rarity 5, $275.00. Photo courtesy of David Surgan.

Plate 189. Perched Parrot (PB), ca. 1925, attr Pompeian Bronze, bronze-clad, 6¾", polychrome, rarity 5*; monochrome, rarity 5; polychrome, $195.00; monochrome, $150.00.

Plate 190. Perky Parrot, ca. 1932 , Littco, gray metal, 7¼", rarity 5, $175.00.

Plate 191. World Atlas, ca. 1922, Pompeian Bronze, bronze-clad, 9", marked Pompeian Bronze, The World Atlas, 106, rarity 4, $175.00.

Birds-Peacocks

Plate 192. Peacock, ca. 1930, iron, 7", rarity 4, $75.00.

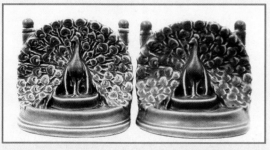

Plate 193. Peacock (Rookwood), 1924, Rookwood, pottery, 5", marked XXIV #2445, rarity 5, $395.00. *Designer: McDonald.*

Plate 194. Peacock Display, ca. 1925, iron, 6¼", rarity 5, $195.00. Photo courtesy of Agris Kelbrants.

Plate 195. Peacock Splendor, ca. 1930, bronze, 5¾", rarity 5, $175.00.

Plate 196. Perched Peacock, ca. 1925, Bradley & Hubbard, iron, 6½", shopmark, rarity 5, $135.00.

Plate 197. Proud Peacock, ca. 1925, iron, 5½", rarity 3, $75.00.

Plate 198. Proud Peacock (X-1), ca. 1930, X-1, gray metal, 5¾", marked #501, rarity 4, $175.00. *Essentially identical piece marketed by Art Metal Works.*

Plate 199. Proud Peacock (WB), ca. 1925, Weidlich Brothers, gray metal, 5¾", shopmark #641, rarity 4, $125.00.

59

Plate 200. Silver Peacock, ca. 1914, Heintz Art Metal, bronze with silver overlay, 5", shopmark, rarity 5, $275.00. Photo courtesy of David Surgan.

Plate 204. Proud Penguin, ca. 1930, Frankart, gray metal, 7", shopmark, rarity 5, $300.00.

Birds-Penguins

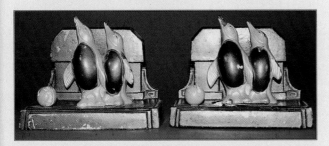

Plate 201. Penguin Family, ca. 1925, gray metal, 4¾", rarity 5, $225.00.

Plate 202. Penguin Play, ca. 1933, gray metal, 3½", rarity 5, $110.00.

Plate 203. Perfect Penguin, ca. 1930, Ronson, gray metal, 5½", company tag #14773, rarity 5, $350.00. Photo courtesy of Richard Weinstein.

Birds-Pigeons

Plate 205. Pigeon, glass, 5¾", rarity 4, $125.00.

Plate 206. Pigeon (Indiana Glass), ca. 1940, Indiana Glass, glass, 5½", amber, rarity 5*; others, rarity 3; amber, $150.00; others, $75.00. Photo courtesy of Michael Horseman.

Plate 207. Variation: Pigeon (Indiana Glass) (amber).

Plate 208. Pouter Pigeon, ca. 1928, gray metal, 6", rarity 5, $75.00.

Plate 209. Pouter Pigeon (Burwood), ca. 1925, Burwood, burwood, 6", paper tag Burwood Company, Traverse City, Michigan, rarity 5, $95.00.

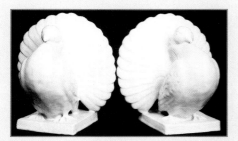

Plate 210. Pouter Pigeon (L & A), ca. 1940, Lotus and Acanthus Studios, ceramic, 6", marked Lotus and Acanthus Studios logo, rarity 5, $500.00.

Birds-Miscellaneous

Plate 211. Beak-to-Beak, ca. 1928, gray metal on marble base, 6", rarity 5*, $175.00. Photo courtesy of Richard's Antiques.

Plate 212. Big Bird, bronze and ivory, 15", marked Bouraine, rarity 5, $3,500.00. Photo courtesy of Miami Beach Convention Center.

Plate 213. Bird Kisses, ca. 1930, attr France, gray metal on marble base, 7", rarity 5*, $175.00.

Plate 214. Birds (K & O), ca. 1930, K & O, gray metal, 5½", shopmark, rarity 5*, $150.00.

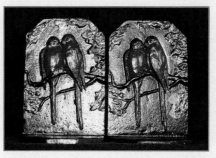

Plate 215. Birds in Love, ca. 1930, iron, 5", rarity 5, $95.00. Photo courtesy of Agris Kelbrants.

Plate 216. Birds on Perch, ca. 1925, bronze on marble base, 7", rarity 5*, $495.00.

Plate 217. Bluebirds (B & H), ca. 1925, Bradley & Hubbard, iron, 5½", shopmark, rarity 5, $295.00.

Plate 218. Bronze Bird, ca. 1920, bronze on marble base, 5", rarity 5*, $400.00.

Plate 219. Cardinal, 1928, Connecticut Foundry, iron, 4", marked Cardinal 1928, rarity 4, $35.00. Photo courtesy of Elizabeth Cody.

Plate 220. Cockatiels, ca. 1920, bronze on wood base, 6", rarity 5*, $550.00. *Made in Austria.*

Plate 221. Crane, ca. 1946, Dodge, gray metal, 6¾", shopmark, rarity 4, $75.00.

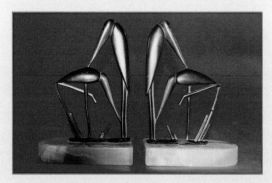

Plate 222. Deco Herons, ca. 1925, bronze on marble base, 6", rarity 5*, $350.00. *Made in Austria.*

Plate 223. Egret, ca. 1920, bronze figure, ivory beak, marble base, 6", rarity 5*, $450.00. *Made in Austria.*

Plate 224. Flowered Bird, ca. 1925, attr Bradley & Hubbard, iron, 6½", marked #1269, rarity 5*, $275.00.

Plate 228. Jaybird, 1929, Rookwood, pottery, 5½", marked #2829, XXIX, rarity 5, $550.00. *Designer: Shirayamadani.*

Plate 225. Graceful Bird, ca. 1928, gray metal on marble base, 7", rarity 5*, $175.00.

Plate 229. Kingfisher, ca. 1928, bronze in marble enclosure, 5¾", rarity 5*, $250.00. *Made in Austria.*

Plate 226. Griffin, ca. 1932, K&O, gray metal, 5¾", shopmark, Yellowstone Park, Holz, polychrome, rarity 5*; monochrome, rarity 5, polychrome, $275.00; monochrome, $150.00. *Not all versions have the "Yellowstone" emblem.*

Plate 230. Kingfisher (Rookwood), 1925, Rookwood, pottery, 5½", marked #2657, XXV, rarity 5, $550.00. *Designer: McDonald.*

Plate 227. Heron, ca. 1925, iron, 7½", rarity 5, $175.00.

Plate 231. Kiwi, ca. 1923, Judd, gray metal figure on bronze base, 5¼", marked J Co, 9688, rarity 5, $295.00.

Plate 232. Long Tail Bird, ca. 1925, attr JB Hirsch, gray metal on polished stone base, 6", rarity 5, $135.00.

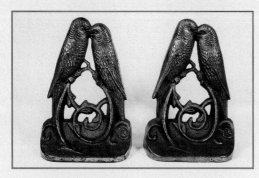

Plate 233. Lovebirds Kissing, ca. 1930, iron, 6", rarity 4, $110.00.

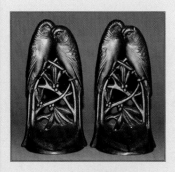

Plate 234. Lovebirds Whispering, ca. 1930, Acorn, iron, 7", #600 shopmark, rarity 4, $150.00.

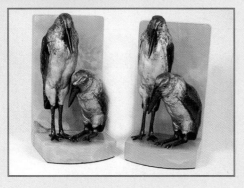

Plate 235. Maribou Storks, ca. 1920, bronze figures on onyx base, 6¾", marked Made in Austria, rarity 5*, $1,500.00.

Plate 236. Maribou Storks (FVM), ca. 1910, FVM, bronze, 6¾", marked FVM, rarity 5*, $2,500.00.

Plate 237. Parakeet, ca. 1920, iron, 6¼", rarity 5*, $175.00. Photo courtesy of Agris Kelbrants.

Plate 238. Pelican, ca. 1925, JB Hirsch, gray metal with celluloid beak on marble base, 7", rarity 5, $175.00. *Such figures were also made into lamps, ashtrays, candy dishes, etc.*

Plate 239. Pelican lamp. *Made with same birds used on bookends above.*

Plate 240. Perky Pheasant, ca. 1932, gray metal on marble base, 6¾", rarity 4, $110.00.

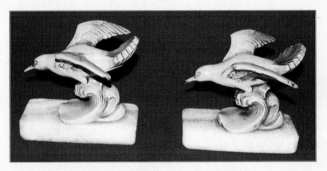

Plate 241. Petrel, ca. 1932, gray metal on marble base, 5", rarity 5*, $135.00.

Plate 242. Pheasant, ca. 1950, gray metal, 6½", rarity 4, $90.00.

Plate 243. Raven, ca. 1925, JB Hirsch, gray metal figure, celluloid beak, polished stone base, 6½", rarity 5, $425.00.

Plate 244. Ready for Flight, ca. 1940, Cambridge Glass, glass, 5½", rarity 4, $160.00. Photo courtesy of Mike Horseman.

Plate 245. Road Runner, ca. 1930, Ronson, gray metal, 4¾", company tag #16065, rarity 4, $150.00.

Plate 246. Rook (Rookwood), ca. 1940, Rookwood, pottery, 5¼", shopmark, IXIII 2275, designer initials of Wm. McDonald, rarity 5, $400.00. Photo courtesy of Sue Benoliel.

Plate 247. Rooster, ca. 1945, glass, rarity 4, $110.00.

Plate 248. Sea Bird, ca. 1934, Frankart, gray metal, 8", shopmark, rarity 5*, $210.00.

Plate 252. Sound of Spring, ca. 1930, gray metal on marble base, 5", marked Tedd (sculptor), rarity 5, $175.00. *Made in France.*

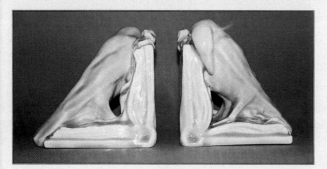

Plate 249. Side-glancing Rook, ca. 1945, Rookwood, pottery, 6", marked #2274 on base; XLV, rarity 5, poly-chrome, $750.00; monochrome, $450.00.

Plate 253. Splendor, ca. 1925, Pompeian Bronze, gray metal, 3¾", marked splendor, PB & Co., rarity 4, $110.00.

Plate 250. Silver Cormorant, ca. 1930, gray metal, 4¼", rarity 5*, $150.00. Photo courtesy of Sue Benoliel.

Plate 254. Springtime, porcelain in brass, marked China, rarity 5, $165.00.

Plate 251. Sleepy, ca. 1925, Albany Foundry, iron, 7½", rarity 4, $95.00.

Plate 255. Standing Tall, ca. 1930, iron, 7", rarity 5*, $325.00. Photo courtesy of Agris Kelbrants.

Plate 256. Toucan, ca. 1925, gray metal figure, Bakelite pebble, marble base, 5¼", marked H Moreau (sculptor), rarity 5, $650.00. *Made in France.*

Plate 257. Toucan Perched, 1933, Crescent Art Novelties, gray metal, 7¾", marked TK 1933 Crescent Art Novelties, Inc, Irvington, NJ, rarity 5*, $395.00.

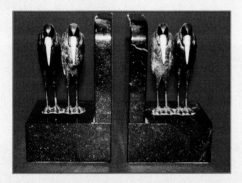

Plate 258. Twins, ca. 1930, gray metal figures, ivory beaks on marble base, 4¾", rarity 5*, $175.00.

Plate 259. Warbler, ca. 1930, Nuart, gray metal, shopmark, rarity 5*, $225.00.

Plate 260. Wings Folded, ca. 1930, Jennings Brothers, gray metal, 6", marked JB #287, rarity 3, $75.00. Photo courtesy of Agris Kelbrants.

Plate 261. Woodpecker, ca. 1930, gray metal figure on marble base, 7", marked Franjou (sculptor), rarity 5*, $175.00. *Made in France.*

Buffalo (Bison)

Plate 262. Bison (Armor Bronze), ca. 1925, Armor Bronze, bronze-clad, 8½", marked JK Krupka (sculptor), Armor Bronze shopmark, rarity 5*, $275.00. Photo courtesy of Ron/Penny Sommerfield.

Plate 263. Bison (B & H), ca. 1925, Bradley & Hubbard, iron, 6½", shopmark, rarity 5, $295.00.

Plate 264. Bison (PB), ca. 1920, Pompeian Bronze, bronze-clad, 5½", marked Paul Herzel, 169 Pompeian, company tag, rarity 5, $300.00. Photo courtesty of Billie Trepanier.

Plate 268. Buffalo (Ronson), 1923, Ronson, gray metal, 4¼", marked LV Aronson 1923, rarity 5, $250.00.

Plate 265. Bowing Buffalo, ca. 1925, bronze, 4", marked Austria, rarity 5*, $295.00.

Plate 269. Buffalo and Arch, ca. 1925, gray metal, 4", rarity 5, $95.00.

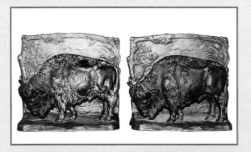

Plate 266. Buffalo, ca. 1920, bronze, 5", marked Austria, rarity 5*, $750.00.

Plate 270. Buffalo Hunt, ca. 1930, bronze, 5½", rarity 4, $150.00.

Plate 267. Buffalo (Eddog), ca. 1920, bronze, 4", marked Eddog (sculptor), made in Austria, rarity 5*, $900.00.

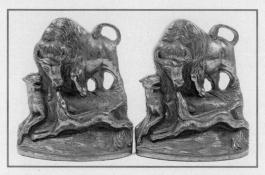

Plate 271. Buffalo Hunt (Gift House), 1926, Gift House, iron, 5¾", marked Gift House Inc, New York 1926 D35, rarity 5, $175.00.

Plate 272. Buffalo Hunt (PB), ca. 1925, attr Pompeian Bronze, bronze-clad, 4¾", marked ©," rarity 5*, $195.00.

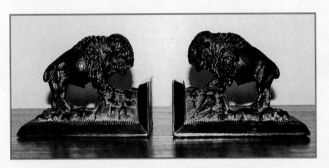

Plate 273. Buffalo on Rocky Terrain, 1922, Ronson, gray metal, 4½", marked LVA ©, rarity 5*, $125.00.
Photo courtesy of Blythe Curry.

Plate 274. Grazing Buffalo, ca. 1925, iron, 4¾", rarity 5, $75.00. Photo courtesy of Blythe Curry.

Plate 275. Shaggy Head, ca. 1920, iron, 3¾", rarity 4, $85.00. Photo courtesy of Agris Kelbrants.

Buildings-Architectural

Plate 276. Alamo, 1930, Alamo Iron Works, iron, 4¼", marked Alamo Iron Works Safety 4/1/30, rarity 5, $195.00.

Plate 277. Angeles Temple, 1928, A E Mitchell Company, iron, 4½", marked © 1928 by AE Mitchell Co, 1907 Waterloo Street, Los Angeles, CA, rarity 5*, $175.00.

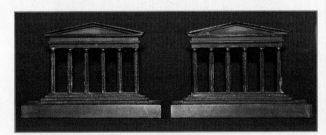

Plate 278. Athens, ca. 1925, Bradley and Hubbard, iron, 4½", shopmark, rarity 4, $90.00.

Plate 279. Berkshire Symphonic Music Shed, ca. 1925, iron, 4½", marked Berkshire Symphonic Music Shed, rarity 5, $75.00.

69

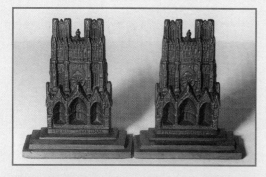

Plate 280. Bishop's Cathedral (variety 1), ca. 1929, iron, 5½", rarity 3, $50.00. Photo courtesy of Agris Kelbrants.

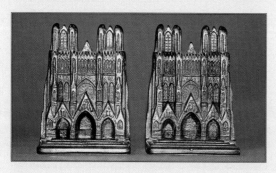

Plate 281. Bishop's Cathedral (variety 2), ca. 1929, iron, 5½", rarity 2, $35.00.

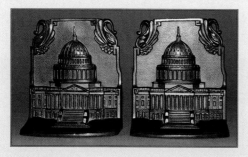

Plate 282. Capitol Building, 1925, X-1, gray metal, 5½", marked #507, rarity 5, $225.00.

Plate 283. Capitol Building (Curtis), ca. 1940, gray metal, 7½", marked Russell Wood Curtis, Arlington, California, rarity 4, $195.00.

Plate 284. Caryatid Columns, ca. 1925, Bradley and Hubbard, iron, 4½", shopmark, rarity 5, $195.00. Photo courtesy of Agris Kelbrants.

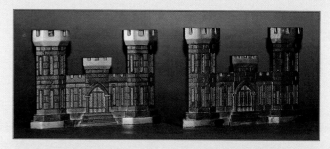

Plate 285. Castle, ca. 1930, bronze, 5¾", rarity 5, $195.00.

Plate 286. Castle Lichtenstein, ca. 1925, Bradley and Hubbard, iron, 5", shopmark, rarity 5, $150.00.

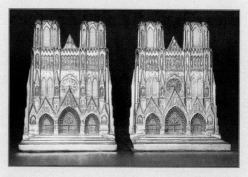

Plate 287. Cathedral, ca. 1927, Ronson, gray metal, 5½", company paper tag #11485, rarity 4, polychrome, $115.00; monochrome, $90.00.

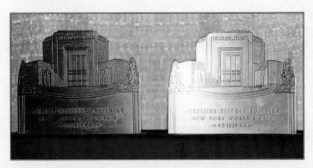

Plate 288. Christian Science Building, 1939, brass, 4¼", marked Christian Science Building, NY Worlds Fair 1939, rarity 4, $95.00.

Plate 289. Church, ca. 1925, iron, 9", rarity 5, $75.00.

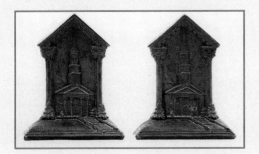

Plate 290. Church (DF), ca. 1925, DF Co, iron, 7", marked DF Co, Patent Pending, rarity 5, $100.00.

Plate 291. Church in Archway, ca. 1925, iron, 5", rarity 4, $125.00.

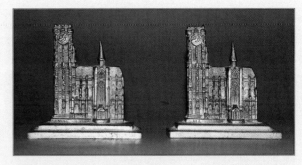

Plate 292. Church with Spire, ca. 1925, MTV, iron, 4¼", rarity 4, $50.00.

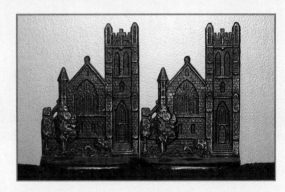

Plate 293. Classic Church, 1931, Champion Hardware, iron, 5", marked #526, 1931, rarity 5, $110.00.

Plate 294. Colonial House, ca. 1928, Solid Bronze, bronze, 5", marked Solid Bronze, rarity 5, $150.00. Photo courtesy of Agris Kelbrants.

Plate 295. Column, 1922, Ronson, gray metal, 4½", marked LV Aronson 1922, rarity 4, $50.00. Photo courtesy of Richard Weinstein.

Plate 296. Cornice, ca. 1925, Bradley and Hubbard, iron, 3½", shopmark, rarity 4, $125.00.

Plate 297. Cottage, ca. 1925, Hubley, iron, 6", rarity 5, $125.00. Photo courtesy of Agris Kelbrants.

Plate 298. Country Cottage, ca. 1924, Hubley, iron, 5", polychrome, rarity 5*; monochrome, rarity 3; polychrome, $225.00; monochrome, $50.00.

Plate 299. Country Cottage (Cliff), ca. 1926, Wilkinson Potteries, pottery, 5¼", marked Hand painted Bizarre by Clarice Cliff Newport Potters, England Wilkinson LTD, England, rarity 5, $600.00.

Plate 300. Country Home, ca. 1925, Bradley and Hubbard, iron, 5", shopmark, rarity 5, $75.00. Photo courtesy of Agris Kelbrants.

Plate 301. Country House, ca. 1925, bronze, 3½", rarity 5, $75.00. Photo courtesy of Agris Kelbrants.

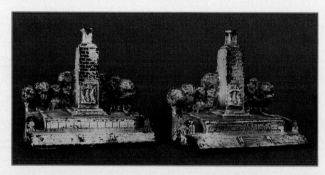

Plate 302. Eternal Light Peace Memorial, ca. 1925, iron, 4¾", marked Eternal Light Peace Memorial, rarity 4, $75.00. *Located in Gettysburg, Pennsylvania.*

Plate 303. Farm House, ca. 1925, iron, 3", rarity 5, $75.00. Photo courtesy of Agris Kelbrants.

Plate 304. Grand Entrance, ca. 1925, iron, 5⅝", rarity 5, $125.00. Photo courtesy of Agris Kelbrants.

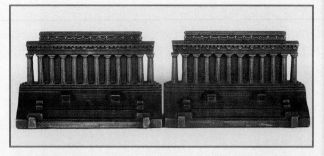

Plate 308. Lincoln Memorial, ca. 1925, Bradley and Hubbard, iron, 3⅝", Lincoln Memorial, shopmark, rarity 4, $150.00.

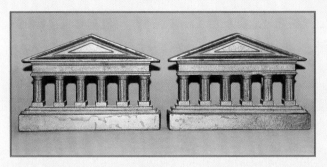

Plate 305. Greek Columns, ca. 1925, Judd, iron, 5", marked 9787, rarity 5, $150.00.

Plate 309. Lincoln's Cabin, ca. 1925, Judd, iron, 3¾", Lincoln's Cabin, rarity 3, $50.00.

Plate 306. Guilford Old Stone House, ca. 1925, brass, Guilford Old Stone House, USA Built 1639, shopmark Solid Brass, rarity 5, $150.00. *Built in 1639, this is the oldest house in Connecticut and the oldest stone house in New England.* Photo courtesy of Henry Whitfield.

Plate 310. Lincoln's Homes, ca. 1920, Gorham, bronze, 5¼", marked Gorham Co Founders 0467, rarity 5, $495.00.

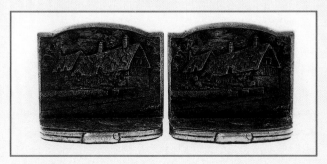

Plate 307. House, ca. 1925, bronze, 3½", rarity 4, $50.00.

Plate 311. Log Cabin, ca. 1925, Bradley and Hubbard, iron, 5", shopmark, rarity 5, $75.00. Photo courtesy of Agris Kelbrants.

Plate 312. Mill, ca. 1925, Verona, iron, 6¾", shopmark, rarity 4, $75.00.

Plate 313. NCR Schoolhouse, 1927, National Cash Register, bronze, 4⅞", marked with contest award to sales person commentary, rarity 5, $400.00. *See page 21 for details.*

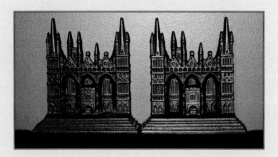

Plate 314. Peterborough Cathedral, 1928, Connecticut Foundry, iron, 1928 shopmark, rarity 5, $135.00. Photo courtesy of Agris Kelbrants.

Plate 315. "Road Home, The," ca. 1925, Bradley and Hubbard, iron, 5", shopmark, rarity 5, $75.00. Photo courtesy of Agris Kelbrants.

Plate 316. Santa Barbara Mission, ca. 1925, Solid Bronze, bronze, 4¼", marked Solid Bronze, rarity 5*, $135.00. *See page 23 for details.*

Plate 317. Shakespeare's House, 1923, Ronson, gray metal, 3⅝", marked LV Aronson 1923, polychrome, rarity 5; monochrome, rarity 4; polychrome, $75.00; monochrome, $45.00.

Plate 318. Shakespeare's House (Hubley), ca. 1925, Hubley, iron, 5¾", marked Stratford-on-Avon, rarity 3, $35.00.

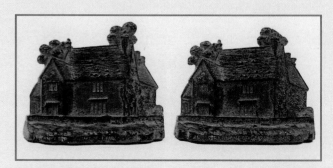

Plate 319. Sulgrave Manor, ca. 1925, iron, 4¼", marked Sulgrave Manor, rarity 4, $80.00. *Ancestral Home of George Washington (England).*

Plate 320. Sulgrave Manor (Hubley), ca. 1925, Hubley, iron, 5¼", rarity 5, $125.00. Photo courtesy of Agris Kelbrants.

Plate 321. Temple of Isis, ca. 1925, Bradley and Hubbard, iron, 4", marked Bradley and Hubbard, rarity 4, $100.00.

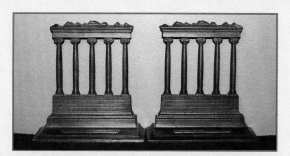

Plate 322. Temple of Saturn, ca. 1925, Bradley and Hubbard, iron, 5½", shopmark, rarity 4, $110.00. Photo courtesy of Agris Kelbrants.

Plate 323. Three Columns, ca. 1925, Bradley and Hubbard, iron, 5¾", shopmark, rarity 5, $175.00. Photo courtesy of Agris Kelbrants.

Plate 324. Welcome Cottage (variety 1), ca. 1925, iron, 4¾", rarity 4, $65.00.

Plate 325. Welcome Cottage (variety 2), ca. 1925, iron, 4¼", marked Welcome, rarity 4, $50.00. Photo courtesy of Agris Kelbrants.

Plate 326. Windmill, ca. 1930, bronze, 6¾", rarity 4, $150.00.

Buildings-Doors and Gates

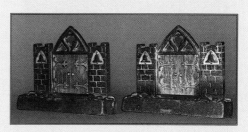

Plate 327. Church Gate, ca. 1925, Judd, iron, 5¾", marked 9737, rarity 4, $125.00.

Plate 328. Colonial House, ca. 1920, Gorham, bronze, 7", marked F Ziegler (sculptor) Gorham Co, rarity 5, $295.00.

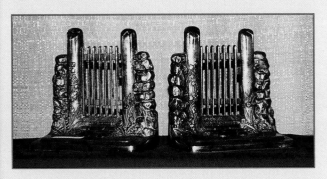

Plate 329. Country Gate, ca. 1935, Bradley and Hubbard, iron, 5", shopmark, rarity 5, $125.00.

Plate 330. Door, ca. 1925, attr Bradley and Hubbard, iron, 6", polychrome, rarity 5; monochrome, rarity 4; polychrome, $175.00; monochrome, $125.00.

Plate 331. Fencepost, ca. 1935, Revere, coiled steel and resin, 5", shopmark, rarity 3, $45.00.

Plate 332. Front Door, ca. 1925, Bradley and Hubbard, iron, 5¾", rarity 4, gray and white, $175.00; other polychrome, $135.00; monochrome, $115.00.

Plate 333. Handel's Door, ca. 1922, Handel, bronze, 7", company paper tag Handel, rarity 5, $400.00.

Plate 334. Iron Gate, ca. 1925, iron, 5", rarity 5, $125.00. Photo courtesy of Kay Ross, White Elephant Antiques.

Plate 335. Mt. Pleasant Front Door, ca. 1925, Bradley and Hubbard, iron, 5½", marked Bradley and Hubbard logo, Mt. Pleasant, rarity 4, $100.00.

Plate 336. Oaken Door, ca. 1985, wood with metal ring, 6", rarity 2, $15.00.

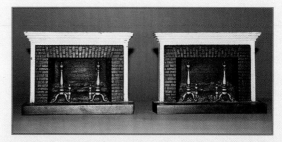

Plate 340. Fireplace (B & H), ca. 1925, Bradley and Hubbard, iron, 4½", rarity 5, $175.00.

Plate 337. Ontario Agricultural College, 1947, iron, 5½", marked OAC (Ontario Agricultural College), Guelph, Canada, ADSA (American Dairy Science Association), rarity 4, $75.00.

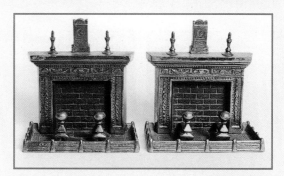

Plate 341. Fireplace (Graham), ca. 1935, Graham Bronze, bronze, 5½", marked Graham Bronze, rarity 5, $175.00.

Buildings-Fireplaces

Plate 338. Brick Fireplace, ca. 1925, iron, 4¾", rarity 3, $75.00. Photo courtesy of Agris Kelbrants.

Plate 342. Homes Hearth, ca. 1935, bronze, 6", rarity 5, $300.00.

Plate 343. Kettle in Fireplace, ca. 1925, iron, 5", rarity 3, $65.00. Photo courtesy of Agris Kelbrants.

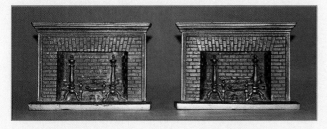

Plate 339. Fireplace, ca. 1925, Solid Bronze, bronze, 4", marked Solid Bronze, rarity 4, $115.00.

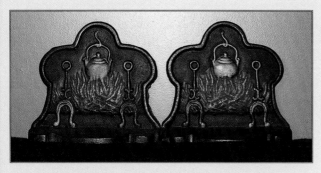

Plate 344. Roaring Fire, ca. 1925, Albany Foundry, iron, 5½", rarity 2, $45.00. Photo courtesy of Agris Kelbrants.

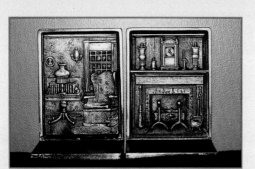

Plate 345. Scenes from Home, ca. 1925, Bradley and Hubbard, iron, 5¼", shopmark, rarity 5*, $175.00. Photo courtesy of Agris Kelbrants.

Camels

Plate 346. Camel, ca. 1930, gray metal, 4½", rarity 5*, $95.00.

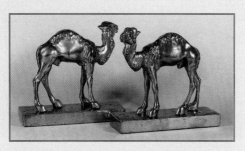

Plate 347. Camel (Armor Bronze), ca. 1925, Armor Bronze, bronze-clad, 7½", company paper tag, rarity 5*, $325.00.

Plate 348. Camel (Judd), ca. 1926, Judd, iron, 6", marked 9971, rarity 5, $175.00.

Plate 349. Camel Resting, ca. 1925, Judd, iron base, gray metal figure, 5¾", rarity 5*, $300.00.

Plate 350. Egyptian Camel, 1928, Connecticut Foundry, iron, 6", marked Connecticut Foundry, Egyptian Camel, © 1924, rarity 4, $95.00.

Plate 351. Ship of the Desert, ca. 1925, Ronson, gray metal, 5½", paper tag #1195M, rarity 5, polychrome, $495.00; monochrome, $350.00.

Plate 352. Shriner Camel, ca. 1930, brass, 4½", rarity 5, $110.00. Photo courtesy of Kay Ross White Elephant Antiques.

Plate 353. Thirsty Camel, ca. 1925, Galvano Bronze, bronze-clad, 6½", rarity 5, $125.00.

Canines

Plate 354. Airedales, ca. 1920, Gorham, bronze, 5½", marked E B Parsons (sculptor) Gorham Co Founders, rarity 5, $1,500.00.

Plate 355. All Ears, 1932, McClelland Barclay, gray metal, 6", marked with signature McClelland Barclay 1932, rarity 5, $175.00.

Plate 356. All Dressed Up, ca. 1930, attr Armor Bronze, bronze-clad, 6", rarity 5, $150.00.

Plate 357. Apologetic Pup, ca. 1920, Gorham, bronze, 5¼", marked R M Mulroney (sculptor), Gorham Co, rarity 5*, $2,500.00.

Plate 358. Auburn Scottie, ca. 1927, gray metal, 4¾", rarity 5, $100.00.

Plate 359. Baby Pup, ca. 1920, Gorham, bronze, 6", marked E B Parsons (sculptor) Gorham Co Founders, rarity 5, $2,500.00.

79

Plate 360. Beagle Dogs, 1929, Rookwood, pottery, 6", shopmark XXIX, rarity 5, $400.00.

Plate 361. Beg, ca. 1920, Gorham, bronze, 7¼", marked E Knauth (sculptor), Gorham Co, rarity 5, $900.00.

Plate 362. Belgian Dogs, ca. 1932, gray metal on marble base, 7", marked Belgium, rarity 5, $175.00.

Plate 363. Best Feet Forward, 1920, Gorham, bronze, 5⅞", marked E Ehrmann (sculptor), Gorham Co., rarity 5*, $2,500.00.

Plate 364. Best Foot Forward, ca. 1970, BMP, gray metal, 4¼", marked BMP, rarity 2, $20.00.

Plate 365. Big Dog, Little Dog, ca. 1930, attr Ronson, gray metal, 5¾", rarity 5*, $195.00.

Plate 366. Boxer, ca. 1930, gray metal, 6¼", rarity 5, $175.00.

Plate 367. Buddy, ca. 1931, gray metal, 6¾", marked Buddy the Original Seeing Eye Dog for the Blind, rarity 5, $195.00.

Plate 368. Buddy (McClelland Barclay), 1931, McClelland Barclay, gray metal, 7", shopmark, rarity 5, $225.00.

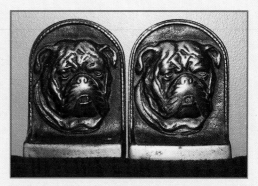

Plate 372. Bull Dog Face, ca. 1925, iron, 5", rarity 5, $165.00. Photo courtesy of Agris Kelbrants.

Plate 369. Bull Dog (JB), ca. 1923, gray metal, 4⅞", rarity 4, $125.00.

Plate 373. Bull Terrier (Gorham), ca. 1920, Gorham, bronze, 7¼", marked EB Parsons (sculptor), Gorham, rarity 5*, $2,500.00.

Plate 370. Bull Dog (Gorham), ca. 1920, Gorham, bronze, 6", marked Belle Johnson (sculptor), Gorham Co, rarity 5*, $2,500.00.

Plate 374. Bust of Scottie, ca. 1925, gray metal, 6½", rarity 5, $85.00. Photo courtesy of Agris Kelbrants.

Plate 371. Bull Dog (JB), ca. 1932, Jennings Brothers, gray metal, 6½", marked JB, rarity 5, $195.00. *Previously called simply BULL DOG, changed to BULL DOG (JB).*

Plate 375. Chow, ca. 1950, iron, 4¼", marked #904, rarity 5, $75.00.

Plate 376. Chrome Scottie, ca. 1930, Ronson, gray metal, 5½", rarity 5*, $325.00. Photo courtesy of Richard Weinstein.

Plate 380. Curious Pup, 1925, Littco, iron, 5", paper tag: Littco, rarity 4, $175.00. Photo courtesy of Joyce Derian.

Plate 377. Cocker Spaniel, ca. 1934, Frankart, gray metal, 6¼", shopmark, rarity 4, $150.00.

Plate 381. Dachshund (PMC), ca. 1965, Philadelphia Metal Craftsman, gray metal, 5", company paper tag, rarity 2, $50.00.

Plate 378. Country Dogs, ca. 1920, bronze, 5", marked Made in Austria, rarity 5*, $475.00. Photo courtesy of Dealer's Choice Antiques.

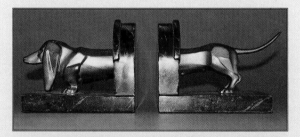

Plate 382. Dachshund Coming and Going, ca. 1925, Ronson, gray metal, 4½", rarity 5, $375.00.

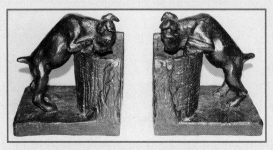

Plate 379. Curious Pooch, ca. 1925, bronze, 5¾", marked ©, rarity 5*, $1,200.00.

Plate 383. Dane Cameo, ca. 1920, gray metal, 6", shopmark (some combination of "M" or "A" and "W") Made in Canada, rarity 5*, $125.00. Photo courtesy of Blythe Curry.

Plate 384. Deco Dog, ca. 1925, chrome-plated iron, 5½", rarity 5*, $475.00.

Plate 385. Dog, ca. 1920, Littlestown Hardware and Foundry (Littco), iron, 4½", company paper tag, rarity 4, $175.00.

Plate 386. Dog (Gift House), 1939, Gift House, Inc, iron, 5¼", marked Gift House, Inc. 1939, rarity 4, $100.00.

Plate 387. Dog (Pompeian Bronze), ca. 1925, Pompeian Bronze, bronze-clad, 7", marked Paul Herzel (sculptor) Pompeian Bronze ©, rarity 5*, $275.00.

Plate 388. Dog and Cat, ca. 1925, attr Armor Bronze, bronze-clad, 6", marked G S Allen (sculptor), rarity 5, $250.00.

Plate 389. Dog and Cat (Gorham), ca. 1920, Gorham, bronze, 6½", marked E Norton (sculptor), Gorham Co, rarity 5*, $2,500.00.

Plate 390. Dog at the Fence, ca. 1930, Frankart, gray metal, 6", shopmark, rarity 5, $195.00.

Plate 391. Dog at the Fence (PMC), ca. 1965, PM Craftsman, gray metal, 6½", company paper tag, rarity 5, $95.00.

83

Plate 392. Dog Chasing Cat, ca. 1930, Pompeian Bronze, bronze-clad, 10¼", marked A Retolatto (sculptor), rarity 5*, $495.00.

Plate 393. Dog Head, 1930, iron, 5⅜", marked J L Drucklieb (sculptor) Progress lounge #38, 1890-1930, ©, rarity 5, $100.00.

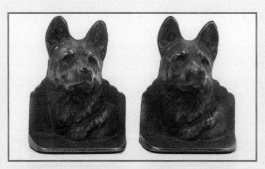

Plate 394. Dog Head (Littco), ca. 1925, Littco, iron, 4¾", company paper tag, rarity 3, $40.00.

Plate 395. Dog House, ca. 1920, attr Hubley, iron, 5½", rarity 5, $150.00.

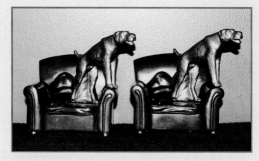

Plate 396. Dog in Chair, ca. 1925, attr Nuart, gray metal, 5", rarity 5, $125.00.

Photo courtesy of Agris Kelbrants.

Plate 397. Dog on the Wall, ca. 1930, attr Pompeian Bronze, bronze-clad, 6", rarity 5, $125.00.

Plate 398. Dog Reading to Cat, ca. 1930, K & O, gray metal, 6", shopmark, rarity 5, $175.00.

Plate 399. Dogs at Play, ca. 1930, PRM, gray metal, 5¾", marked 430 B, rarity 5, $100.00.

Plate 400. Ears Up and Down, ca. 1920, Gorham, bronze, marked FS Godwin (sculptor), Gorham, rarity 5*, $2,500.00.

Plate 401. English Bulldog, ca. 1930, K & O, gray metal, 3½", shopmark, rarity 5*, $225.00. Photo courtesy of Agris Kelbrants.

Plate 402. English Pointer, ca. 1930, Ronson, gray metal, 3¼", company paper tag #14766, rarity 5, $110.00.

Plate 403. Favorite Mutt, ca. 1922, Frankart, gray metal, 5¼", marked Frankart, Pat Applied For, rarity 5*, $275.00.

Plate 404. Fido, ca. 1925, Bronzart, gray metal, 6½", shopmark, rarity 4, $165.00. *Figure of dog partially covers shopmark on base.*

Plate 405. Five Pups, ca. 1925, gray metal, 4¼", rarity 5, $110.00. Photo courtesy of Agris Kelbrants.

Plate 406. Fox and Grapes, ca. 1925, bronze, 6½", rarity 5, $195.00.

Plate 407. Fox and Grapes (Fontinelle), ca. 1930, (French), bronze on marble base, 8", marked L Fontinelle (sculptor), Made in France #6603, rarity 5*, $1,250.00.

Plate 408. Fox and Grapes (Le Verrier), ca. 1925, Le Verrier, bronze on marble base, 9", marked M. Le Verrier (sculptor), rarity 5, original, $795.00; current production, $495.00. *See page 18 for details.*

Plate 409. Fox Heads, ca. 1925, brass, 5¾", rarity 5, $150.00. Photo courtesy of Agris Kelbrants.

Plate 410. Fox Terrier, ca. 1925, Spencer, iron, 5", marked Spencer, Reg US Pat Off, Guilford, Conn, rarity 5, $175.00. Photo courtesy of Nancy Middleton.

Plate 411. Fox Terrier (B & H), ca. 1925, Bradley and Hubbard, iron, 5¼", shopmark, rarity 5, $125.00. Photo courtesy of Agris Kelbrants.

Plate 412. Frisky Terrier, 1930, iron, 6", marked #247, rarity 4, $75.00. Photo courtesy of Agris Kelbrants.

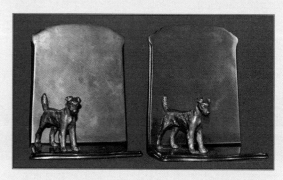

Plate 413. Frisky Airedales, ca. 1925, Ronson, gray metal, 4¼", company paper tag #14473, rarity 5, $110.00.

Plate 414. German Shepherd, ca. 1928, iron, 4¾", rarity 3, $45.00.

Plate 415. German Shepherd (JB), ca. 1930, Jennings Brothers, gray metal, 6", marked JB 2408, rarity 5, $175.00.

Plate 416. German Shepherd (Nuart), ca. 1930, Nuart, gray metal, 7", shopmark, rarity 4, $100.00. Photo courtesy of Sue Benoliel.

Plate 417. German Shepherd (Pompeian Bronze), ca. 1920, Pompeian Bronze, bronze-clad, 8½", marked Paul Herzel (sculptor) ©, rarity 5, $250.00. Photo courtesy of Billie Trepanier.

Plate 418. German Shepherd Standing, ca. 1920, Pompeian Bronze, bronze-clad, 8½", marked Paul Herzel (sculptor) ©, rarity 5, $350.00. Photo courtesy of Billie Trepanier.

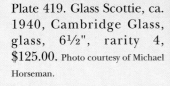

Plate 419. Glass Scottie, ca. 1940, Cambridge Glass, glass, 6½", rarity 4, $125.00. Photo courtesy of Michael Horseman.

Plate 420. Graceful Dane, ca. 1920, bronze, 6½", marked Austria, rarity 5*, $750.00.

Plate 421. Great Dane, ca. 1928, JF Company, gray metal, 7¾", shopmark, rarity 5, $195.00.

Plate 422. Great Dane (Frankart), ca. 1930, Frankart, gray metal, 6¾", marked Frankart Inc, Patent Applied For, rarity 4, $175.00.

Plate 423. Great Dane (Great Dane Trailers), ca. 1930, bronze, 7", marked Great Dane Trailers, Inc. Savannah Georgia, rarity 5, $175.00.

87

Plate 424. Greyhound, ca. 1925, gray metal on marble base, 7½", rarity 5, $375.00.

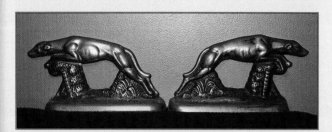

Plate 425. Greyhound Leaping, ca. 1925, bronze, 4", rarity 5, $200.00. Photo courtesy of Agris Kelbrants.

Plate 426. Greyhound Twins, ca. 1925, Nuart, gray metal, 5", shopmark, rarity 5, $135.00.

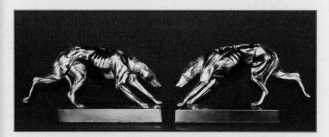

Plate 427. Greyhounds, ca. 1938, attr Jennings Brothers, gray metal, 4¼", rarity 5, $175.00.

Plate 428. Guard Dog, ca. 1930, Jennings Brothers, gray metal , 5", shopmark, rarity 5, $135.00.

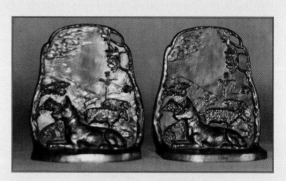

Plate 429. Guarding the Flock, ca. 1925, X-1, gray metal, 5½", marked #610, rarity 5, $175.00.

Plate 430. Hair in His Eyes, ca. 1925, gray metal, 5½", rarity 5, $75.00. Photo courtesy of Agris Kelbrants.

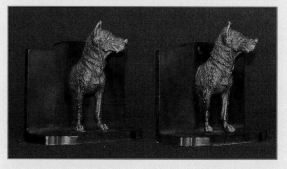

Plate 431. Half-Breed, ca. 1920, Bradley and Hubbard, iron, 6", company paper tag, rarity 5*, $250.00.

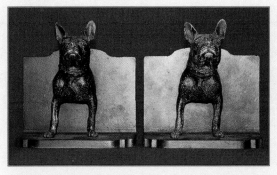

Plate 432. Halfway Out, ca. 1920, Bradley and Hubbard, iron, 6", company paper tag, rarity 5*, $250.00.

Plate 433. Head Dog, ca. 1928, Frankart, gray metal, 6", marked Frankart, Pat Applied For, rarity 5, $175.00.

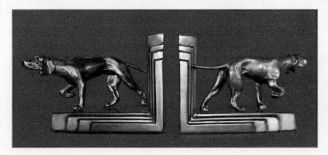

Plate 434. Hound, ca. 1930, Ronson, gray metal, 5¾", company paper tag, rarity 4, $150.00.

Plate 435. Hound and Bird, ca. 1930, Frankart, gray metal, 5", marked Frankart Inc, Patent Applied For, rarity 4, $195.00.

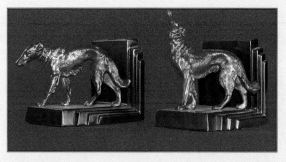

Plate 436. Hounds Up and Down, ca. 1930, Ronson, gray metal, 5", company paper tag, rarity 5, $150.00.

Plate 437. Hunting Dog, ca. 1930, gray metal on marble base, 5¼", rarity 4, $165.00.

Plate 438. I Hear You, ca. 1930, gray metal, 6", rarity 5, $150.00.

Plate 439. I Hear You (Nuart), ca. 1925, Nuart, gray metal, 6", shopmark, rarity 5, $150.00.

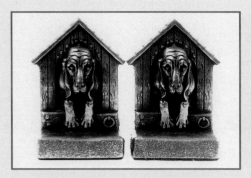

Plate 440. In the Dog House, ca. 1925, bronze-clad, 6¾", rarity 5*, $175.00.

Plate 441. Jasper, ca. 1929, Art Colony Industries, iron, 5¾", rarity 3, $50.00.

Plate 442. Latticework and Dog, 1930, Creation Company, iron, 6", marked C Co 1930 ©, rarity 5, $200.00.

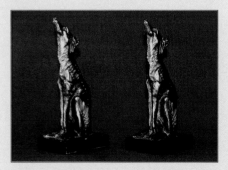

Plate 443. Le Loup (The Wolf), ca. 1925, JB Hirsch, gray metal on polished stone base, 10", rarity 5, $275.00.

Plate 444. Leaping Greyhounds, ca. 1928, bronze on marble base, 3", rarity 5, $175.00.

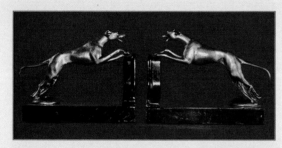

Plate 445. Leaping Greyhounds (Ronson), ca. 1930, Ronson, gray metal, 5½", company tag #12314, rarity 5, $195.00. Photo courtesy of Richard Weinstein.

Plate 446. Listening Pooch, ca. 1920, Gorham, bronze, 4¾", marked HS Davis (sculptor), Gorham Co, rarity 5*, $1,000.00.

Plate 447. Man's Best Friend, ca. 1920, bronze-clad, 5½", rarity 5, $175.00.

Plate 448. Man's Best Friend (Ronson), 1932, Ronson, gray metal, 5", marked Ronson 1932 Newark, rarity 4, $100.00.

Plate 449. Mastiff, ca. 1926, Bradley and Hubbard, iron, 5¼", shopmark, rarity 4, $125.00.

Plate 450. Me and My Dog House, ca. 1929, Verona, iron, 6", Verona, rarity 5, $110.00. Photo courtesy of Henrietta Milan.

Plate 451. Mickey, ca. 1920, Pompeian Bronze, bronze-clad, 7", marked Paul Herzel ©(sculptor), Mickey, rarity 5, $150.00. Photo courtesy of Billie Trepanier.

Plate 452. Mostly Ears, ca. 1920, SC Tarrant, bronze-clad, 7", company paper tag: Galvano bronze, the SC Tarrant Co, Inc NY, rarity 5, $195.00.

Plate 453. Mountain Shepherd, ca. 1925, Hubley, iron, 5¾", marked #297, rarity 4, $125.00.

Plate 454. Mutt, ca. 1930, Bronzart, gray metal, 6", Bronzart, rarity 5, $100.00. Photo courtesy of Judy Hawk.

Plate 455. On Alert, ca. 1930, brass, 6¼", rarity 4, $125.00.

Plate 456. On Point, ca. 1925, Jennings Brothers, gray metal, 5", marked JB 1601, rarity 5*, $250.00.

Plate 457. Orphans, ca. 1923, iron, 4½", #272, rarity 5, $150.00.

Plate 458. Paired Wolfhounds, ca. 1930, Ronson, gray metal, 4½", rarity 5, $110.00.

Plate 459. Parted Pooch, ca. 1925, bronze-clad, 6", marked Bristol (sculptor), rarity 5, $175.00.

Plate 460. Pal, 1930, Connecticut Foundry, iron, 6½", Pal 1930, shopmark, rarity 5, $110.00.

Plate 461. Pekingese, 1926, NY Brass Co, iron, 5", marked NY Brass Co, 1926, rarity 5*, $250.00.

Plate 462. Pekingese Peek-A-Boo, ca. 1925, Ronson, gray metal on marbleized base, 5½", company paper tag, rarity 5, $200.00.

Plate 463. Pekingese Pups, ca. 1930, Ronson, gray metal, 5¼", company paper tag #16601, rarity 5, $175.00. Photo courtesy of Richard Weinstein.

Plate 464. Pensive Hound, ca. 1930, Ronson, gray metal, 3¼", company paper tag #16031, rarity 3, $95.00. Photo courtesy of Richard Weinstein.

Plate 465. Perched Puppies, ca. 1925, Ronson, gray metal, 5", marked AMW Newark, New Jersey, rarity 4, $150.00. Photo courtesy of Dave Udstuen.

Plate 466. Plains Wolf, 1923, Ronson, gray metal, 4¼", marked LV Aronson 1923, rarity 4, $125.00.

Plate 467. Playful Pups, 1920, Kunst Foundry, bronze, 6¾", marked EB Parsons (sculptor); A Kunst Bronze Foundry, NY, rarity 5, $1,300.00.
Photo courtesy of Billie Trepanier.

Plate 468. Playful Terriers, 1914, Zoppo Foundry, bronze, 7", marked EB Parsons 1914, B Zoppo Foundry, NY, rarity 5, $1,200.00. Photo courtesy of Billie Trepanier.

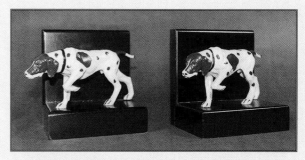

Plate 469. Pointers, ca. 1950, gray metal, 5", rarity 5*, $95.00.

Plate 470. Pointers (Hubley), ca. 1925, Hubley, iron, 4¼", polychrome, rarity 4; monochrome, rarity 3; polychrome, $95.00; monochrome, $75.00. Photo courtesy of Sue Benoliel.

Plate 471. Police Dogs, ca. 1925, Jennings Brothers, gray metal, 5½", marked JB 1922, rarity 5, $275.00.

Plate 472. Pooch on Pedestal, ca. 1925, iron, 5½",
marked #945, rarity 5, $110.00. Photo courtesy of Agris Kelbrants.

Plate 476. Puppy, ca. 1930, gray metal, rarity
5, $75.00.

Plate 473. Pooch Profile, ca. 1925, iron, 5½",
rarity 5, $195.00. Photo courtesy of Agris Kelbrants.

Plate 477. Puppy Triplets, ca. 1925, Ronson,
gray metal, 6", company paper tag, rarity 4,
$175.00.

Plate 474. Prancing Greyhounds, ca. 1930,
Ronson, gray metal, 6", rarity 5*, $325.00.

Plate 478. Pups in a Basket, 1936, K & O, gray metal,
4½", shopmark, rarity 5, $175.00. Photo courtesy of Agris Kelbrants.

Plate 475. Prestigious Pooch, ca.
1925, iron, 6½", rarity 5, $150.00.

Plate 479. Retriever Dog, ca. 1925, bronze, marked
with English Registry #694237, rarity 5, $175.00. Photo
courtesy of Sue Benoliel.

Plate 480. Retrievers (Armor Bronze), ca. 1925, attr Armor Bronze, bronze-clad, 4¼", marked ©, rarity 5*, $175.00.

Plate 481. Retrievers (Bruce Fox), 1950, Bruce Fox, aluminum, 6½", marked Bruce Fox (sculptor), rarity 5, $125.00.

Plate 482. Retrievers (Ronson), 1923, Ronson, gray metal, 4¼", marked LV Aronson 1923, rarity 5, $150.00.

Plate 483. Retro Scottie, ca. 1930, Frankart, gray metal, 4½", shopmark, rarity 5, $150.00.

Plate 484. Russian Wolfhound, 1929, Connecticut Foundry, iron, 5¼", marked Russian Wolfhound, #933, shopmark 1929, rarity 4, $125.00.

Plate 485. Scot, ca. 1929, gray metal, 7½", rarity 2, $35.00.

Plate 486. Scotch Twins, ca. 1925, Art Colony Industries, iron, 5¼", rarity 3, $90.00.

Plate 487. Scottie (Ronson), ca. 1925, Ronson, gray metal, 6", rarity 5, $195.00.

Plate 488. Scottie at the Fence, ca. 1925, Bradley and Hubbard, iron, 6", shopmark, rarity 4, $125.00.

Plate 489. Scottie on Fence, ca. 1928, bronze, 6", rarity 5, $195.00.

Plate 490. Scottie Pair, ca. 1934, Nuart, gray metal, 5", shopmark, rarity 2, $35.00.

Plate 491. Scottie Pair (Frankart), ca. 1930, Frankart, gray metal, 4¼", marked Frankart, inc Pat Applied For, rarity 5, $225.00.

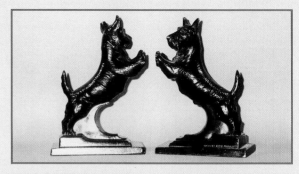

Plate 492. Scottie Terrier, 1932, Crescent Metal Works, gray metal, 6¼", marked Crescent Metal Works 1932, rarity 5*, $150.00 Photo courtesy of Billie Trepanier.

Plate 493. Scottie: One Ear Up, ca. 1930, Ronson, gray metal, 5", company paper tag, rarity 5, $175.00.

Plate 494. Scottish Terrier, 1929, Connecticut Foundry, iron, 5½", shopmark, Scottish Terrier, 1929, rarity 4, $65.00.

Plate 495. Scotty (Connecticut Foundry), 1929, Connecticut Foundry, iron, 5½", marked 1929 Connecticut Foundry, shopmark, rarity 4, $95.00.

Plate 496. Scotty (Gorham), ca. 1920, Gorham, bronze, 4¾", CC Davis (sculptor), Gorham Co, rarity 5*, $2,500.00.

Plate 500. Scotty and Terrier Friends, ca. 1925, Hubley, iron, 5½", marked #280, rarity 5, $150.00.

Plate 497. Scotty (Hubley), ca. 1925, Hubley, iron, 5", rarity 3, $50.00. Photo courtesy of Sue Benoliel.

Plate 501. Scotty Dog Sitting Up, ca. 1934, Ronson, gray metal, 4", company paper tag #16038, rarity 5, $95.00. Photo courtesy of Agris Kelbrants.

Plate 498. Scotty (Littco), ca. 1925, Littco, iron, 5", rarity 4, $110.00.

Plate 502. Scotty Dogs, ca. 1928, gray metal on marble base, 5¾", rarity 4, $95.00.

Plate 499. Scotty (Verona), ca. 1925, Verona, iron, 5⅜", Verona, rarity 4, $95.00.

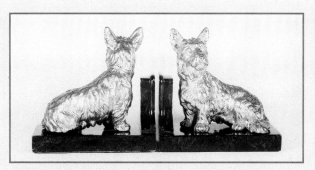

Plate 503. Scotty Dogs (Ronson), ca. 1932, Ronson, gray metal, 6", company paper tag, rarity 5, $225.00.

Plate 504. Scotty Standing, ca. 1920, Gorham, bronze, 8", marked Marguerite Kirmse (sculptor), Gorham Co, rarity 5*, $3,500.00.

Plate 505. Seated Shepherd, ca. 1925, bronze, 5½", rarity 4, $100.00.

Plate 506. Setter Dog, 1922, Ronson, gray metal, 3¼", marked LVA 1922, rarity 5, $125.00.

Plate 507. Setters, ca. 1925, Littco, iron, 5", company paper tag, rarity 4, $115.00.

Plate 508. Setters (Judd), ca. 1925, Judd, iron, 3½", rarity 5, $175.00.

Plate 509. Shepherd, ca. 1932, bronze, 9", rarity 4, $175.00.

Plate 510. Shepherd (B&H), ca. 1925, Bradley and Hubbard, iron, 6", shopmark, rarity 5, $150.00.

Plate 511. Shepherd (Gotham Art bronze), ca. 1930, Gotham Art bronze, bronze-clad, 8¾", company paper tag, rarity 5, $195.00.

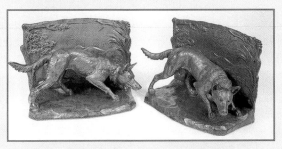

Plate 512. Shepherd (Hirschler), ca. 1920, bronze, 4¼", marked Heinrich W Hirschler, Made in Austria, rarity 5, $800.00.

Plate 516. Silver Scotties, ca. 1929, Jennings Brothers, gray metal, 5¼", shopmark, rarity 5, $125.00.

Plate 513. Shepherd (Hubley), ca. 1925, Hubley, iron, 5", rarity 4, $125.00.

Plate 517. Silver Scotty Pair, ca. 1929, Jennings Brothers, gray metal, 5¼", company paper tag, rarity 5, $175.00. Photo courtesy of Dave Udstuen.

Plate 514. Shepherd (Salat), ca. 1920, bronze, 5¼", marked Salat (sculptor), Made in Austria, rarity 5, $400.00.

Plate 518. Sitting Up, ca. 1930, Ronson, gray metal, 6", rarity 5, $125.00.

Plate 515. Shepherd on Log, ca. 1930, gray metal on onyx base, 7", rarity 5, $175.00.

Plate 519. Sleeping Fox, ca. 1930, gray metal, 4", rarity 5, $125.00.

Plate 520. Smiling Pup, ca. 1920, Gorham, bronze, 4½", marked Mrs George Benney (sculptor), Gorham Co, rarity 5*, $750.00.

Plate 524. Sportsman's Friend, ca. 1925, iron, 6½", marked England, rarity 5, $125.00.

Plate 521. Spaniel, ca. 1930, iron, 5¼", rarity 5, $110.00. Photo courtesy of Agris Kelbrants.

Plate 525. Sportsman's Friend (Hann), ca. 1925, iron, 6½", marked Hann (sculptor), Sportsman's Friend, rarity 5, $175.00.

Plate 522. Spaniel (JB), ca. 1930, Jennings Brothers, gray metal, 4½", marked JB, rarity 5, $125.00.

Plate 526. Spunky Pup, ca. 1930, McClelland Barclay, gray metal, 5", marked McClelland Barclay ©, rarity 5*, $250.00.

Plate 523. Speed Pup, ca. 1920, Gorham, bronze, 4¼", marked E B Parsons (sculptor), Gorham Co Founders, rarity 5*, $2,500.00.

Plate 527. Spunky Spaniel, ca. 1930, gray metal, 5", rarity 4, $100.00. Photo courtesy of Sue Benoliel.

Plate 528. Squatty Scottie, ca. 1940, glass, 5", rarity 3, $75.00.

Plate 529. Standing Tall, ca. 1925, iron, 3½", rarity 5, $75.00. Photo courtesy of Agris Kelbrants.

Plate 530. Tail to Spare, ca. 1925, iron, 3", rarity 5, $65.00. Photo courtesy of Agris Kelbrants.

Plate 531. Terriers, ca. 1925, Ronson, Schreiber Cintio, bronze, 4½", rarity 5*, $165.00.

Plate 532. Thirsty Pooch, ca. 1925, gray metal on marble base, 4⅛", rarity 5, $75.00.

Plate 533. Three Muttketeers, ca. 1930, Jennings Brothers, gray metal, 6", marked JB 1926, rarity 5, $175.00.

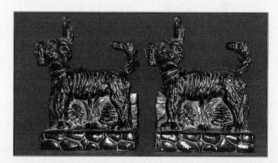

Plate 534. Tiperari Dog, ca. 1930, Ronson, gray metal, 6", company paper tag # 1073, rarity 5, $195.00.

Plate 535. Too Cute, ca. 1930, Nuart, gray metal, 5", shopmark, rarity 5, $75.00.

Plate 536. Two Scotties, ca. 1930, Nuart, gray metal, 4¼", shopmark, rarity 5, $125.00.

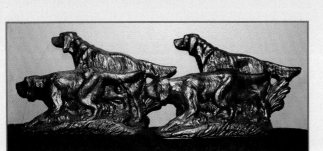

Plate 537. Two Setters, ca. 1930, gray metal, 5½", rarity 4, $135.00. Photo courtesy of Agris Kelbrants.

Plate 538. Vagrants, ca. 1920, Gorham, bronze, 5⅞", marked E B Parsons (sculptor), Gorham Co Founders, rarity 5*, $2,500.00.

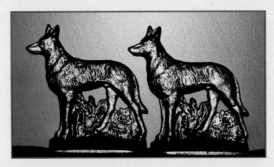

Plate 539. Vigilant Shepherds, ca. 1925, iron, 6", rarity 4, $75.00.

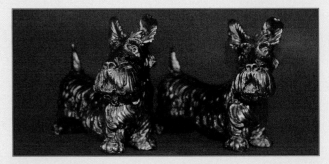

Plate 540. Whiskers, ca. 1930, gray metal, 5", rarity 5*, $250.00.

Plate 541. Wire Terrier, 1929, Connecticut Foundry, iron, 5¾", Wire Terrier 1929 shopmark, rarity 4, $85.00.

Plate 542. Wirehaired Fox Terrier, ca. 1925, brass, 5", English registry mark, rarity 5*, $95.00.

Plate 543. Wirehaired Fox Terrier (Hubley), ca. 1925, Hubley, iron, 6", rarity 5, polychrome, $195.00.

Plate 544. Wolfhound, ca. 1940, New Martinsville Glass, glass, 7", rarity 4, $200.00.

Plate 548. Coach (Hubley), ca. 1925, Hubley, iron, 3⅞", marked Hubley #379, rarity 4, polychrome, $125.00; monochrome, $75.00.

Carriages

Plate 545. Carriage, Private, 1928, iron, 3½", shopmark, rarity 4, $75.00. Photo courtesy of Blythe Curry.

Plate 549. Coaches, ca. 1930, bronze, 5⅞", marked Genuine Solid Bronze, rarity 5, $150.00.

Plate 546. Carriage (Judd), ca. 1925, Judd, iron, 2¾", marked #9653, rarity 4, $75.00. Photo courtesy of Agris Kelbrants.

Plate 550. Coaxing the Horses, ca. 1925, Hubley, iron, 6", shopmark, rarity 5, $175.00.

Plate 547. Carriage and Castle, ca. 1925, iron, 3¾", rarity 5*, $75.00. Photo courtesy of Agris Kelbrants.

Plate 551. Empty Coach, 1931, Champion, iron, 3¼", shopmark, Geneva 1931, rarity 3, $35.00.

Plate 552. English Coach, ca. 1930, WH Howell & Co, iron, 4", marked WH Howell, ©, rarity 4, $75.00.

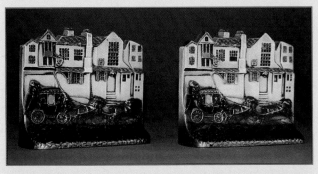

Plate 556. Old Stagecoach, 1934 (pictured in Wallenstein & Meyer catalog, 1934), iron, 4", rarity 4, $95.00.

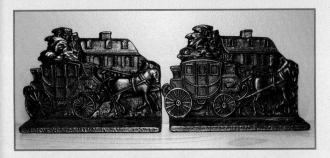

Plate 553. English Stage Coach, ca. 1925, iron, 4¼", rarity 4, $95.00. Photo courtesy of Agris Kelbrants.

Plate 557. Olde English Coach, ca. 1930, K & O, gray metal, 5¼", shopmark, polychrome, rarity 5; monochrome, rarity 4; polychrome, $165.00; monochrome, $110.00.

Plate 554. In Colonial days, ca. 1925, Bradley & Hubbard, iron, 4½", shopmark, rarity 5, $175.00.

Plate 558. Royal Coach, ca. 1925, WH Howell & Co, iron, 5¼", marked © WH Howell & Co, rarity 4, $75.00.

Plate 555. Old Coaching Days, ca. 1925, Armor Bronze, bronze-clad, 5¼", rarity 4, $95.00.

Plate 559. Stage Coach, ca. 1932, Jennings Brothers, gray metal, 4½", marked JB 3149 Pat Applied For, rarity 5, $225.00.

Plate 560. Ye Olde Coaching Days, ca. 1924, Jennings Brothers, gray metal, 4¼", shopmark #2385, rarity 3, $65.00.

Plate 564. Baby Asleep Under Tree, ca. 1920, Gorham, bronze, 5½", marked D Rich (sculptor), Gorham Co., rarity 5*, $3,500.00.

Plate 561. Ye Olde Inne, ca. 1940, Syracuse Ornamental, Syrocowood, 6½", company paper tag, rarity 3, $45.00.

Plate 565. Basket Case, ca. 1925, Armor Bronze, bronze-clad, 5½", rarity 4, $125.00.

Children

Plate 562. Apple Tree Girl and Boy, ca. 1950, Hummel, porcelain and wood, 6", shopmark, rarity 4, $250.00.

Plate 566. Best Friends, ca. 1920, Gorham, bronze, 7¾", marked M T Bradley (sculptor), Gorham Co., rarity 5*, $3,500.00.

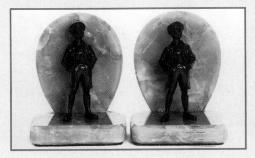

Plate 563. Austrian Boy, ca. 1925, bronze on marble base, 5½", rarity 5*, $550.00.

Plate 567. Birthday Suit, ca. 1930, Bronzart, gray metal, 8¾", marked Bronzart, rarity 5, $225.00.

105

Plate 568. Blenko Girl, ca. 1970, Blenko, glass, 8", rarity 3, $40.00.

Plate 569. Boy, 1918, Gorham, bronze, 8¾", marked K Gruppe (sculptor), © 1918, Gorham Co., rarity 5*, $5,000.00.

Plate 570. Boy and Girl (Backer), ca. 1960, Alexander Backer Company, resin, 9½", marked Alexander Backer Company, rarity 3, $35.00

Plate 571. Boy and Girl (Everstyle), ca. 1930, Everstyle, gray metal, 7", marked Everstyle, rarity 5, $110.00.

Plate 572. Boy and Girl (Nuart), ca. 1930, Nuart, gray metal, 5", marked Nuart Creations, NYC, Made in USA, rarity 4, $125.00.

Plate 573. Boy and Girl (Viking), ca. 1950, Viking Glass, glass, 8", rarity 4, $75.00.

Plate 574. Boy and Girl Cupid, ca. 1912, Griffoul, bronze, 6¾", marked M Peinlich (sculptor), Cast by Griffoul, Newark, NJ, Theodore Starr Inc., NY, rarity 5, $800.00.

Plate 575. Boy on Donkey, ca. 1915, bronze, 6¾", marked Heinrich (sculptor), rarity 5*, $950.00.

Plate 576. Boy on World, ca. 1930, gray metal, 6", rarity 4, $115.00.

Plate 577. Boy with Frog, ca. 1925, bronze-clad, 5½", marked 181 ©, rarity 5, $200.00.

Plate 578. Boy with Frog (Armor Bronze), 1914, Armor Bronze, bronze-clad, 7½", S Morani (sculptor), shop-mark 1914, rarity 4, $250.00.

Plate 579. Boys with Puppies, ca. 1930, McClelland Barclay, gray metal, 6¼", marked McClelland Barclay, rarity 4, $225.00.

Plate 580. Cherub & Butterfly, ca. 1924, Ronson, gray metal, 6¼", company tag #7072, polychrome, rarity 5; monochrome, rarity 4; polychrome, $250.00; monochrome, $150.00.

Plate 581. Cherub (Verona), ca. 1925, Verona, iron, 8", shopmark, rarity 5, $210.00.

Plate 582. Cherub Reading, ca. 1914, Armor Bronze, bronze-clad, 6", S Morani (sculptor), shopmark, polychrome, rarity 5; monochrome, rarity 4; polychrome, $250.00; monochrome, $150.00.

Plate 583. Cherubs, ca. 1925, various, gray metal, 5½", 1903, rarity 4, $175.00. *This bookend was extraordinarily popular and manufactured by a variety of makers. The earliest version dated 1903.*

Plate 584. Cherubs and Garlands, ca. 1925, K & O, gray metal, 5", shopmark, rarity 5, $150.00.

Plate 585. Cherubs in Book, ca. 1918, Kathodian Bronze Works, bronze-clad, 5¼", marked KBW ArtBronz, rarity 5*, $295.00.

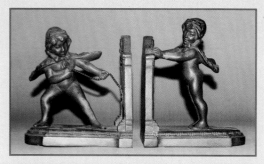

Plate 586. Cherub's Play, ca. 1900, gray metal, 7", France, rarity 5, $400.00.

Plate 587. Chick Girl and Playmates (Hummel), ca. 1950, Hummel, porcelain and wood, 6", shopmark, rarity 4, $275.00.

Plate 588. Child Reading, ca. 1928, Frankart, gray metal, 6½", rarity 5, $325.00.

Plate 589. Child with Book, ca. 1920, Gorham, bronze, 6", marked A Austin (sculptor), Gorham Co, rarity 5*, $1,400.00.

Plate 590. Child with Rabbit, 1926, American Encaustic Tile Co, ceramic, 4½", marked American Encaustic Tile Co, 1926, rarity 5, $300.00.

Plate 957. Lion of Lucerne, ca. 1934, gray metal, 4¼", marked Antonio Canova 1757 – 1822 (sculptor), rarity 4, $135.00.

Pate 961. Lion of Lucerne (Judd), ca. 1920, Judd, iron, 5", rarity 5, $175.00. Photo courtesy of Rick Kushon, Etna Antiques.

Plate 958. Lion of Lucerne (B & H), ca. 1925, Bradley and Hubbard, gray metal figure on iron base, 6", company paper tag, rarity 5, $225.00.

Plate 962. Lion of Lucerne (Littco), ca. 1928, Littco, iron, 4", marked Lion of Lucerne, rarity 3, $65.00.

Plate 959. Lion of Lucerne (JB), ca. 1925, Jennings Brothers, gray metal, 6", shopmark, #1570, rarity 4, $125.00.

Plate 963. Lion of Lucerne (Nuart), ca. 1930, Nuart, gray metal, 4", marked Nuart Creations, NYC, rarity 5, $135.00.

Plate 960. Lion of Lucerne (JB) Petite, ca. 1930, Jennings Brothers, gray metal, 4½", marked JB #2146, rarity 4, $125.00.

Plate 964. Lion on Rocky Terrain, 1922, Ronson, gray metal, 4½", marked LVA 1922, rarity 4, $165.00.

155

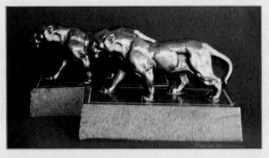

Plate 965. Lioness, ca. 1925, Judd, gray metal figure on iron base, 5½", rarity 5, $300.00. Photo courtesy of Agris Kelbrants.

Plate 969. Menacing Tiger, ca. 1925, bronze-clad, 4½", rarity 5, $125.00. Photo courtesy of Agris Kelbrants.

Plate 966. Lioness and Gazelle, 1914, Gorham, bronze, 7", marked RG Paine (sculptor), Gorham Co, rarity 5*, $6,000.00.

Plate 970. Mountain Lion, ca. 1932, K & O, gray metal, 4", shopmark, rarity 4, $135.00.

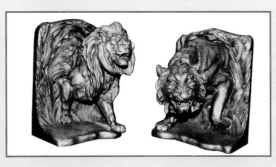

Plate 967. Lions on the Prowl, ca. 1925, Bradley and Hubbard, bronze, 6⅝", shopmark, rarity 5, $525.00.

Plate 971. Mountain Lion on Rocks, ca. 1925, iron, 4", rarity 5, $75.00. Photo courtesy of Agris Kelbrants.

Plate 968. Lions on the Prowl (Glass), ca. 1925, Bradley and Hubbard, bronze with glass eyes, 6⅝", shopmark, rarity 5, $75.00.

Plate 972. Mythic Lion, ca. 1925, brass, 6", Austria, rarity 5, $275.00.

Plate 973. Nubian and Panther, 1946, Russwood, bronze, 6¼", marked Original Russwood © 1946, rarity 4, $175.00.

Plate 974. On The Prowl, ca. 1925, iron, 4", rarity 5, $75.00.

Plate 975. Panther (Frankart), ca. 1930, Frankart, gray metal, 4", marked Frankart, rarity 5, $125.00.

Plate 976. Panther (Rookwood), ca. 1940, Rookwood, pottery, 5¼", shopmark, XLVI 2564, initials of designer, William P. McDonald, rarity 5, $450.00. Photo courtesy of Sue Benoliel.

Plate 977. Rookwood Panther with clock.

Plate 978. Panther Pair, ca. 1925, Ronson, gray metal on marbleized base, 10", rarity 5*, $350.00. Photo courtesy of Richard Weinstein.

Plate 979. Playful Cat, ca. 1932, brass, 5½", rarity 3, $100.00, currently reproduced $10.00.

Plate 980. Roar of the Tiger, ca. 1925, Ronson, gray metal, 7½", company tag #8172, rarity 4, $175.00.
Photo courtesy of Richard Weinstein.

Plate 981. Roaring Tiger, ca. 1925, Galvano Bronze, bronze-clad, 8", rarity 5*, $175.00.
Photo courtesy of Billie Trepanier.

Plate 982. Roaring Tiger (Armor Bronze), ca. 1925, Armor Bronze, bronze-clad, 5½", shopmark, rarity 5*, $175.00.

Plate 983. Roaring Tiger (Henry), 1940, Henry, gray metal, 3¾", shopmark ©, rarity 5, $185.00.
Photo courtesy of Agris Kelbrants.

Plate 984. Santa Cat, ca. 1998, iron, 6", rarity 2, $15.00.

Plate 985. Screaming Tiger, ca. 1925, Ronson, gray metal, 4", company paper tag, rarity 5, $175.00.

Plate 986. Seated Lion, ca. 1928, Jennings Brothers, gray metal, 8", marked C Vieth (sculptor) JB, rarity 5, $195.00.

Plate 987. Stalking Lion, ca. 1925, iron, 3½", rarity 4, $75.00.

Plate 988. Stealthy Lion (JB), ca. 1930, Jennings Brothers, gray metal, 5", marked JB 2038, rarity 5, $225.00.

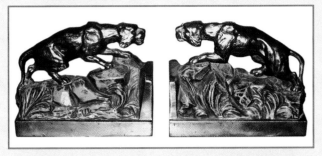

Plate 989. Stealthy Tiger, ca. 1930, attr Ronson, gray metal, 4½", rarity 5*, $170.00.

Plate 993. Talons Bared, 1930, iron, 5¾", marked Copr 1930, rarity 4, $150.00.

Plate 990. Surveying His Kingdom, ca. 1925, bronze, 5½", rarity 4, $125.00.

Plate 994. Tiger (New Martinsville), ca. 1940, New Martinsville, glass, 6½", rarity 5, $325.00. Photo courtesy of Michael Horseman.

Plate 991. Surveying His Kingdom (Gift House), 1925, Gift House, iron, 5¾", marked © 1925 Gift House Inc NYC, rarity 4, $110.00.

Plate 995. Tiger and Snake, 1928, Connecticut Foundry, iron, 5", shopmark, Tiger and Snake, 1928, rarity 4, $65.00.

Plate 992. Surveying the Prey, ca. 1920, Gorham, bronze, 5½", marked E Fiero (sculptor), Gorham Co, rarity 5*, $2,000.00.

Plate 996. Two Big Cats, ca. 1925, iron, 5", rarity 5, $135.00.

Plate 997. Two Lions, ca. 1926, iron, 4", rarity 4, $50.00.

Plate 998. Unlikely Playmates, ca. 1940, gray metal, 6", marked Japan, rarity 5, $95.00. *Made in Japan.*

Plate 999. Wild Beast, ca. 1950, gray metal, 4⅞", rarity 4, $50.00. Photo courtesy of Agris Kelbrants.

Female Figures

Plate 1000. Anchor Lady, ca. 1929, JB Hirsch, gray metal figure, celluloid face and hands, marble base, 8½", rarity 5, $275.00.

Plate 1001. Aphrodite, ca. 1928, Galvano Bronze, bronze-clad, 6½", company paper tag, rarity 5, polychrome, $425.00; monochrome, $350.00. Photo courtesy of Billie Trepanier.

Plate 1002. Arching Dancer, ca. 1925, gray metal, 6", rarity 5*, $375.00.

Plate 1003. Arching Nude, 1927, Armor bronze, bronze-clad, 7", marked Armor Bronze Corp 1927, rarity 5, $375.00. Photo courtesy of Billie Trepanier.

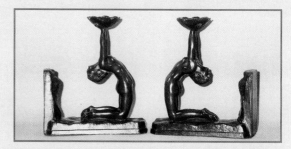

Plate 1004. Arching Nude with Bowl, ca. 1930, AP Famm, bronze-clad, 6¾", marked AP Famm, rarity 5*, $350.00. Photo courtesy of Billie Trepanier.

Plate 1005. Art Deco Nude, ca. 1932, X-1, gray metal, 8¾", marked #518, rarity 5, $250.00.

Plate 1006. Shopmark

Plate 1010. Aztec Archer, ca. 1925, iron, 7½", rarity 5, $150.00.

Plate 1007. As With Wings, ca. 1925, iron, 9", rarity 5, iron, $295.00; bronze, $425.00.

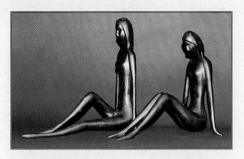

Plate 1011. Back to Back Girls, ca. 1940, brass, 7¾", rarity 5*, $175.00.

Plate 1008. Asian Lady, ca. 1920, Gorham, bronze, 7", marked I Coll (sculptor), rarity 5*, $1,500.00.

Plate 1012. Bad News for M'Lady, ca. 1925, Bradley and Hubbard, iron base, gray metal figure, 7¼", shopmark, rarity 5, $425.00.

Plate 1009. Asian Maiden on the Wall, ca. 1925, iron, 5", rarity 5, $125.00.

Plate 1013. Baker's Chocolate, ca. 1925, iron, 6", rarity 4, $100.00.

161

Plate 1014. Balancing Act, ca. 1927, attr Armor Bronze, bronze-clad, 8¾", rarity 5*, $595.00.

Plate 1018. Bathing Beauty (WB), ca. 1930, Weidlich Brothers Manufacturing, gray metal, 8", shopmark, #665; © USA, rarity 5, $395.00. Photo courtesy of John Gustav Delly.

Plate 1015. Ballerina, ca. 1930 (attr French Maker, due to style of base covering and mold casting ports in figure), gray metal on polished stone base, 7¼", rarity 5*, $175.00.

Plate 1019. Beach Lass, ca. 1930, Jennings Brothers, gray metal, 3½", marked JB 1924, rarity 5, $225.00. Photo courtesy of Charles J Bushman, Antique Elegance.

Plate 1016. Bather, ca. 1925, Kathodion Bronze Works, bronze-clad, 8", marked KBW, rarity 5, $250.00.

Plate 1020. Belly Dancer, ca. 1930, gray metal, 6¾", rarity 5, $300.00.

Plate 1017. Bathing Beauty, ca. 1930, X-1, gray metal, 8½", marked #514, polychrome, rarity 5*; monochrome, rarity 5; polychrome, $350.00; monochrome, $275.00.

Plate 1021. Bonnet Lady, ca. 1924, Armor Bronze, bronze-clad, 9", shopmark, rarity 5*, $450.00.

Plate 1022. Butterfly Dancer, ca. 1925, bronze, 7½", rarity 5, $800.00. *This piece is also produced in gray metal with gold finish by K&O.*

Plate 1023. Butterfly Dancer (K & O), ca. 1930, K & O, gray metal, 7¾", shopmark, rarity 5, polychrome, $495.00; monochrome, $375.00.

Plate 1024. Butterfly Dancer different color.

Plate 1025. Butterfly Dancer rear view.

Plate 1026. Butterfly Girl, ca. 1927, X-1, gray metal, 7", marked #63, rarity 5, polychrome, $375.00; monochrome, $325.00.

Plate 1027. Butterfly Girl (iron), ca. 1925, iron, 5⅞", rarity 5*, $295.00.

Plate 1028. Cameo Girls, 1926, iron, 4¼", rarity 4, $125.00.

Plate 1029. Campfire Girls of America, ca. 1925, Kathodion Bronze Works, bronze-clad, 7½", marked © ArtBronz KBW, rarity 5, $400.00.

Plate 1030. Castanet Dancer, ca. 1925, gray metal figure, marble base, celluloid face and arms, 6½", rarity 5, $495.00.

Plate 1031. Collecting Flowers, ca. 1920, Gorham, bronze, 8½", marked M T Myers (sculptor), Gorham Co, rarity 5*, $3,000.00.

Plate 1032. Curtsey, ca. 1926 , JB Hirsch, gray metal figure, celluloid face, marble or polished stone base, 8¼", rarity 5, $195.00.

Plate 1033. Curtseying Girl, ca. 1920, bronze, 5½", marked Austria, rarity 5*, $2,500.00.

Plate 1034. Curtseying Lady, ca. 1925, X-2, iron, 7½", marked #52, rarity 5, $195.00.

Plate 1035. Dance Pose, ca. 1932, K & O, gray metal, 6¾", shopmark, rarity 5, $175.00.

Plate 1036. Dancer, ca. 1929, Art Colony Industries, iron, 4¾", rarity 4, $175.00.

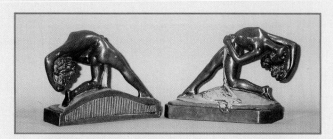

Plate 1037. Dancer (Galvano), ca. 1930, Galvano bronze, bronze-clad, 4¾", rarity 5*, polychrome, $275.00; monochrome, $225.00. Photo courtesy of Billie Trepanier.

Plate 1038. Dancer (GM), ca. 1930, gray metal, 5", rarity 4, $175.00.

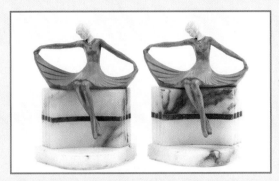

Plate 1039. Displaying Her Dress, ca. 1925, gray metal on marble base, 6¼", rarity 5, $275.00.

Plate 1040. Dancer in Wreathe, ca. 1928, iron, 5", marked #53, rarity 5, $175.00.

Plate 1041. Dancer with Peacock, ca. 1925, Armor Bronze, bronze-clad, 11", shopmark, company paper tag, rarity 5*, $795.00.

Plate 1042. Dancing Girl (Gorham), 1921, Gorham, bronze, 5¾", marked F Ziegler (sculptor), Gorham Co, rarity 5, $795.00.

Plate 1043. Dancing Girl (Hubley), ca. 1928, Hubley, iron, 5½", marked #295, rarity 5, $110.00.

Plate 1044. Dancing Girl (Pompeian Bronze), ca. 1925, attr Pompeian bronze, bronze-clad, 7¼," rarity 5, $375.00.

Plate 1045. Dancing Girl (Ronson), ca. 1924, Ronson, gray metal, 5", polychrome, rarity 5*; monochrome, rarity 5; polychrome, $495.00; monochrome, $350.00.

165

Plate 1046. Dancing Girl (Ronson), polychrome.

Plate 1050. Dawn, ca. 1920, iron, 4¼", rarity 5, $150.00.

Plate 1047. Dancing Ladies with Drape, ca. 1926, attr X-2, bronze, 6½", marked 51, rarity 5, $175.00.

Plate 1051. Deco Bust, 1947, Abbot, gray metal, 7¼", marked Abbot Schy 47, rarity 5, $150.00.

Plate 1048. Dancing Nymph, ca. 1928, Art Colony Industries, iron, 8¾", rarity 4, $175.00.

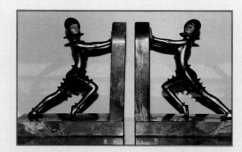

Plate 1052. Deco Warm-up, ca. 1925, gray metal figure, celluloid face, marble base, 6", rarity 5*, $600.00.

Plate 1049. Dancing with the Moon, 1930, Creation Company, iron, 6", marked © 1930 C CO, #217, rarity 5, $175.00.

Plate 1053. Demure, ca. 1928, gray metal, 4½", rarity 5, $175.00.

Plate 1054. Diversion, ca. 1925, bronze-clad, 8½", rarity 5*, $295.00.

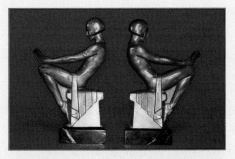

Plate 1055. Diversion (Le Verrier), ca. 1925, Le Verrier Foundry, bronze, 8¼", marked M Le Verrier, rarity 5, original, $1,500.00; current production, $600.00.

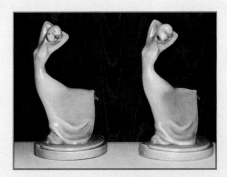

Plate 1056. Dreaming, ca. 1930, gray metal, 7", rarity 5, $150.00.

Plate 1057. Drug Trip, ca. 1930, Nuart, gray metal, 6", shopmark, rarity 5, $250.00.

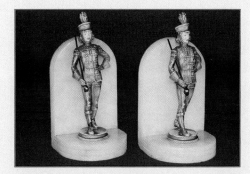

Plate 1058. Drum Majorette, ca. 1925, attr JB Hirsch, gray metal figure, celluloid head, marble base, 7", rarity 5, $195.00.

Plate 1059. Duclos Deco, ca. 1930, Duclos, gray metal, 7½", marked Duclos, rarity 5*, $275.00.

Plate 1060. Dutch Girl, ca. 1925, iron, 5½", rarity 5, $225.00.

Plate 1061. Echo, ca. 1925, Armor Bronze, bronze-clad, 9½", marked Ruhl (sculptor); ECHO, shopmark, rarity 5, polychrome, $450.00; monochrome, $395.00.

167

Plate 1062. Ecstasy, ca. 1925, Le Verrier Foundry, bronze, 6½", marked Fayral (sculptor) Le Verrier, Paris, rarity 5, $1,200.00.

Plate 1063. Ecstasy (Pompeian Bronze), ca. 1926, Pompeian Bronze, bronze-clad, 6½", rarity 5, $325.00.Photo courtesy of Billie Trepanier.

Plate 1064. Egyptian Dancer, ca. 1920, Gorham, bronze, 10¾", marked Mrs. Harry Bingham (sculptor), Gorham Co, rarity 5*, $1,200.00.

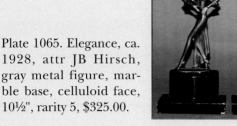

Plate 1065. Elegance, ca. 1928, attr JB Hirsch, gray metal figure, marble base, celluloid face, 10½", rarity 5, $325.00.

Plate 1066. Eve, ca. 1925, iron, 6¾", rarity 5, $150.00.

Plate 1067. Eve and Apple, ca. 1925, iron, 6¾", rarity 4, $110.00. *Eve is very similar to "Eve and Apple."*

Plate 1068. Exotic Lady, ca. 1925, attr JB Hirsch, gray metal figure, celluloid face on polished stone base, 5¾", rarity 5, $250.00.

Plate 1069. Feeding Her Friends, ca. 1925, gray metal figure on marble base, 4½", rarity 5, $300.00.

Plate 1070. Feeding the Fawns, ca. 1930, Creation Company, iron, 6", marked © 1930 C Co #234, rarity 5, $125.00.

Plate 1074. Flower Ladies, ca. 1910, bronze on granite base, 11¾", rarity 5*, $1,400.00. *Made in France.*

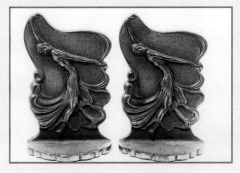

Plate 1071. Flamenco Dancers, ca. 1928, iron, 7¾", marked © JL Drucklieb (sculptor), patent applied for, rarity 5, $175.00.

Plate 1075. Flowery Pose, ca. 1925, bronze, 6", rarity 5, $175.00.

Plate 1072. Flapper, ca. 1930, gray metal on marble base, 9", rarity 5*, $300.00.

Plate 1076. Forest Maiden, ca. 1925, McClelland Barclay, gray metal, 5¾", marked McClelland Barclay, rarity 5, $275.00.

Plate 1073. Flower Girl, ca. 1925, iron, 5", rarity 5, $150.00. Photo courtesy of Agris Kelbrants.

Plate 1077. Fountain, ca. 1926, Galvano bronze, bronze-clad, 5½", marked Kilen (sculptor) The Fountain, rarity 5, polychrome, $195.00; monochrome, $150.00.

169

Plate 1078. Frolic, ca. 1920, Gorham, bronze, 11½", marked E I Spencer (sculptor), Gorham Co, rarity 5*, $7,500.00.

Plate 1079. Fruit Gatherer, ca. 1930, Le Verrier, bronze, 6½", M. Le Verrier, rarity 5, 1930, $1,100.00; current production, $500.00. *See page 29 for details.*

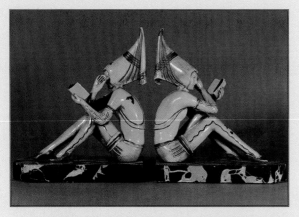

Plate 1080. Gerdago Girl, ca. 1927, JB Hirsch, gray metal with celluloid face on marble face, 7¼", rarity 5, $375.00. *This figure was also produced by Jennings Brothers.*

Plate 1081. Girl and Fawn, ca. 1928, bronze-clad, 9½", rarity 5*, $425.00.

Plate 1082. Girl at Fountain, ca. 1923, X-1, gray metal, 5", marked #503, rarity 5, $225.00.

Plate 1083. Girl at Fountain, reverse side.

Plate 1084. Girl in the Circle, ca. 1925, X-2, iron, 5¼", marked #17, rarity 5, $250.00.

Plate 1085. Girl in Wreath, ca. 1929, X-2, iron, 6¼", rarity 5, $250.00.

Plate 1086. Girl on Bench, ca. 1925, attr JB Hirsch, gray metal figure, marble base, celluloid face, 6⅛", rarity 5, $350.00.

Plate 1087. Girl on Bench (lamp version), ca. 1925, attr JB Hirsch, gray metal figure, marble base, celluloid face, rarity 5, $300.00.

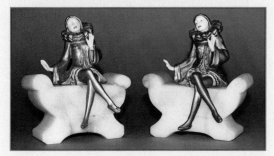

Plate 1088. Girl on Divan, ca. 1925, JB Hirsch, gray metal figure, marble base, celluloid face, 5¾", rarity 5, $325.00.

Plate 1089. Girl Posing, ca. 1947, Dodge, gray metal, 7", company paper tag, rarity 5, $175.00.

Plate 1090. Girl Reflecting, ca. 1920, Gorham, bronze, 6¼", marked N Thompson (sculptor), Gorham Co, rarity 5*, $2,000.00.

Plate 1091. Girl Scout, ca. 1925, iron, 6½", rarity 5, $200.00.

Plate 1092. Girl with a Globe, ca. 1925, Bradley and Hubbard, cast nickel with bronze flashing, 6¼", triangular shopmark, rarity 5*, $300.00.

171

Plate 1093. Girls with Deer, ca. 1925, Galvano Bronze, bronze-clad, 5", company paper tag, rarity 5, $150.00.

Plate 1097. Gymnast, ca. 1920, bronze, 6¼", marked Made in Austria, Ergzgiesserei A.G Wien, rarity 5*, $1,500.00. *Made in Austria.*

Plate 1094. Goddess, ca. 1920, bronze, 6¾", Made in Austria, shopmark, rarity 5*, $1,295.00.

Plate 1098. Gymnastic, ca. 1925, Frankart, 7½", marked Frankart Pat Appld For, rarity 5*, $395.00. Photo courtesy of Vicki Nolten-Mair.

Plate 1095. Golden Nudes, ca. 1930, Frankart, gray metal, 7", marked Frankart, Inc Pat Appld For, rarity 5, $400.00. Photo courtesy of Billie Trepanier.

Plate 1099. Hair bow, ca. 1925, iron, 6", rarity 5, $95.00. Photo courtesy of Agris Kelbrants.

Plate 1096. Good Fairy, ca. 1923, Armor Bronze, bronze-clad, 7½", company paper tag, The Good Fairy, rarity 5, polychrome, $225.00; monochrome, $175.00.

Plate 1100. Hands Down, ca. 1925, iron, 5¾", marked #323, rarity 4, $95.00.

Plate 1101. Hanging the Moon, ca. 1930, gray metal figure on marble, 5½", rarity 5*, $275.00.

Plate 1102. Harp Player, JB Hirsch, plated white metal on stone base, 6¾", marked with inscription patent pending, $275.00.

Plate 1103. Hindu Dancer, ca. 1925, attr JB Hirsch, gray metal figure, marble base, celluloid face, 9", rarity 5*, $395.00. *Modeled after a figure by Chiparus.*

Plate 1104. Hoop-Skirted Belle, ca. 1920, iron, 5½", rarity 5, $295.00.

Plate 1105. Hoop-Skirted Belle (Littco), ca. 1925, Littco, iron, 6⅞", company paper tag, rarity 5*, $195.00.

Plate 1106. In The Clouds, ca. 1925, X-2, iron, 6", marked #73, rarity 5, $150.00.

Plate 1107. Indochina Beauty, ca. 1939 (French Indochina), bronze, 8½", marked Made in French Indochina, rarity 5*, $275.00. *See page 18 for details.*

Plate 1108. Innocence, ca. 1926, Kathodion Bronze Works, bronze-clad, 9½", marked KBW Art bronze, rarity 5, $395.00. *Sales catalog description reads "Girlhood–simple, innocent and beautiful, is here portrayed in slender, lithe grace to hold your books."*

Plate 1109. Jean Harlow, ca. 1938, Greist, gray metal, 6¾", marked Greist, New Haven Pat Pend, rarity 5, $450.00. *Jean Harlow: March 3,1911 to June 7,1937.*

Plate 1110. Jeanne D'Arc (Solid Bronze), ca. 1928, Solid Bronze, bronze, 3½", marked Solid Bronze, rarity 5, $90.00.

Plate 1111. Jeanne D'Arc (JB), ca. 1928, Jennings Brothers, gray metal, 6", marked JB 1876, rarity 5, $175.00. Photo courtesy of Judy Hawk.

Plate 1112. Joan of Arc, ca. 1925, iron, 4", rarity 4, $50.00.

Plate 1113. Joan of Arc (Armor Bronze), ca. 1926, Armor Bronze, bronze-clad, 8½", Gregory Allen (sculptor) shopmark, rarity 5, $175.00.

Plate 1114. Joan of Arc (DAL), ca. 1926, Decorative Arts League, iron, 4½", marked DAL, rarity 3, $35.00.

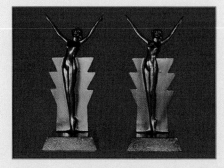

Plate 1115. Julian's Girls, 1929, Crescent Metal Works, gray metal, 8¼", marked Crescent Metal Works 1929, rarity 5, $425.00.

Plate 1116. Just One Tiptoe, ca. 1924, Ronson, gray metal, 10¾", rarity 5, polychrome, $425.00; monochrome, $375.00.

Plate 1120. Kneeling Gerdago Girl (JB), ca. 1925, Jennings Brothers, gray metal, 6¾", marked JB, rarity 5, $325.00.

Plate 1117. Just Shoes, ca. 1920, bronze on wood base, 9", sculptor signature, foundry mark, rarity 5, $695.00. *Made in Italy.*

Plate 1121. Kneeling Nude, ca. 1933, gray metal, 5", rarity 4, $110.00.

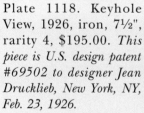

Plate 1118. Keyhole View, 1926, iron, 7½", rarity 4, $195.00. *This piece is U.S. design patent #69502 to designer Jean Drucklieb, New York, NY, Feb. 23, 1926.*

Plate 1122. Kneeling Nude (Nuart), ca. 1930, attr Nuart, gray metal, 5", rarity 5, $125.00. Photo courtesy of Agris Kelbrants.

Plate 1119. Kneeling Gerdago Girl, ca. 1925, gray metal on marble base, 6¾", rarity 5, $400.00.

Plate 1123. Knowledge (Armor Bronze), ca. 1926, Armor Bronze, bronze-clad, 8", C.A. Johnson (sculptor), shopmark, rarity 5, polychrome, $325.00; monochrome, $275.00.

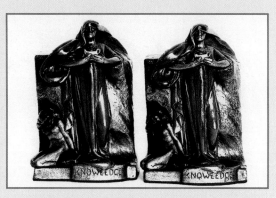

Plate 1124. Knowledge (Galvano), ca. 1926, Galvano bronze, bronze-clad, 7½", marked V Carano (sculptor), Knowledge, rarity 5, polychrome, $395.00; monochrome, $295.00.

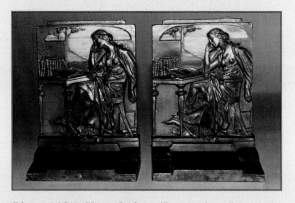

Plate 1125. Knowledge (Pompeian Bronze), 1925, Pompeian Bronze, gray metal, 4¼", marked Knowledge PB, rarity 4, $125.00.

Plate 1126. Knowledge Makes Free, ca. 1920, Gorham, bronze, 6⅝", marked F F Ziegler (sculptor), Knowledge Makes Free Gorham, rarity 5, $695.00.

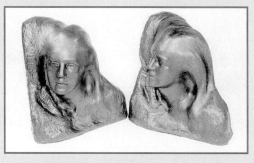

Plate 1127. Lady, ca. 1925, Ideal Casting, bronze, marked Ideal Casting Company, Providence, RI, F Wigglesworth (sculptor), rarity 5*, $800.00.

Plate 1128. Lady Face, ca. 1940, New Martinsville, glass, 5¼", rarity 5, $200.00.

Plate 1129. Lady Godiva, ca. 1925, iron, 5½", rarity 5, $150.00.

Plate 1130. Lady Godiva (Gasser), ca. 1925, bronze, 6", marked Gasser, rarity 5, $195.00.

Plate 1131. Lady Godiva (Haley), ca. 1940, Haley, glass, 6", rarity 4, $125.00.

Plate 1135. Lady Reading, ca. 1935, plaster-filled plastic, 7", rarity 5, $200.00.

Plate 1132. Lady in Red, ca. 1932, Crescent Metal Works, gray metal, 9", company tag, rarity 5*, $425.00.

Plate 1136. Lady with Dog, ca. 1940, pottery, 5¼", marked XS680A, rarity 5, $100.00.

Plate 1133. Lady of the Theatre, ca. 1924, Jennings Brothers, gray metal, 5", marked JB 1529, rarity 5, $275.00. *Seen in signed (CVV) and unsigned formats.*

Plate 1137. Lady with Globe, ca. 1925, Jennings Brothers, gray metal, 8", marked C Vieth (sculptor) JB 1523, rarity 5, $225.00.

Plate 1134. Lady on Divan, ca. 1920, Gorham Bronze, bronze, 9½", marked H K Bush-Brown (sculptor), Gorham Co, rarity 5*, $7,500.00.

Plate 1138. Lady Pirates, ca. 1925, JB Hirsch, gray metal figure, marble base, celluloid face, 6½", rarity 5, $295.00. Photo courtesy of Tom Boniface.

177

Plate 1139. Lancelette, ca. 1929, JB Hirsch, gray metal figure, celluloid head, polished stone base, 6", rarity 4, $250.00. *This pair was produced in a variety of formats, including marble, metal, and polished stone bases, none particularly more or less valuable than another.*

Plate 1140. Learning, ca. 1920, Gorham, bronze, 7½", marked E E Codman (sculptor), Gorham Co, rarity 5*, $900.00.

Plate 1141. Little Red Riding Hood, 1924, Ronson, gray metal, 5", marked LV Aronson 1924, rarity 5, $450.00.

Plate 1142. Loie, 1927, X-1, gray metal, 7", #500, rarity 4, polychrome, $300.00; monochrome, $200.00. *Also manufactured by Art Metal Works (AMW).*

Plate 1143. Loie (monochrome).

Plate 1144. Lorenzl Lady (Jennings Brothers), ca. 1930, Jennings Brothers, gray metal, 9", company paper tag, rarity 5, $295.00. Photo courtesy of R. Joiner.

Plate 1145. Lorenzl Lady, ca. 1924, bronze on marble base, 9", rarity 5*, $7,500.00. - *Made in Austria.*

Plate 1146. Lorenzl Lady, Petite, 1937, Ronson, gray metal, 5¾", company tag #16532, rarity 5, $225.00. *Although usually unsigned, this pair has been seen signed "Art."*

Plate 1147. Maiden and Dolphin, ca. 1925, Bradley and Hubbard, iron base, gray metal figure, 6½", shopmark, rarity 5, $395.00.

Plate 1148. Maiden's Fountain, ca. 1928, iron, 5½", polychrome, rarity 5; monochrome, rarity 3; polychrome, $150.00; monochrome, $75.00.

Plate 1149. Maiden's Fountain (Solid Bronze), ca. 1928, Solid Bronze, bronze, 5½", marked Solid Bronze, rarity 5, $150.00.

Plate 1150. Maidservant, ca. 1932, attr JB Hirsch, chalk on polished stone base, 6", rarity 5, $50.00.

Plate 1151. March Girl, ca. 1925, Acorn, iron, 7", shopmark, March Girl, #601, rarity 5, $225.00.

Plate 1152. Martha Washington, ca. 1920, bronze, 6½", rarity 5*, $175.00.

Plate 1153. Meditation (Le Verrier), ca. 1925, Le Verrier, bronze on marble base, 8", shopmark Fayral, rarity 5, original, $795.00; current production, $450.00.

Plate 1154. Meditation (Gorham), ca. 1920, Gorham, bronze, 7", marked E E Codman (sculptor), Gorham Co, rarity 5*, $900.00.

Plate 1155. Meditation (PB), ca. 1925, Pompeian Bronze, gray metal, 5¼", marked Pompeian Bronze, Meditation, 1925, rarity 4, $175.00.

Plate 1156. Men at Her Feet, ca. 1925, bronze, 6½", rarity 5, $125.00. Photo courtesy of Wilkinson Antiques.

Plate 1157. Minerva, ca. 1925, Judd, iron, 5¾", marked 9726, rarity 5, $125.00. Also seen as expandable, rarity 5, $100.00.

Plate 1158. Minerva Goddess of Wisdom, ca. 1925, iron, 4", marked 581, rarity 4, $50.00. Photo courtesy of Agris Kelbrants.

Plate 1159. Minerva Profile, ca. 1925, Judd, iron, 4¾", marked 9659, rarity 4, $75.00. Photo courtesy of Agris Kelbrants.

Plate 1160. Mirror, Mirror, ca. 1925, gray metal on marble base, 6½", marked France, signature, rarity 5*, $750.00.

Plate 1161. Miss and Pooch, ca. 1930, attr JB Hirsch, gray metal figure, marble base, celluloid face, rarity 5*, $375,00.

Plate 1162. Miss Moderne, ca. 1929, iron, 6½", marked Miss Moderne, rarity 4, $115.00.

Plate 1163. Model Student, ca. 1930, gray metal, 6", rarity 5*, $295.00.

Plate 1164. Modern Nudes, ca. 1930, Frankart, gray metal, 7½", marked Frankart Inc Patent Applied For, rarity 5, $300.00. Photo courtesy of Billie Trepanier.

Plate 1165. Modest Maiden, ca. 1930, X-1, gray metal, 7", marked #520, rarity 5, $295.00.

Plate 1166. Modest Maiden polychrome.

Plate 1167. Modesty, ca. 1920, Ronson, gray metal, 5", rarity 5, polychrome, $495.00; monochrome, $395.00.

Plate 1168. Modesty (marbelized), ca. 1920, Ronson, gray metal on marbleized base, 6½", company paper tag, rarity 5, $495.00.

Plate 1169. Mother and Child, ca. 1930, gray metal, 6", rarity 5, $125.00.

Plate 1170. Mournful Lady, ca. 1928, Littco, iron, 6", company paper tag, rarity 5, bronze patina, $195.00; others, $165.00.

Plate 1171. Nefruari, ca. 1928, attr JB Hirsch, gray metal figure, celluloid face and hands, marble base, 9", rarity 5*, $395.00. *Figure modeled after Chiparus.*

Plate 1172. Niobe, ca. 1925, Judd, iron base, gray metal figure, 6½", rarity 5, $350.00. *The original paper tag reads: "A goddess who was proud of her numerous family, six daughters and six sons. She boasted of her superiority to her friend Leto (goddess) and the mother of only two children Apollo and Artemis. As a punishment Apollo slew her sons and Artemis her daughters. Their bodies lay for nine days unburied for Zeus had changed the people to stone. On the tenth day they were buried by the gods. Out of pity for her grief the gods changed Niobe herself into a rock. In which form she continued to weep."*

Plate 1173. Not Quite Bookish, ca. 1930, K & O, gray metal, 8", shopmark, rarity 5, $350.00.

Plate 1174. Nouveau Dance, ca. 1920, iron, 5¼", marked #306, rarity 5, $175.00.

Plate 1175. Nouveau Lady Reading, ca. 1920, Zoppo Foundry, bronze, 6", marked Needham (sculptor) B Zoppo Foundries, NY, rarity 5*, $1,750.00.

Plate 1176. Nude Arching With Drape, ca. 1920, Pompeian Bronze, bronze-clad, 7", company paper tag, rarity 5*, $495.00. Photo courtesy of Billie Trepanier.

Plate 1177. Nude Arching with Drape (GAB), ca. 1920, Gotham Art bronze, bronze-clad, 7", company paper tag: Galvano Bronze, Gotham Art Bronze, rarity 5, $295.00.

Plate 1178. Nude Bather, ca. 1925, attr Armor Bronze, bronze-clad, 5", marked ©, rarity 5, $225.00.

Plate 1182. Nude on Book, ca. 1929, Littco, iron, 8", shopmark, rarity 4, $175.00.

Plate 1179. Nude Dancer, ca. 1930, Ronson, gray metal, 5", rarity 5*, $400.00.

Plate 1183. Nude on One Knee, ca. 1932, Jennings Brothers, gray metal, 7", marked JB, rarity 5*, $275.00.
Photo courtesy of Billie Trepanier.

Plate 1180. Nude Dancer with Sash, ca. 1925, iron, 6", rarity 4, $195.00.

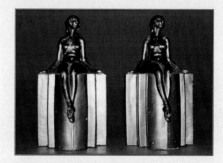

Plate 1184. Nude on Pedestal, ca. 1933, gray metal, 8", rarity 4, $175.00.

Plate 1181. Nude Kneeling on Pedestal, ca. 1933, Bronzart, gray metal, 7", shopmark, rarity 4, $175.00.

Plate 1185. Nude on Wall, ca. 1930, gray metal, 5¾", rarity 5, $225.00.

Plate 1186. Nude Resting, ca. 1925, bronze-clad, 6½", marked M Stizyt (sculptor), rarity 5*, $325.00.

Plate 1190. Nude with Mirror, ca. 1922, attr Pompeian Bronze, bronze-clad, 6½", rarity 5, $175.00.

Plate 1187. Nude With Dogs, ca. 1925, Art Colony Industries, iron, 7", marked © #269, rarity 5, $195.00.

Plate 1191. Nude with Outstretched Arms, ca. 1920, bronze-clad, 5¼", rarity 5*, $350.00. Photo courtesy of Billie Trepanier.

Plate 1188. Nude with Drape, ca. 1928, Verona, iron, 6¾", shopmark, rarity 4, $95.00.

Plate 1192. Nude with Sash (multi-tier pedestal), ca. 1929, X-2, iron, 5½", marked Des Patent Appl For, rarity 5, $275.00.

Plate 1189. Nude with Hounds, ca. 1930, attr Creation Company, iron, 6", rarity 5, $175.00.

Plate 1193. Nude with Sash (single-tier), ca. 1929, X-2, iron, 5", rarity 4, $175.00.

184

Plate 1194. Nude with Tambourine, 1927, Armor Bronze, bronze-clad, 5½", company paper tag, rarity 5, $350.00. Photo courtesy of Billie Trepanier.

Plate 1195. Nude with Tambourine Backarching, 1927, Armor Bronze, bronze-clad, 6½", company paper tag, rarity 5*, $450.00. Photo courtesy of Billie Trepanier.

Plate 1196. Nudes (Gorham), ca. 1920, Gorham, bronze, 11", marked EB Parsons (sculptor), Gorham Co Founders OBWY, rarity 5*, $8,000.00.

Plate 1197. Nudes (Nock), ca. 1920, bronze, 5", marked LF Nock (sculptor), rarity 5*, $650.00.

Plate 1198. Nudes with Elk, ca. 1922, Marion Bronze, bronze-clad, 4¾", company paper tag: Manufactured by Marion Bronze, Metuchen, NJ, rarity 5, $100.00.

Plate 1199. Nymph and Dryad, ca. 1925, Hubley, iron, 5", rarity 5, $150.00, Photo courtesy of Jocelyn Serbe.

Plate 1200. Nymph and Goat, ca. 1925, Hubley, iron, 5½", marked #327, rarity 5, $110.00.

Plate 1201. Nymph on Dolphin, ca. 1929, gray metal, 5¾", rarity 5, $195.00.

185

Plate 1202. Nymph on Skull, ca. 1922, Frankart, gray metal, 7¾", marked ©, rarity 5*, $600.00. Photo courtesy of Billie Trepanier.

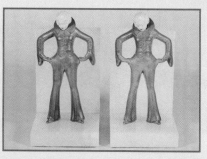

Plate 1206. Pauvre, ca. 1925, attr JB Hirsch, gray metal figure, celluloid face, on marble base, 5¾", rarity 5, $225.00.

Plate 1203. Offering, The, ca. 1920, gray metal figure with celluloid bowl on marble base, 7", rarity 5, $500.00.

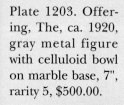

Plate 1207. Peace, ca. 1926, Armor Bronze, bronze-clad, 8½", S Morani (sculptor) shopmark, rarity 5, polychrome, $395.00; monochrome, $325.00.

Plate 1204. Offering, ca. 1930, gray metal, 7", marked Made in Germany, rarity 5, $225.00. *Tag on base reads "Whitmore's New Art Galleries, 1517 Dodge St, Omaha." This would be the site of sale.*

Plate 1208. Perfect Symmetry, ca. 1925, Glauber, bronze, 8⅞", marked Glauber, rarity 5, $895.00.

Plate 1205. Outrageous, ca. 1930, Gotham Art Bronze, bronze-clad, 6½", company paper label, rarity 5, $350.00. Photo courtesy of Sue Benoliel.

Plate 1209. Pink Lady, ca. 1943, JB Hirsch, chalk on polished stone base, 5½", marked JBH, rarity 5, $125.00.

Plate 1210. Pin-up Girl, ca. 1930, gray metal, 7", marked EPC, rarity 5, $295.00.

Plate 1211. Pioneer Woman, 1927, Jennings Brothers, gray metal, 8½", marked JB 8355 Bryant Baker, rarity 5, $300.00.

Plate 1212. Pixie Girl, ca. 1927, attr JB Hirsch, gray metal on marble base, 5¼", rarity 5, $200.00. *Sculptor: Gerdago.*

Plate 1213. Platinum Girls, ca. 1927, attr Greist Inc, gray metal, 7", rarity 5, $300.

Plate 1214. Pleased to Meet You, ca. 1925, attr JB Hirsch, gray metal figure, celluloid face, on marble base, 6¾", rarity 5, $195.00.

Plate 1215. Plenty to Think About, ca. 1925, attr Judd, bronze, 6⅜", marked 9888, rarity 5, $175.00.

Plate 1216. Poetry & Thought, 1911, attr Roman Bronze Works, bronze, 9", marked I. Konti (sculptor) 1911, rarity 5, $3,800.00.

Plate 1217. Portrait of a Lady, ca. 1930, Ronson, gray metal, 6½", company paper tag #16176, rarity 5, polychrome, $375.00, monochrome, $300.00.

187

Plate 1218. Preparation, ca. 1930, gray metal, 7", rarity 5, $195.00.

Plate 1219. Pretty as a Picture, ca. 1920, bronze on marble base, 10½", marked CH Manginot (sculptor), rarity 5*, $2,000.00. *Made in France.*

Plate 1220. Pretty in Pleats, ca. 1925, gray metal figure, celluloid head, chrome base, 6¼", rarity 5, $195.00.

Plate 1221. Priscilla, ca. 1925, gray metal, 6½", marked F Cliffe, rarity 5, $175.00. Photo courtesy of Agris Kelbrants.

Plate 1222. Profile, 1925, Gorham, bronze, 6¾", marked F Wigglesworth (sculptor), Gorham Co, rarity 5*, $1,500.00.

Plate 1223. Promenade, ca. 1945, Dodge Inc., gray metal with copper-flashed finish, 7", rarity 5*, $150.00.

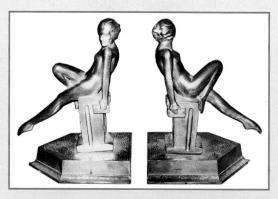

Plate 1224. Quite the Pose, ca. 1927, Nuart, gray metal, 7", shopmark, rarity 5, $250.00.

Plate 1225. Read to Me, ca. 1925, X-1, gray metal, 5½", marked #509, polychrome, rarity 5; monochrome, rarity 4, polychrome, $175.00; monochrome, $125.00.

Plate 1226. Reading Girl, 1920, Roman Bronze Works, bronze, 6¾", marked Adeles Hammond (sculptor) RBW Jan 1920, rarity 5*, $1,200.00.

Plate 1230. Renaissance Storybook Woman, ca. 1934, gray metal, 4¼", rarity 5, $75.00. *The style of hat worn by this woman is known as a "Hennin hat." You can also see the same style worn by Gerdago Girl.*

Plate 1227. Ready for the Big Screen, ca. 1930, Greist, gray metal, 7½", marked Greist, rarity 5, $225.00.

Plate 1231. Repose on Tapestry, ca. 1925, Ronson, gray metal, 7¾", paper tag #12835, rarity 5*, $450.00.

Plate 1228. Red Ribbon Pose, ca. 1930, Crescent Metal Works, gray metal, 7", paper tag: Crescent Metal Works, rarity 5, polychrome, $250.00; monochrome, $150.00.

Plate 1232. Sailor Girl, ca. 1925, gray metal on marble base, 8¾", rarity 5*, $500.00.

Plate 1229. Reflection, ca. 1920, Gorham, bronze, 4⅝", marked L H Treadway (sculptor), Gorham Co, rarity 5*, $2,000.00.

Plate 1233. Sauciness, ca. 1925, Le Verrier, bronze, 7", Janle (sculptor), Le Verrier (Foundry), shopmark, rarity 5, original, $1,500.00; current production, $600.00.

189

Plate 1234. Scarf Dance, ca. 1920, X-2, iron, 6½", marked #15, rarity 4, $175.00.

Plate 1235. Science and Knowledge, 1921, Gorham, bronze, 6⅝", marked FF Ziegler (sculptor), 1921, Science, Knowledge Makes Free, Gorham, rarity 5, $695.00.

Plate 1236. Sea Mist Nymph, ca. 1925, bronze, 5", rarity 5, $175.00.

Plate 1237. Seated & Standing Ladies, ca. 1925, iron, 5" and 8", marked THEW, rarity 5, $250.00.

Plate 1238. Seated Pose, ca. 1930, gray metal, 6¾", marked Made in USA, rarity 5, polychrome, $375.00; monochrome, $295.00.

Plate 1239. Sharing a Book, ca. 1920, Gorham, bronze, 6½", marked Phiny Rogers (sculptor), Gorham Co, rarity 5*, $750.00.

Plate 1240. She's Holding Up the Books, ca. 1930, gray metal on marble base, 6", rarity 5, $275.00.

Plate 1241. Silence, ca. 1926, Armor Bronze, bronze-clad, 8", S Morani (sculptor) shopmark, rarity 5, $275.00.

Plate 1242. Sitting Lady, ca. 1925, Judd, iron base, gray metal figure, 7¼", marked Judd, #9750, rarity 5, $550.00.

Plate 1243. Sitting Pretty, ca. 1927, X-1, gray metal, 6", marked #519, rarity 5, polychrome, $375.00; monochrome, $275.00. Photo courtesy of Billie Trepanier.

Plate 1244. Sleeping Beauty, ca. 1927, Ronson, gray metal, 5⅜", rarity 5, polychrome, $350.00; monochrome, $225.00.

Plate 1245. Smelling the Flowers , ca. 1925, gray metal, 5", rarity 5, $110.00.

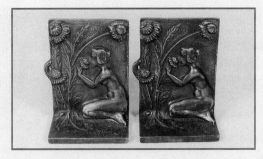

Plate 1246. Smelling the Flowers (X-1), ca. 1925, X-1, gray metal, 4¾", rarity 5, $125.00.

Plate 1247. Smiling Girl, 2003, British reproduction, metal figure, ivorine head, marble base, 8½", marked Lorenzl, rarity 1, $35.00. *These bookends are seen with various sculptors names, and are currently reproduced in England.*

Plate 1248. Sophisticated Lady, ca. 1925, attr JB Hirsch, gray metal figure, marble base, celluloid face, 8¾", rarity 5, $475.00.

Plate 1249. Sophisticated Lady, Petite, ca. 1925, attr JB Hirsch, gray metal figure, marble base, celluloid face, 6¼", rarity 5*, $375.00.

191

Plate 1250. Southern Belle, ca. 1930, attr JB Hirsch, gray metal figure, marble base, celluloid face, 7½", rarity 5, $295.00.

Plate 1254. Spinning Wheel, ca. 1925, JB Hirsch, gray metal figure, celluloid face and hands, marble or polished stone base, 6½", marked JBH, rarity 5, $375.00.

Plate 1251. Spanish Dancer, ca. 1930, Pompeian Bronze, bronze-clad, 10¾", marked Paul Herzel (sculptor), rarity 5, $195.00.

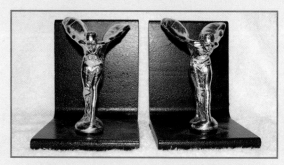

Plate 1255. Spirit of Ecstasy, various 1911 to 1950, Rolls Royce, nickel, 5¼", rarity 5, $650.00. *See page 24 for details.*

Plate 1252. Speed, ca. 1925, gray metal, 6", marked A-S (Andersen-Starr), rarity 5, $225.00. *It is unclear why this figure, which closely resembles Dancing Girl (Ronson) is named "Speed"; nonetheless, the Ronson catalogue reflects the name Dancing Girl, and several citations for this figure are named "Speed."*

Plate 1256. Standing Colonial Woman, 1920, Rookwood, pottery, 6", marked McDonald #2185, rarity 5, $400.00.

Plate 1253. Spinning Scene, ca. 1930, attr Bradley and Hubbard, iron, 4⅞", rarity 3, $50.00.

Plate 1257. Standing for Knowledge, ca. 1918, Gorham, bronze, 7", marked Gorham, rarity 5, $2,000.00.

Plate 1258. Sunday in the Park, ca. 1930, K & O, gray metal, 7", shopmark, rarity 5, $175.00.

Plate 1259. Sword Dancer, ca. 1930, gray metal figure on marble base, 9", rarity 5*, $650.00.

Plate 1260. Take a Bow, ca. 1930, gray metal figure on marble base, 6", rarity 5, $150.00.

Plate 1261. Tambourine Girl, 1926, Gift House Inc, iron, 5¼", marked Gift House, Inc 1926, rarity 4, $125.00. *Same figure is made in bronze by Tiffany.*

Plate 1262. Tango Dancer, ca. 1935, attr Dodge, gray metal, 6¾", rarity 4, $140.00.

Plate 1263. Tango Deco, 1930, Creation Company, iron, 6", marked C Company 1930, rarity 5, $225.00.

Plate 1264. Tapestry Dancer, ca. 1925, iron, 7¼", rarity 5, $175.00.

Plate 1265. Thespian, ca. 1925, iron, 5½", marked #140, rarity 4, $115.00.

193

Plate 1266. Thought, ca. 1920, Gorham, bronze, 7", marked E E Codman (sculptor), Gorham Co, rarity 5*, $1,200.00.

Plate 1267. Thought and Progress, ca. 1920, Gorham, bronze, 10", marked I Konti (sculptor), Gorham Co, rarity 5*, $7,500.00.

Plate 1268. Tip Toes, ca. 1925, Pompeian Bronze, bronze-clad, 10", shopmark, rarity 5, $495.00.

Plate 1269. Traditional Nude, ca. 1925, bronze, 5½", rarity 5, $110.00.

Plate 1270. Travail, ca. 1920, Gorham, bronze, 3¼", marked W Stratton (sculptor), Gorham Co, rarity 5*, $750.00.

Plate 1271. Truth, ca. 1925, Kathodion Bronze Works, bronze-clad, 7", marked KBW, rarity 5, $275.00.

Plate 1272. Umbrella Girls, ca. 1925, X-1, gray metal, 5", marked #62, rarity 5, $275.00.

Plate 1273. Under the Shade Tree, ca. 1925, iron, 4¾", marked #70, rarity 5*, $150.00. Photo courtesy of Agris Kelbrants.

Plate 1274. Under the Shade Tree (Solid Bronze), ca. 1925, bronze, 5¼", marked Solid Bronze, rarity 5*, $175.00.

Plate 1278. Wait Here, ca. 1926, JB Hirsch, gray metal figure, celluloid face and fan, marble or polished stone base, 6¾", rarity 5, $275.00.

Plate 1275. Victorian Miss, ca. 1920, gray metal, 5¼", marked CV Vaeremberl (sculptor), rarity 5*, $225.00.

Plate 1279. Waiting to Dance, ca. 1925, attr Armor Bronze, bronze-clad, 5½", rarity 5, $150.00.

Plate 1276. Vine Entwined Lady, 1928, Armor Bronze, bronze-clad, 6", marked P Beneduce (sculptor) 1928, rarity 5, $295.00.

Plate 1280. Walking Her Dog, ca. 1925, attr Pompeian Bronze, bronze-clad, 8", rarity 5*, $475.00. Photo courtesy of Jay Mendlovitz.

Plate 1277. Virginia, ca. 1930, gray metal, 9", marked HW Hahn, rarity 5, $275.00.

Plate 1281. Walking in Style, 1925, bronze on marble base, 7", marked B Zach, rarity 5*, $4,500.00. *Made in Austria.*

Plate 1282. Water Sprite, ca. 1925, Acorn, iron, 5⅜", marked #604 Watersprite, rarity 4, $195.00.

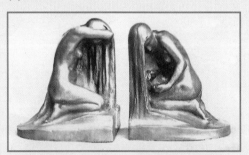

Plate 1283. Waterfall of Hair, ca. 1920, Gorham, bronze, 7¼", marked E W Keyser (sculptor), Gorham Co, rarity 5*, $2,500.00.

Plate 1284. Webbed Cape, ca. 1925, gray metal with celluloid face on marble base, 6", rarity 5, $300.00.

Plate 1285. Well of Wisdom, 1929, Connecticut Foundry, iron, 6", shopmark, Well of Wisdom, 1929, rarity 5, $195.00.

Plate 1286. Whistler's Mother, ca. 1932, JB Hirsch, gray metal figure, celluloid face and hands, marble base, 6½", marked JBH, rarity 5, $225.00. *Numerous metal formats seen, all of similar value.*

Plate 1287. Whistler's Mother, different finish.

Plate 1288. Whistler's Mother, plaster, rarity 5, $150.00. *Similar to the two previous Whistler's Mothers this piece is made of plaster, produced approximately 10 years after the original, but from the same molds.*

Plate 1289. Windswept Nude, ca. 1924, Pompeian Bronze, bronze-clad, 9¼", marked Pompeian Bronze, rarity 5, polychrome, $795.00; monochrome, $695.00. Photo courtesy of Billie Trepanier.

Plate 1290. Winged Nymph, ca. 1925, Ronson, gray metal, 5", company paper tag #11782, rarity 5, polychrome, $495.00; monochrome, $395.00.

Plate 1294. Woman at the Wall, ca. 1925, attr Armor Bronze, bronze-clad, 6", rarity 5, $295.00.

Plate 1291. Woman and Book, 1913, Gorham, bronze, 5¾", marked Lillian Baer (sculptor), Gorham Co 1913, rarity 5*, $3,500.00.

Plate 1295. Womanhood, ca. 1932, Comet Metal Craft, gray metal, 5½", rarity 3, $75.00. Photo courtesy of Agris Kelbrants.

Plate 1292. Woman and Child, ca. 1922, Pompeian Bronze, bronze-clad, 6½", rarity 5, $165.00.

Plate 1296. Woman in Flight (Ronson), ca. 1920, Ronson, gray metal, 8", marked LV Aronson, 1920, company tag, rarity 5*, $450.00.

Plate 1293. Woman and Child (Gorham), ca. 1920, Gorham, Bronze, 6", marked W D Paddock, rarity 5*, $2,000.00.

Plate 1297. Woman in Flight, ca. 1920, (Le Verrier), bronze, 8", shopmark, rarity 5, original, $950.00; current production, $450.00.

197

Plate 1298. Woman on Couch, ca. 1930, JB Hirsch, gray metal with celluloid face, 4¾", marked JBH, rarity 5, $300.00.

Plate 1302. Boy Scouts, ca. 1970, gray metal, 6½", rarity 3, $50.00.

Plate 1299. Wood Nymph, 1927, Armor Bronze, bronze-clad, 7½", marked Armor Bronze, rarity 5, $425.00.

Plate 1303. BPOE Design, 1922, Ronson, gray metal, 3¼", marked LV Aronson 1922, rarity 3, $75.00.

Plate 1300. Your Book, Sir, 1924, Ronson, gray metal, 5½", marked LV Aronson 1924, rarity 5, $150.00.

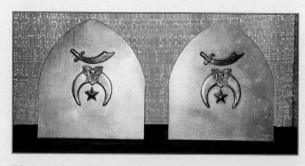

Plate 1304. Brass Shriners, ca. 1935, Robbins Co, brass, 5½", shopmark (Attleboro), rarity 5, $85.00.

Fraternal Order

Plate 1301. American Legion, ca. 1939, bronze, 8", rarity 5, $115.00.

Plate 1305. Eastern Star, 1922, Ronson, gray metal, 4¼", marked LV Aronson 1922, polychrome, rarity 5; monochrome, rarity 4, polychrome, $125.00; monochrome, $100.00.

Plate 1306. Ebony Elks, ca. 1925, iron, 3½", rarity 4, $50.00.

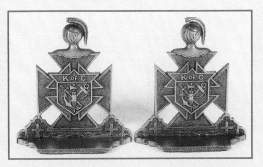

Plate 1310. Knights of Columbus (Ronson), 1922, Ronson, gray metal, 3¼", marked LV Aronson 1922, rarity 3, $85.00.

Plate 1307. Elks, ca. 1920, Judd, iron, 5¼", rarity 5, $115.00.

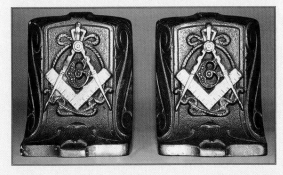

Plate 1311. Masonic Emblem, ca. 1928, Judd, iron, 5¼", rarity 4, $100.00.

Plate 1308. Elks (B & H), ca. 1925, Bradley and Hubbard, iron, 6", shopmark, rarity 4, $125.00.

Plate 1312. Masons, ca. 1925, gray metal, 6½", rarity 5, $125.00.

Plate 1309. Knights of Columbus, ca. 1925, bronze, 6½", rarity 4, $125.00.

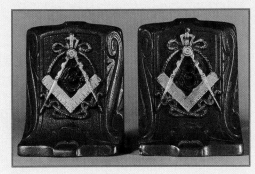

Plate 1313. Masons (Judd), ca. 1920, Judd, iron, 5¼", rarity 5, $115.00.

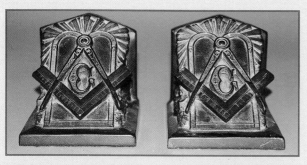

Plate 1314. Masons (Ronson), 1922, Ronson, gray metal, 4¼", marked LV Aronson 1922, rarity 5, $95.00.

Plate 1318. Shriner Crescent, 1922, Ronson, gray metal, 3¼", marked LV Aronson 1922, rarity 4, $95.00.
Photo courtesy of Richard Weinstein.

Plate 1315. Moose Lodge, 1922, Ronson, gray metal, 4¼", marked LV Aronson 1922, rarity 5, $125.00.

Plate 1319. Shriner Saber, ca. 1920, iron, 4¾", rarity 5, $85.00.

Plate 1316. Oddfellows, ca. 1935, Vergne Artware (West Coast Industries, Oakland, CA), bronze, 6¼", marked #119, rarity 4, $125.00.

Plate 1320. Shriners and Stars, ca. 1925, Judd, iron, 5¼", rarity 4, $110.00.

Plate 1317. Scottish Rite, 1922, Ronson, gray metal, 3¼", marked LV Aronson 1922, rarity 3, $85.00.

Plate 1321. Shriners Fez, ca. 1922, Ronson, gray metal, 3¼", marked LV Aronson 1922, rarity 3, $75.00.

Plate 1322. Syria Temple, ca. 1930, gray metal, 5½", rarity 5, $75.00.

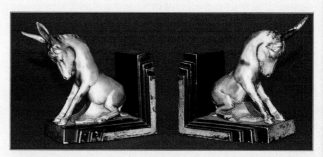

Plate 1326. Deco Horse, ca. 1940, bronze, 7", rarity 5, $125.00.

Horses, Donkeys, Mules, and Burros

Plate 1323. Burro, ca. 1925, Hubley, iron, 4", marked Made in USA #492, rarity 5, $150.00.

Plate 1327. Donkey, 1932, Ronson, gray metal , 6", company paper tag, rarity 5*, $225.00.

Plate 1324. Caricature Pony, ca. 1935, K & O, gray metal, 5½", shopmark, rarity 5*, $150.00.

Plate 1328. Flicka, ca. 1935, attr Dodge, gray metal, 6", rarity 4, $85.00. Photo courtesy of Agris Kelbrants.

Plate 1325. Chariot Horses, ca. 1934, Frankart, gray metal, 5", marked Frankart Inc. Pat Appl. For, rarity 4, $150.00.

Plate 1329. Good Luck Horse, ca. 1930, Jennings Brothers, gray metal, 7¼", marked JB 1714, rarity 5*, $195.00. Photo courtesy of Agris Kelbrants.

Plate 1330. Graceful Horse, ca. 1930, gray metal, 7¼", rarity 4, $100.00.

Plate 1334. Horse (Chase), ca. 1935, Chase, bronze, 6¼", rarity 5, $600.00.

Plate 1331. Grand Horse Head, ca. 1930, Frankart, gray metal, 8", marked Frankart Inc. Pat Appl. For, rarity 5, $175.00.

Plate 1335. Horse (New Martinsville), ca. 1940, New Martinsville Glass, glass, 7½", rarity 4, $150.00. Photo courtesy of Michael Horseman.

Plate 1332. Grazing Pony, ca. 1930, gray metal, 5¼", rarity 4, $110.00.

Plate 1336. Horse (New Martinsville), different version.

Plate 1333. Head Up Horse, ca. 1940, New Martinsville Glass, glass, 8", rarity 5, $190.00.
Photo courtesy of Michael Horseman.

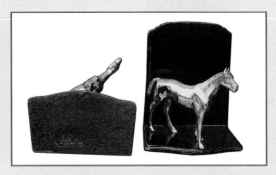

Plate 1337. Horse (Ronson), ca. 1925, Ronson, gray metal, 4½", company paper tag, rarity 5, $95.00.

Plate 1338. Horse (Smith), ca. 1925, Smith Glass, glass, 8", rarity 3, $50.00. Photo courtesy of Mary Collins.

Plate 1339. Horse (Smith) Stable, ca. 1925, Smith Glass, glass, 8", various.

Plate 1340. Horse and Pup, ca. 1930, Frankart, gray metal, 6", marked Frankart Inc. Pat Appl. For, rarity 5, $150.00.

Plate 1341. Horse, Cat, and Dog, ca. 1930, K & O, gray metal, 6", shopmark, rarity 5, $175.00.

Plate 1342. Horse at the Gate, ca. 1925, Bradley and Hubbard, iron base, gray metal figure, 6", shopmark, rarity 5, $175.00.

Plate 1343. Horse Family, ca. 1930, Judd Company, iron, 5¼", shopmark #09855, rarity 5, $95.00.

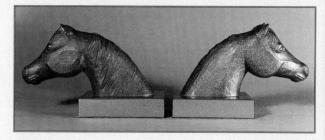

Plate 1344. Horse Head, ca. 1935, bronze, 5", rarity 5*, $175.00.

203

Plate 1345. Horse Head (Dodge), ca. 1930, Dodge, gray metal, 7", company paper tag, rarity 4, $125.00.

Plate 1349. Horse Head (Gladys Brown), 1946, Dodge, gray metal, 6", marked Gladys Brown (sculptor) Dodge Inc 46, rarity 3, $95.00.

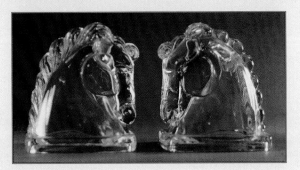

Plate 1346. Horse Head (Federal), ca. 1940, Federal Glass, glass, 5½", rarity 1, $10.00. Photo courtesy of Michael Horseman.

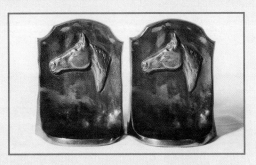

Plate 1350. Horse Head (Graham Bronze), ca. 1935, Graham Bronze, bronze, 5¾", marked Graham Bronze, rarity 4, $140.00.

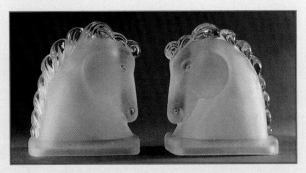

Plate 1347. Horse Head (Federal), frosted version.

Plate 1351. Horse Head (Heisey), ca. 1946, Heisey, glass, 6½", rarity 4, $240.00.

Plate 1348. Horse Head (Frankart), ca. 1930, Frankart, gray metal, 5¾", marked Frankart Inc. Pat Appl. For, rarity 5, $150.00.

Plate 1352. Horse Head (Indiana Glass), ca. 1940, Indiana Glass, glass, 6", rarity 3, $50.00.

Plate 1353. Horse Head (Kraftware), ca. 1950, Kraftware, gray metal, 5½", marked Kraftware, rarity 4, $50.00. Photo courtesy of Agris Kelbrants.

Plate 1354. Horse Head (McClelland and Barclay), ca. 1930, McClelland and Barkley, gray metal, 6¼", marked McClelland and Barclay, rarity 4, $225.00.

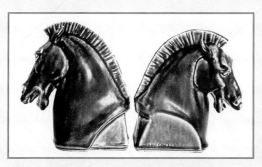

Plate 1355. Horse Head (Rookwood), 1929, Rookwood, pottery, marked XXIX #6014 McDonald, rarity 4, $500.00.

Plate 1356. Horse in Horseshoe, ca. 1930, Ronson, gray metal, 4⅝", company paper tag #16513, rarity 4, $95.00. Photo courtesy of Richard Weinstein.

Plate 1357. Horse on Arc, ca. 1947, Dodge, gray metal, 5½", company paper tag, rarity 4, $95.00.

Plate 1358. Horse on the Loose, ca. 1930, Jennings Brothers, gray metal, 6½", shopmark, rarity 5, $195.00. *The horses' reins are quite fragile and easily broken. Intact sets are uncommon.* Photo courtesy of Jay Mendlovitz.

Plate 1359. Horses, ca. 1930, Nuart Creations, gray metal, 5¼", marked Nuart Creations NYC, rarity 3, $135.00.

Plate 1360. Horses (Drucklieb), ca. 1926, H Company, gray metal, 5¾", marked artist signature Jeanne L. Drucklieb ©, rarity 5*, $165.00. Photo courtesy of Sue Benoliel.

Plate 1361. In His Stable, ca. 1925, iron, 5", marked 2, rarity 5, $125.00. Photo courtesy of Agris Kelbrants.

Plate 1365. Leaping Horse (Nuart), ca. 1934, Nuart, gray metal, 5¾", shopmark, rarity 4, $110.00.

Plate 1362. Jumper, ca. 1930, Jennings Brothers, gray metal, 5", rarity 5, $145.00. *This piece has been altered, although skillfully done, and I did not detect it at the time of purchase. Subsequently, seeing an intact piece indicates a short tail was present. Likely, the tail was damaged on one piece, requiring some "adjustment" to make a suitable pair, hence the new tail.*

Plate 1366. Listening to the Wind, ca. 1930, Armor Bronze, bronze-clad, 6¼", shopmark, rarity 5, $125.00.

Plate 1363. Jumping Horse, ca. 1940, attr Cambridge Glass, glass, 8", rarity 4, $100.00.

Plate 1367. Looking Back, ca. 1950, gray metal, 6½", marked Kraftware, rarity 3, $110.00. Photo courtesy of Sue Benoliel.

Plate 1364. Lady Godiva, ca. 1940, Haley Glass, glass, 6", rarity 4, $135.00.

Plate 1368. Mare and Colt, ca. 1925, bronze-clad, 6", marked Paul Herzel (sculptor) ©, rarity 5*, $275.00. Photo courtesy of Agris Kelbrants.

Plate 1369. Miniature Horse, ca. 1930, Sellright Gift Corporation, gray metal, 4¼", company paper tag: SRG Sellright Giftwares Brooklyn NY, rarity 4, $65.00.

Plate 1370. Mustang, ca. 1920, Pompeian Bronze, bronze-clad, 8½", marked Paul Herzel, rarity 5, $195.00. Photo courtesy of Billie Trepanier.

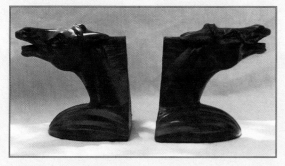

Plate 1371. Neighing, ca. 1930, gray metal, 5½", rarity 3, $50.00. Photo courtesy of Mary Collins.

Plate 1372. Over the Top, 1947, Haley Glass, glass, 7½", rarity 4, $110.00.

Plate 1373. Ponies in Storm, ca. 1925, Hubley, iron, 5", marked Hubley Manufacturing Co. #175, rarity 4, $125.00. Photo courtesy of Agris Kelbrants.

Plate 1374. Pony, ca. 1926, Littco, iron, 6", rarity 4, $110.00.

Plate 1375. Prancers, ca. 1932, K & O, gray metal, 10", rarity 5*, $125.00. Photo courtesy of Agris Kelbrants.

Plate 1376. Prancing Horse (Frankart), ca. 1934, Frankart, gray metal, 5¾", marked "Frankart Inc. Patient Applied For" shopmark, rarity 4, $125.00.

Plate 1377. Rearing Horse (Heisey), 1980, Heisey (re-issue), glass, rarity 5*, $400.00.

Plate 1381. Thoroughbred, ca. 1925, bronze-clad, 7¾", ©, rarity 5, $200.00.

Plate 1378. Rearing Horse, ca. 1925, gray metal, 6¾", rarity 3, $50.00. *The painted finish on these is often of poor quality.*

Plate 1382. Thoroughbred (Hubley), ca. 1925, attr Hubley, gray metal, 6", rarity 5, $125.00.

Plate 1379. Riderless Horse, ca. 1930, various, bronze, 4¾", bronze, rarity 5; iron, rarity 3, bronze, $110.00; iron, $45.00.

Plate 1383. Thoroughbred (Littco), ca. 1928, Littco, iron, 5½", company paper tag, rarity 4, $100.00.

Plate 1380. Rough Rider, ca. 1925, iron, 5½", rarity 4, $100.00. Photo courtesy of Sue Benoliel.

Plate 1384. Thorough-bred Horse Head, ca. 1930, Ronson, gray metal, 4⅛", company paper tag #16339, rarity 4, $95.00.

Plate 1385. Twin Horses, ca. 1930, Ronson, gray metal, 3½", company paper tag #16417, rarity 4, $100.00.
Photo courtesy of Richard Weinstein.

Plate 1389. Wild Horses, 1926, Gift House, iron, 4⅝", marked © 1926 Gifthouse Inc NYC, rarity 5, $150.00.

Plate 1386. Up to My Neck, ca. 1940, glass, 5", rarity 4, $75.00.

Lamps

Plate 1390. Double Flamed Lamp, ca. 1928, Judd, iron, 4⅜", marked #9749, rarity 5, $125.00.

Plate 1387. Whipper, The, ca. 1925, Hubley, iron, 4¾", marked Hubley #415, rarity 4, $150.00.

Plate 1391. Lamp, ca. 1925, iron, 4¾", rarity 5, $75.00. Photo courtesy of Agris Kelbrants.

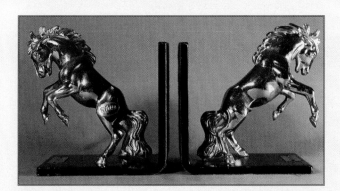

Plate 1388. White Horse, ca. 1935, gray metal on iron base, 6¼", marked White on rear haunch, rarity 5, $150.00.

Plate 1392. Lamp and Book, 1942, Ronson, gray metal, 5", marked LVA 1942, rarity 4, $125.00.

Plate 1393. Lamp of Knowledge, ca. 1925, iron, 3¼", rarity 3, $45.00. Photo courtesy of Agris Kelbrants.

Plate 1394. Lamp, Books, and Quill, ca. 1928, Weidlich Brothers, gray metal, 5", WB shopmark, rarity 4, $110.00.

Plate 1395. Lamp, Books, and Quill (B & H), ca. 1928, Bradley and Hubbard, iron, 5", shopmark, rarity 5, $125.00. Photo courtesy of Agris Kelbrants.

Plate 1396. Oil Lamp, 1947, Dodge, gray metal, 4½", marked Dodge, Inc, rarity 4, $75.00.

Lincoln

Plate 1397. Abe's Profile, ca. 1925, iron, 5¾", rarity 5, $75.00. Photo courtesy of Agris Kelbrants.

Plate 1398. Abraham Lincoln, ca. 1925, Solid Bronze, bronze, 4¾", marked Solid Bronze, rarity 4, $100.00. Photo courtesy of Agris Kelbrants.

Plate 1399. Borglum Lincoln (Solid Bronze), ca. 1930, Solid Bronze, bronze, 3¾", marked Solid Bronze, rarity 3, $90.00.

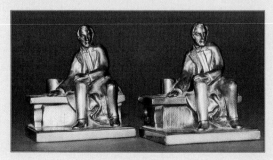

Plate 1400. Borglum's Lincoln, 1931, Ronson, gray metal, 4½", company tag #14149, rarity 4, $90.00. *Also comes in 5½", company tag #16561 and 6½", company tag #16250.*

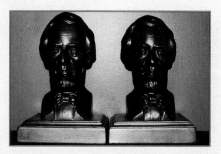

Plate 1401. Bow-tie Lincoln, ca. 1950, gray metal, 7½", rarity 3, $65.00. Photo courtesy of Agris Kelbrants.

Plate 1402. Emancipator, 1928, Connecticut Foundry, iron, shopmark, 1928, rarity 4, $75.00. Photo courtesy of Agris Kelbrants.

Plate 1403. French's Lincoln, ca. 1924, Gift House, Inc., iron, 6", marked D 57, NYC, rarity 5, $195.00.

Plate 1404. Great Emancipator, 1925, Pompeian Bronze, gray metal, 5½". marked The Emancipator PB & Co., rarity 5, $175.00.

Plate 1405. Lincoln, ca. 1925, iron, 7", rarity 4, $65.00.

Plate 1406. Lincoln (Bronzmet), ca. 1925, Bronzmet, iron, marked D42L, Bronzmet shopmark, rarity 5, $125.00.

Photo courtesy of Agris Kelbrants.

Plate 1407. Lincoln (Galvano), ca. 1918, Galvano Bronze, bronze-clad, 8¾", marked Lincoln, rarity 4, $175.00.

Plate 1408. Lincoln (Gift House), 1929, Gift House, Inc., iron, 6½", marked © 1929 Gift House Inc NYC, rarity 5, $135.00.

Plate 1409. Lincoln (Greenblatt), 1923, A M Greenblatt, gray metal, 6", marked © 1923 AM Greenblatt, rarity 4, $80.00.

Plate 1413. Lincoln Bust (Marion Bronze), ca. 1950, Marion Bronze, bronze-clad, 8¼", rarity 5, $135.00.

Plate 1410. Lincoln at Gettysburg, ca. 1930, K&O, gray metal, 7¾", marked Lincoln at Gettysburg, rarity 5*, $225.00. *Reissue by PMC, post 1964 also seen, rarity 4, $75.00.*

Plate 1414. Lincoln Bust (PMC), ca. 1960, PM Craftsman, gray metal, 6", marked PM Craftsman, rarity 5, $45.00. Photo courtesy of Agris Kelbrants.

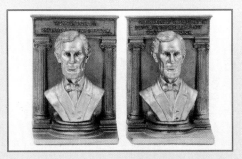

Plate 1411. Lincoln Bust (B & H), ca. 1925, Bradley and Hubbard, gray metal figure, iron base, 8", shopmark, rarity 5, $285.00.

Plate 1415. Lincoln Bust (Verona), ca. 1928, Verona, iron, 6½", shopmark, rarity 3, $65.00.

Plate 1412. Lincoln Bust (g), ca. 1925, bronze-clad, 8¾", rarity 5*, $250.00.

Plate 1416. Lincoln Bust on Pedestal, ca. 1930, gray metal, 6", rarity 5, $50.00. Photo courtesy of Agris Kelbrants.

Plate 1417. Lincoln, Head and Shoulders, ca. 1930, K&O, gray metal, 4", shopmark, rarity 5, $75.00. Photo courtesy of Agris Kelbrants.

Plate 1418. Lincoln in Chair, ca. 1935, gray metal, 6", rarity 5, $125.00.

Plate 1419. Lincoln: Log Cabin to White House, ca. 1918, Griffoul, bronze, 6", marked Griffoul, rarity 5, $195.00.

Plate 1420. Lincoln Medallion, 1921, Ronson, gray metal, 4¾", marked LV Aronson, 1921, rarity 3, $90.00. Photo courtesy of Richard Weinstein.

Plate 1421. Lincoln Monument, ca. 1930, WB, gray metal, 5½", shopmark, 1924, rarity 4, $150.00. Photo courtesy of John Asfor.

Plate 1422. Lincoln Profile, ca. 1925, iron, 5¼", rarity 3, $65.00. Photo courtesy of Jay Mendlovitz.

Plate 1423. Lincoln Profile (CF), 1930, Connecticut Foundry, iron, 6", Lincoln, 1930, shopmark, rarity 4, $110.00.

Plate 1424. Lincoln Profile (CT), ca. 1925, CT, iron, 6", marked CT ©, rarity 4, $110.00.

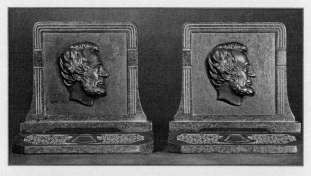

Plate 1425. Lincoln Profile (Judd), ca. 1926, Judd, iron, 5½", marked #9747, rarity 4, $110.00.

Plate 1429. Lincoln: With Malice Toward None (Gorham), ca. 1921, Gorham, bronze, 5¼", marked M Peinlich (sculptor) Gorham Co New York, rarity 5, $350.00.

Plate 1426. Lincoln Tad, 1922, iron, 7½", marked P Muller (sculptor) 1922 ©, rarity 4, $110.00.

Plate 1430. Seated Lincoln, 1924, Nuart, gray metal, 6½", shopmark, 1924, rarity 4, $110.00.

Plate 1427. Lincoln Thinking, ca. 1925, Judd, iron, 4½", marked Judd, #9674, rarity 5, $85.00. Photo courtesy of Agris Kelbrants.

Plate 1431. Seated Lincoln (Galvano), 1921, Galvano Bronze, bronze-clad, 8", marked P Beneduce (sculptor) © 1921, rarity 5, $175.00.

Plate 1428. Lincoln: With Malice Toward None, 1915, Griffoul, bronze, 5⅜", marked A Lincoln 1809 – 1865© 1915 Cast by Griffoul Newark NJ Distributor Marshall Field and Co. Chicago, rarity 5, $250.00.

Plate 1432. Young Lincoln, ca. 1930, bronze, 6¾", rarity 5*, $195.00.

Plate 1433. Young Lincoln (Connecticut Foundry), ca. 1928, Connecticut Foundry, iron, 5", shopmark, #906, rarity 5, $95.00. Photo courtesy of Agris Kelbrants.

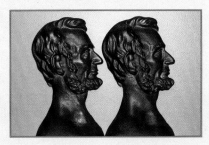

Plate 1434. Young Lincoln Profile, ca. 1925, iron, 5⅞", marked EMIG, #1568, rarity 5, $95.00. Photo courtesy of Agris Kelbrants.

Literary

Plate 1435. Auld Lang Syne, 1925, K & O, gray metal, 4¾", shopmark, rarity 5, polychrome, $175.00; monochrome, $110.00. *Pictured in 1925 AC Becken Jewelers Catalogue.*

Plate 1436. Bacon and Johnson, ca. 1930, brass, 6½", rarity 4, $110.00. *This is an expandable book rack.*

Plate 1437. Blest Be the Man, 1953, bronze, 7", marked England #694236, rarity 5, $150.00. Photo courtesy of Agris Kelbrants.

Plate 1438. Book, ca. 1930, Frankart, gray metal, 5½", shopmark, rarity 5*, $175.00. *This bookend has been seen with a girl on top of the book. It is unclear whether the figure was ever actually marketed as a book alone, or the girl simply removed.*

Plate 1439. Bookcase, ca. 1920, iron, 5¼", marked #1014, rarity 3, $65.00. Photo courtesy of Agris Kelbrants.

Plate 1440. Bryant and Holmes, ca. 1926, Bradley and Hubbard, iron, 6", company paper tag, rarity 4, $75.00.

215

Plate 1441. Bryant and Whittier, ca. 1926, Bradley and Hubbard, iron, 6", company paper tag, rarity 4, $75.00.

Plate 1442. Charles Dickens, 1926, X-3, iron, 6", rarity 4, $95.00.

Plate 1443. Colonial Librarian, ca. 1930, K & O, gray metal, 6", shopmark, rarity 5, $150.00.

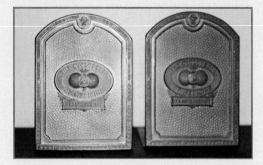

Plate 1444. Cyclopedia of Medicine, ca. 1930, HF Grimes and Sons Inc, brass, 8", marked FA Davis Company, rarity 5, $125.00.

Plate 1445. Dickens, ca. 1929, Jennings Brothers, gray metal, 6¼", shopmark #2062, rarity 5, $125.00.

Plate 1446. Dickens and Shakespeare, ca. 1926, Bradley and Hubbard, iron, 6", shopmark, rarity 4, $75.00.

Plate 1447. Dickens Bust, ca. 1925, Armor Bronze, bronze-clad, 5¼", shopmark, rarity 4, polychrome, $125.00; monochrome, $95.00.

Plate 1448. Field and Riley, ca. 1925, Bradley and Hubbard, iron, 5½", shopmark, rarity 4, $75.00.

Plate 1449. Hall's Bookcase, ca. 1928, S W Hall, Bakelite, 5¾", marked Design © September 1928 to Samuel W Hall, rarity 5*, $350.00.

Plate 1450. Henry W Longfellow, ca. 1930, K & O, gray metal, 5¼", shop-mark, rarity 5, $100.00.

Plate 1451. Holmes, ca. 1925, Bradley and Hubbard, iron, 6¼", shopmark, rarity 5, $125.00.

Plate 1452. Huck Finn, ca. 1930, Armor Bronze, bronze-clad, 7¾", rarity 4, $175.00.

Plate 1453. James Whitcomb Riley, ca. 1925, Bradley and Hubbard, iron, 5½", rarity 4, $75.00.

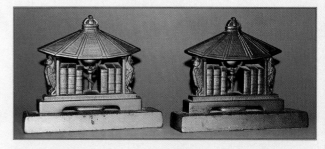

Plate 1454. Lamp of Knowledge, ca. 1925, Judd, iron, 4¾", marked 9986, rarity 4, $100.00.

Plate 1455. Limp Grained Leather, 1933, Ronson, gray metal, 4½", marked AMW 1933, rarity 3, $50.00.

Plate 1456. Longfellow, ca. 1925, Bradley and Hubbard, iron, 6¼", shopmark, rarity 5, $195.00.

Plate 1457. Longfellow (Judd), ca. 1925, Judd, iron base, gray metal figure, 5¼", marked 9991, rarity 4, $150.00.

Plate 1458. Longfellow and Emerson, 1917, Gorham, bronze, 6½", marked W C Noble (sculptor), Gorham Co, rarity 5*, $300.00.

Plate 1459. Mark Twain (Nuart), ca. 1930, Nuart, gray metal, 5¾", shopmark, rarity 5, $150.00.

Plate 1460. Mark Twain (WB), ca. 1925, Weidlich Brothers, gray metal, 6½", marked Mark Twain © USA WB, rarity 5, $175.00.

Plate 1461. Mark Twain (X-3), ca. 1926, X-3, iron, 6", rarity 4, $95.00.

Plate 1462. Mark Twain and Tom Sawyer, ca. 1936, Jennings Brothers, gray metal, 7¾", marked JB 707© company paper tag reads "Mark Twain and Tom Sawyer," rarity 5, $275.00. *See page 19 for details.*

Plate 1463. Merchant of Venice, ca. 1925, iron, 4", marked Merchant of Venice, rarity 4, $45.00.

Photo courtesy of Agris Kelbrants.

218

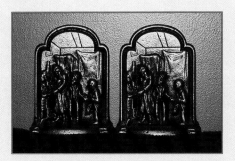

Plate 1464. Oliver Twist, ca. 1930, iron, 4", marked #47, rarity 5, $75.00.
Photo courtesy of Agris Kelbrants.

Plate 1468. Quixote and Panza, ca. 1950, plaster, 7½", rarity 5, $75.00.

Plate 1465. Peter Pan, ca. 1965, Marion Bronze, bronze-clad, 7½", shopmark, rarity 5, $175.00.

Plate 1469. Ralph Waldo Emerson, ca. 1925, Galvano Bronze, bronze-clad, 7½", rarity 4, $135.00.

Plate 1466. Plato, ca. 1926, Armor Bronze, bronze-clad, 7", shopmark, rarity 5, $150.00.

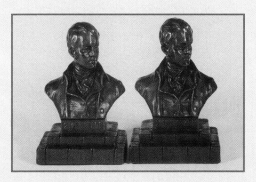

Plate 1470. Rob Burns, ca. 1925, Galvano Bronze, bronze-clad, 5¼", rarity 5, $125.00.

Plate 1467. Pope and Young, ca. 1925, Bradley and Hubbard, iron, 5½", shopmark, rarity 5, $150.00.

Plate 1471. Sajous Cyclopedia, ca. 1925, iron, 6½", rarity 5, $75.00.

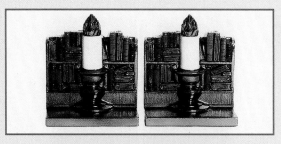

Plate 1472. Volumes and Candlelight, ca. 1930, Ronson, gray metal, 4¼", company paper tag #11484, polychrome, rarity 4; other, rarity 3, polychrome, $90.00; other, $65.00.

Plate 1473. Will Rogers, ca. 1925, Great Falls Iron Works, iron, 6¾", marked Great Falls Iron Works, rarity 5, $195.00.

Plate 1474. Tolstoy, ca. 1925, iron, 5½", rarity 5, $125.00. Photo courtesy of Agris Kelbrants.

Male Figures

Plate 1475. Ancients, ca. 1930, bronze, 8", rarity 5, $95.00. Photo courtesy of Agris Kelbrants.

Plate 1476. Asleep at Mid-Story, ca. 1929, K & O, gray metal, 4¼", shopmark, rarity 4, $175.00.

Plate 1477. Athlete, ca. 1928, Armor Bronze, bronze-clad, 9", Meliodon (sculptor) shopmark, rarity 5, $175.00.

Plate 1478. Atlas, ca. 1932, JB Hirsch, chalk on polished stone base, 7¾", shopmark, rarity 5*, $100.00.

Plate 1479. Back to Work, ca. 1926, gray metal on marble base, 6¼", rarity 5, $300.00.

Plate 1480. Bearded Man, ca. 1925, bronze-clad, 7½", rarity 5*, $450.00.

Plate 1481. Bending Backwards, ca. 1925, iron, 6", rarity 4, $75.00.

Plate 1482. Bird Watchers, ca. 1925, gray metal, 7", rarity 5, $475.00.

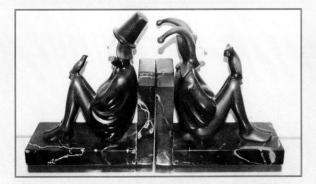

Plate 1483. Bird Watchers (R. Paris), ca. 1925, bronze & ivory on marble base, 6½", marked Roland Paris (sculptor), rarity 5*, $6,500.00.

Plate 1484. Blacksmith (American Chain Company), ca. 1930, American Chain Co, gray metal, 4½", rarity 5, $95.00. *This piece, unmarked but identical otherwise has been seen with logo "American Chain Co."*

Plate 1485. Blacksmith, ca. 1925, Littco, iron, 5", rarity 5, $175.00.

Plate 1486. Blacksmith (Pompeian Bronze), ca. 1920, Pompeian Bronze, bronze-clad, 7¼", marked Paul Herzel (sculptor); PB Co., rarity 5, $500.00. Photo courtesy of Billie Trepanier.

Plate 1487. Blue Boy, ca. 1925, bronze, rarity 5, $95.00.

221

Plate 1488. Book Load, ca. 1925, JB Hirsch, gray metal figure on marble base, 5¼", rarity 5, $300.00.

Plate 1489. Bookworm, 1931, Nuart, gray metal, 6¾", shopmark (faint), ©, rarity 4, $110.00. *The description of this bookend, in the 1931 catalog reproduction reprinted by Art Deco by design, PO Box 1321, Dearborn, Michigan 48121 – 1321 reads "Book Worm bookends: A rare combination of humor and dignity that should be appreciated by every connoisseur of books." Originally priced at $300.00 per pair.*

Plate 1490. Boss, ca. 1925, iron, 4½", marked No 510, rarity 5, $225.00.

Plate 1491. Buccaneer, 1930, Connecticut Foundry, iron, 7¼", shopmark, Buccaneer, 1930, rarity 5, $125.00.

Plate 1492. Buccaneer (Armor Bronze), ca. 1928, Armor Bronze, bronze-clad, 6¾", marked Paul Herzel (sculptor), rarity 4, $125.00.

Plate 1493. Buccaneer (Marion Bronze), ca. 1965, Marion Bronze, bronze-clad, 6¾", marked MB, rarity 4, $125.00.

Plate 1494. Builder, ca. 1925, bronze-clad, 7½", marked The Builder, rarity 5, $250.00.

Plate 1495. Butler, ca. 1990, aluminum alloy, 7", rarity 5, $20.00.

Plate 1496. Castaways, ca. 1920, Pompeian Bronze, bronze-clad, 9½", marked Pompeian Bronze Co, rarity 5, $425.00. Photo courtesy Billie Trepanier.

Plate 1497. Cavalier, ca. 1928, attr Armor Bronze, bronze-clad, 5½", marked Paul Herzel (sculptor), rarity 5*, $250.00. Photo courtesy of Sue Benoliel.

Plate 1498. Chase Sentinel, 1940, Chase, bakelite and brass, 7¼", shopmark, rarity 5, $275.00.

Plate 1499. Checking the Treasure, ca. 1930, Armor Bronze, bronze-clad, 5¼", rarity 4, $110.00.

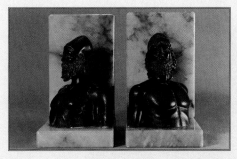

Plate 1500. Classical Men, ca. 1975, bronze on marble base, 6", rarity 5*, $150.00. *See page 17 for details.*

Plate 1501. Clown Dancers, ca. 1920, Pompeian bronze, bronze-clad, 9", marked Pompeian Bronze Co, rarity 5, $225.00. Photo courtesy of Billie Trepanier.

Plate 1502. Clowns, ca. 1925, bronze, 10", signature, rarity 5*, $750.00.

Plate 1503. Clowns (Cartier), ca. 1923, bronze on marble base, 7¼", marked Jacques Cartier (sculptor), rarity 5, $1,200.00.

Plate 1507. Cornell Flux, ca. 1950, Cornell Flux, aluminum, 4", rarity 5, $35.00.

Plate 1504. Clowns (Nuart), ca. 1932, Nuart Creations Inc, gray metal, 6¾", rarity 4, $90.00.

Plate 1508. Cyrano de Bergerac, ca. 1920, Pompeian Bronze, bronze-clad, 9½", marked Pompeian Bronze Co, rarity 5, $295.00. Photo courtesy of Billie Trepanier.

Plate 1505. Coca Cola Man, ca. 1925, iron, rarity 5, $100.00. *These were purchased as bookends, but are of uncertain derivation.*

Plate 1509. D'Artagnan, ca. 1928, Kathodion Bronze Works, bronze-clad, 7¾", marked KBW ArtBronz, rarity 5, $225.00.

Plate 1506. Contemplation, ca. 1920, Gorham, bronze, 7", marked D Melicoo (sculptor), Gorham Co, rarity 5*, $750.00.

Plate 1510. Deep in Thought, ca. 1925, attr JB Hirsch, gray metal on polished stone base, 6", marked J. Ruhl (sculptor), rarity 5, $275.00.

Plate 1511. Don Quixote , ca. 1925, attr Hubley, iron, 5¾", rarity 4, $100.00. Photo courtesy of Zeth Kuritzky.

Plate 1512. Don Quixote and Sancho Panza, ca. 1960, WW, stone-resin complex, 9", marked WW, rarity 5*, $125.00.

Plate 1513. Don Quixote's Respite, ca. 1930, Le Verrier, bronze, 11", marked Janle (sculptor signature), Le Verrier, foundry mark, rarity 5, original, $1,200.00; current production, $550.00. *See page 17 for details.*

Plate 1514. Drinking Man, ca. 1965, Marion Bronze, bronze, 8", marked MB, rarity 5, $95.00.

Plate 1515. Father Knickerbocker, ca. 1925, Judd, iron base, gray metal figure, 5¾", paper tag: Father Knickerbocker; #9936, rarity 5, $195.00.

Plate 1516. Fireside Comfort, ca. 1930, Armor Bronze, bronze-clad, 7¾", Fireside Comfort, shopmark, rarity 4, polychrome, $195.00; monochrome, $175.00.

Plate 1517. Foundry Worker, ca. 1974, bronze, 5¾", rarity 4, $95.00. *Numerous foundries within the last three decades have used this figure for their advertising in a variety of metals.*

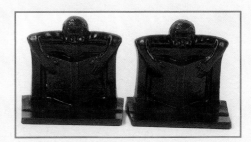

Plate 1518. G Kelley, ca. 1918, Griffoul, bronze, 4¾", marked Cast by Griffoul Newark NJ, Real Solid Bronze, rarity 5, $300.00

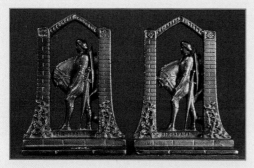

Plate 1519. Galahad in Archway, ca. 1925, Art Colonies Industries, iron, 6", rarity 3, $50.00.

Plate 1520. Galley Slaves, ca. 1925, iron, 5", marked Galley Slaves, rarity 3, $65.00.

Plate 1521. Gentleman, ca. 1925, Bradley and Hubbard, iron, 6¼", company paper tag, rarity 5, $125.00.

Plate 1522. Gladiator (KBW), ca. 1926, Kathodion Bronze Works, bronze-clad, 6½", marked ArtBronze KBW, ©, rarity 5, $350.00.

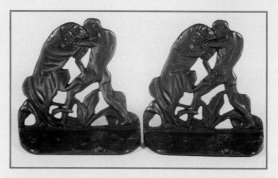

Plate 1523. Gladiator and The Lion, ca. 1930, iron, 5⅜", marked Gladiator, rarity 3, $75.00.

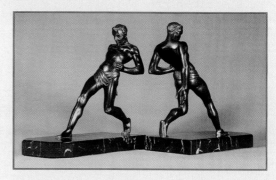

Plate 1524. Gladiators, ca. 1932, gray metal on marble base, 7¾", rarity 5, $500.00.

Plate 1525. Gnome in Library, ca. 1924, Bradley and Hubbard, iron base, gray metal figure, 5", shopmark, rarity 5, $195.00.

Plate 1526. Graphic Arts, ca. 1925, Pompeian Bronze, bronze-clad, 4½", marked Graphic Arts 106 Pompeian Bronze ©, rarity 4, $195.00.

Plate 1527. Greek Athlete, ca. 1927, Ronson, gray metal on marbleized base, 5½", company tag #11945M, rarity 5, $300.00.

Plate 1528. Grooming the Lion, ca. 1922, Marion Bronze, bronze-clad, 6", rarity 5*, $300.00.

Plate 1529. H L Menken, ca. 1928, gray metal, 7", rarity 5, $175.00. Photo courtesy of G. Houle.

Plate 1530. Hold Those Books, ca. 1932, JB Hirsch, gray metal figure, celluloid head, on marble or polished stone base, 7", rarity 4, $225.00.

Plate 1531. Hold Those Books (Dodge), ca. 1929, Dodge, gray metal, 7½", marked Dodge Inc, company paper tag, rarity 4, $195.00.

Plate 1532. Hunters, 1930, bronze, 8¾", marked Laboy Trauy (sculptor) 1930, rarity 5*, $1,000.00.

Plate 1533. Ironworker, 1922, Pompeian Bronze, bronze-clad, 6¾", marked PM © 1922, rarity 5*, $225.00.

Plate 1534. Jester, 1925, Armor Bronze, bronze-clad, 6½", Ruhl (sculptor), shopmark, rarity 5, polychrome, $295.00; monochrome, $225.00.

Plate 1535. John Harvard, ca. 1928, Jennings Brothers, gray metal, 7", marked Daniel C. French (sculptor) JB #2654, rarity 5, $350.00.

Plate 1536. Kneeling Man (Gorham), ca. 1911, Gorham, bronze, 6½", marked I Konti (sculptor), Gorham Foundry, rarity 5*, $3,500.00.

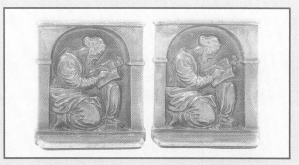

Plate 1537. Kneeling Reader, ca. 1925, Decorators Art League, iron, 4¼", marked DAL, rarity 4, $50.00.

Plate 1538. Knight, ca. 1925, bronze-clad, 6½", rarity 5*, $275.00.

Plate 1539. Knight Errant, ca. 1925, bronze, 6¼", rarity 4, $95.00.

Plate 1540. Knight in Archway, 1931, Gorham, bronze, 8", marked Gorham; The Traveler's Convention, Palm Beach Florida, 1931, rarity 5, $425.00.

Plate 1541. Laborer, ca. 1930, gray metal figure on marble base, 5", rarity 5, $375.00.

Plate 1542. Lazy Pedro, ca. 1930, Hubley, iron, 6¼", rarity 5, $175.00.

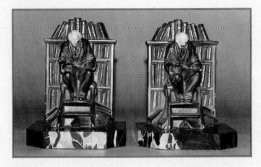

Plate 1543. Librarian, ca. 1932, JB Hirsch, gray metal figure, celluloid head, on marble or polished stone base, 6¼", marked JBH, rarity 5, $225.00.

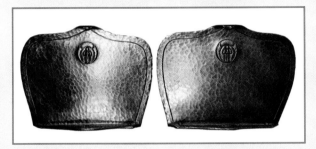

Plate 1544. Little Man Emblem, ca. 1922, Old Mission Koppercraft, copper, 5", shopmark, rarity 5, $195.00.

Plate 1545. Little Prince, ca. 1960, gray metal, 7½", rarity 3, $50.00.

Plate 1546. Lorenzo il Magnificao, ca. 1920, gray metal on marble base, 7", marked Paris, Made in France, rarity 5*, $350.00.

Plate 1547. Man at Globe, ca. 1965, PM Craftsman, gray metal, 5", company paper tag, rarity 4, $65.00.

Plate 1548. Man Flexing, ca. 1930, iron, 6¼", rarity 3, $50.00.

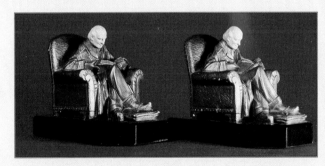

Plate 1549. Man Reading, ca. 1932, JB Hirsch, gray metal figure, celluloid head, on marble or polished stone base, 4½", marked J Ruhl (sculptor), JBH, rarity 4, metal, $295.00; chalk, $125.00.

Plate 1550. Man Reading (Handel), ca. 1928, Handel Lamps, bronze, 6¾", marked John Burroughs (sculptor), rarity 5*, $675.00.

229

Plate 1551. Man Reading (JB), ca. 1930, Jennings Brothers, gray metal, 7", marked JB1925, rarity 4, $175.00.

Plate 1552. Man Reading (MB), ca. 1965, Marion Bronze, bronze-clad, 8", marked MB, rarity 4, $95.00.

Plate 1553. Man with Scroll, ca. 1922, Marion Bronze, bronze-clad, 6", rarity 5*, $300.00.

Plate 1554. Miles Standish, ca. 1930, gray metal, 7", rarity 5, $125.00.

Plate 1555. Minute Men (SOA), ca. 1925, bronze, 6¼", marked SOA, rarity 5, $175.00.

Plate 1556. Morning Paper, ca. 1930, Jennings Brothers, gray metal, 8", marked JB2869, rarity 5, $175.00.

Plate 1557. Mr. Pecksniff, ca. 1927, Jennings Brothers, gray metal, 4½", marked JB, rarity 5, $125.00.

Plate 1558. Mr. Pickwick, ca. 1927, Jennings Brothers, gray metal, 8½", marked JB 2231, rarity 5, $275.00.

Plate 1559. Mr. Winkle's First Shot, 1953, bronze, 4¾", marked Mr. Winkle's First Shot; British Registry #698709; England, rarity 5, $150.00. *See page 20 for details.*

Plate 1560. Musketeers, ca. 1932, attr Pompeian Bronze, bronze-clad, 10¾", marked Paul Herzel (sculptor) ©, rarity 5, $325.00.

Plate 1561. Nude Runner, ca. 1930, bronze, 8½", rarity 5*, $500.00.

Plate 1562. Olympian Athletes, ca. 1925, Ronson, gray metal on marbleized base, 8¾", company paper tag, rarity 5, $300.00.

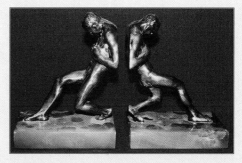

Plate 1563. Olympian Pose, ca. 1925, gray metal on marble base, 6¾", marked C, rarity 5*, $325.00.

Plate 1564. Pennsylvania State Police, 1946, brass, 6¼", marked CJR Steward (sculptor) 1946, rarity 5, $125.00.

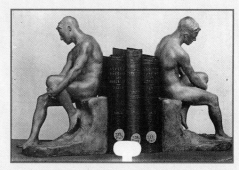

Plate 1565. Pensive, ca. 1920, Gorham, bronze, 13½", marked Edna Spencer (sculptor), Gorham Co, rarity 5*, $8,500.00.

Plate 1566. Pilgrim, 1915, Armor Bronze, bronze-clad, 10½", Ruhl (sculptor), shopmark, rarity 5, $395.00.

Plate 1567. Pipe Smoker, ca. 1925, bronze-clad, 7½", rarity 5, $175.00.

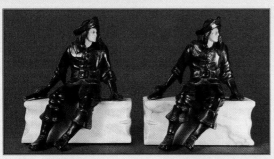

Plate 1568. Pirate, ca. 1925, JB Hirsch, gray metal figure, celluloid face, on marble base, 6½", rarity 4, $250.00.

Plate 1569. Pirate Couple (Hirsch), ca. 1925, JB Hirsch, gray metal figure, marble base, celluloid face, 6½", rarity 5, $325.00. Photo courtesy of Louis & Janet Dianni.

Plate 1570. Pirate Couple (K & O), ca. 1932, K & O company, gray metal, 10½", rarity 4, $195.00.

Plate 1571. Pirate Couple and Treasure Chest, ca. 1932, JB Hirsch, gray metal figure, celluloid face, on gray metal chest, 6½", rarity 5, $295.00.

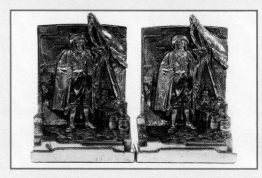

Plate 1572. Pirate Guarding the Treasure, ca. 1927, Pompeian Bronze, bronze-clad, 7", marked Pompeian Bronze Company ©, rarity 5, polychrome, $195.00; monochrome, $150.00.

Plate 1573. Pirates (Armor Bronze), ca. 1928, Armor Bronze, bronze-clad, 10½", company paper tag, rarity 4, $175.00.

Plate 1574. Pirate Booty, ca. 1925, Hubley, iron, 4¾", rarity 3, $65.00.

Plate 1575. Pirate Booty (Littco), ca. 1925, Littco, iron, 6½", company paper tag, rarity 3, $75.00.

Plate 1576. Pirate at the Bow, ca. 1925, attr Pompeian Bronze, bronze-clad, 11", rarity 5*, $500.00.

Plate 1577. Pirate Carrying Booty, ca. 1927, attr Galvano Bronze, bronze-clad, 8", marked P Beneduce (sculptor), rarity 5*, $495.00.

Plate 1578. Pirate (Pompeian Bronze), ca. 1925, Pompeian Bronze, bronze-clad, 10", marked © Pompeian Bronze, rarity 5, $300.00.

Plate 1579. Pirate Stands Alone, ca. 1928, Littco, iron, 7", company paper tag, rarity 3, $95.00.

Plate 1580. Pirate: Sword Ready, ca. 1928, attr Pompeian Bronze, bronze-clad, 7", marked ©, rarity 5, $95.00.

Plate 1581. Pirate (Verona), ca. 1928, Verona, iron, 6¼", marked Verona, rarity 5, $175.00.

Plate 1582. Pirate with Musket, ca. 1920, Pompeian Bronze, bronze-clad, 9¼", marked Pompeian Bronze, rarity 5, $150.00. Photo courtesy of Billie Trepanier.

Plate 1583. Pirate with Sword and Musket, ca. 1930, K & O, gray metal, 8½", shopmark, rarity 5, $175.00.

Plate 1584. Pirate with Chest, ca. 1928, Littco, iron, 5¼", company paper tag, rarity 4, $75.00.

Plate 1585. Policeman, ca. 1925, Littco, iron, 6¾", rarity 5, $250.00.

Plate 1586. Potter, ca. 1928, Armor Bronze, bronze-clad, 8", Ruhl (sculptor), shopmark, rarity 5, polychrome, $295.00; monochrome, $225.00.

Plate 1587. Primitive Sculptor, ca. 1922, Marion Bronze, bronze-clad, 6", rarity 5*, $300.00.

Plate 1588. Puritan, ca. 1924, Jennings Brothers, gray metal, 9¼", marked Puritan, rarity 5, $275.00.

Plate 1589. Pushing Men, ca. 1911, Gorham, bronze, 6½", marked I Konti (sculptor), Gorham Foundry, Q474, ©, rarity 5, $2,000.00.

Plate 1590. Pushing Men (Frishmuth), 1912, Gorham, bronze, 7¾", marked H Frishmuth (sculptor), Gorham Co, rarity 5*, $7,000.00.

Plate 1591. Reading, ca. 1920, Gorham, bronze, 8½", marked N J Murphy (sculptor), Gorham Co, rarity 5*, $1,700.00.

Plate 1595. Roman Scribe, ca. 1922, Pompeian Bronze, bronze-clad, 7", shopmark, rarity 4, polychrome, $275.00; monochrome, $175.00.

Plate 1592. Reader, 1927, Rookwood, pottery, 6", marked 1927 Hastwell (sculptor), rarity 5, $700.00.

Plate 1596. Roman Scribe Seated, ca. 1922, Pompeian Bronze, bronze-clad, 7", shopmark, rarity 5, $195.00.

Plate 1593. Robinson Crusoe, ca. 1920, Pompeian Bronze, bronze-clad, 9½", marked Pompeian Bronze, rarity 5, $350.00. Photo courtesy of Billie Trepanier.

Plate 1597. Rudolph Valentino, ca. 1925, bronze-clad, 4", rarity 5*, $295.00. *This is the style of dress for which Valentino was famous in such movies as (1921) The Sheik.* Photo courtesy of Agris Kelbrants.

Plate 1594. Roman and Scroll, ca. 1932, K & O, gray metal, 5¼", J Ruhl (sculptor), shopmark, rarity 4, $110.00.

Plate 1598. Sands of Time, ca. 1925 , Marion Bronze, bronze-clad, 6", rarity 5*, $300.00.

235

Plate 1599. Scholar, ca. 1925, Armor Bronze, bronze-clad, 7½", CS Allen (sculptor), shopmark, rarity 4, $195.00.

Plate 1603. Variation of Sir Francis Drake.

Plate 1600. Servant, ca. 1925, gray metal on marble base, 7", marked GS Allen, rarity 5*, $350.00. Photo courtesy of Jim Philllips.

Plate 1604. Sir Galahad, ca. 1923, gray metal, 6½", rarity 5, $150.00.

Plate 1601. Servant of Knowledge, ca. 1930, attr JB Hirsch, gray metal figure on polished stone base, 5", rarity 5, $300.00.

Plate 1605. Sisyphus, ca. 1925, McClelland Barclay, gray metal, 6½", marked McClelland Barclay, rarity 5, $375.00.

Plate 1606. Skull Study, ca. 1922, Marion Bronze, bronze-clad, 6", rarity 5*, $300.00.

Plate 1602. Sir Francis Drake, ca. 1925, Jennings Brothers, gray metal, 3", marked JB 2310, rarity 4, $50.00.

Plate 1607. Slashing Samurai, ca. 1930, Ronson, gray metal, 7⅛", company tag #14581, rarity 5, $325.00.

Plate 1611. St. George & the Dragon (Acorn), ca. 1925, Acorn, bronze, 6½", shopmark, #606, St. George and the Dragon, rarity 5*, $175.00.

Plate 1608. Soldier with Saber, ca. 1931, JB Hirsch, gray metal figure, celluloid face and knee, on marble or polished stone base, 8¼", rarity 5, $275.00.

Plate 1612. St. George & the Dragon (Hubley), ca. 1925, Hubley, iron, 5½", marked #312, rarity 3, $85.00.

Plate 1609. Solitude, ca. 1928, Galvano Bronze, bronze-clad, 5", marked ©, rarity 5, $195.00.

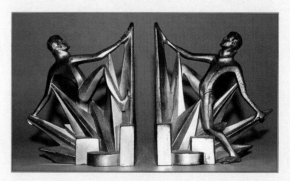

Plate 1613. Star Climber, ca. 1930, gray metal, 5½", rarity 5, $175.00.

Plate 1610. Spanish Conquistadors, ca. 1925, Solid Bronze, bronze, 5", marked Solid Bronze, rarity 5*, $300.00.

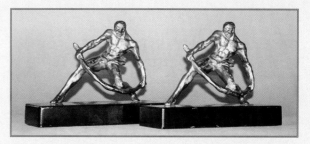

Plate 1614. Strength of Steel, ca. 1920, gray metal figure on polished stone base, 4", rarity 5, $300.00.

Plate 1615. Struggle, ca. 1925, gray metal, 5½", rarity 4, $100.00.

Plate 1616. Student, ca. 1925, Judd, iron, 6", marked #9741, rarity 4, $165.00.

Plate 1617. Study (B & H), ca. 1925, Bradley and Hubbard, iron, 5½", company paper tag, rarity 4, $125.00.

Plate 1618. Study (KBW), ca. 1924, Kathodian Bronze Works, bronze-clad, 6¼", marked KBW, rarity 5*, $250.00.

Plate 1619. Study and Science, ca. 1925, Bradley and Hubbard, iron, 5½", company paper tag, rarity 4, $125.00.

Plate 1620. Surrounded by Books , ca. 1925, Bradley and Hubbard, iron, 5¼", marked Bradley and Hubbard, rarity 5, $150.00.

Plate 1621. Swash-buckler, ca. 1940, Dodge, gray metal , 7¾", Paul Herzel (sculptor), shop-mark, rarity 5, $110.00.

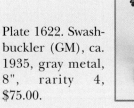

Plate 1622. Swash-buckler (GM), ca. 1935, gray metal, 8", rarity 4, $75.00.

Plate 1623. Swash-buckler (large), ca. 1928, Pompeian Bronze, bronze-clad, 9½", Paul Herzel (sculptor), ©, shop-mark, rarity 5, $175.00.

Plate 1624. Swash-buckler (standard), 1928, Pompeian Bronze, gray metal, 7¾", marked Paul Herzel © 1928 Pompeian Bronze, rarity 5, $150.00.

Plate 1625. Think Figuratively, ca. 1925, Ronson, gray metal, 6", company paper tag #11375, rarity 4, $75.00.

Plate 1626. Thinker (Armor Bronze 6"), ca. 1926, Armor Bronze, bronze-clad, 5¾", company paper tag, rarity 4, $125.00.

Plate 1627. Thinker (Armor Bronze 8"), ca. 1922, Armor Bronze, bronze-clad, 7¾", marked Le Penseur Par Rodin, rarity 4, $175.00.

Plate 1628. Thinker (Church), ca. 1925, GFC, iron, 5¾", marked GFC, rarity 3, $35.00. *Note: church inscribed in background.*

Plate 1629. Thinker (Connecticut Foundry), 1929, Connecticut Foundry, iron, 5¾", marked The Thinker Copr 1929, shopmark, rarity 4, $95.00.

Plate 1630. Thinker (Doric Columns), ca. 1930, gray metal, 5½", marked #103, rarity 4, $50.00.

Plate 1631. Thinker (Pompeian Bronze 7"), ca. 1931, Pompeian Bronze, bronze-clad, 6¾", marked Pompeian Bronze Company, rarity 4, $125.00.

Plate 1632. Thinker (Ronson), ca. 1930, Ronson, gray metal, 5½", company tag #11237, rarity 5, $125.00.

Plate 1633. Thinker (Solid Bronze), ca. 1925, Solid Bronze, bronze, 5½", marked Solid Bronze, rarity 4, $100.00.

Plate 1634. Thinker (Verona), ca. 1925, Verona, iron, 6", marked Verona, rarity 3, $50.00.

Plate 1635. Thinker (WB), ca. 1925, Weidlich Brothers, gray metal, 5½", marked #624, rarity 5, $100.00.

Plate 1636. Thinker Profile, ca. 1925, iron, 4", marked #582, rarity 2, $25.00.

Plate 1637. Thinker Shrine, ca. 1927, iron, 5¼", marked Thinker, rarity 2, $35.00.

Plate 1638. Three Graduates, ca. 1932, K & O, gray metal, 5½", shopmark, rarity 5, $110.00.

Plate 1639. Three Musketeers, ca. 1930, Jennings Brothers, gray metal, 5¾", marked JB Alexandre Dumas, rarity 5, $250.00.

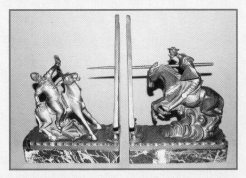

Plate 1640. Tilting at Windmills, ca. 1925, bronze on marble base, 8½", marked R.W.Lange R.U.M., rarity 5, $1,900.00.

Plate 1641. Tire Worker, ca. 1920, bronze, 6¾", rarity 5*, $275.00.

Plate 1642. Tony Weller, ca. 1925, iron, 4⅛", rarity 4, $40.00.

Plate 1643. Town Crier, ca. 1932, K & O, gray metal, 7½", shopmark, rarity 5, $175.00.

Plate 1644. Town Crier (PM Craftsman), ca. 1965, PM Craftsman, gray metal, 7½", company paper tag, rarity 3, $50.00.

Plate 1645. Vanderbilt, ca. 1915, bronze-clad, 8¾", marked ©, rarity 5, $225.00.

Plate 1646. Warming Up, ca. 1935, bronze, 5¾", marked A. G. Bunge (sculptor) ENTWUREL Germany, rarity 5*, $475.00.

241

Plate 1647. Warrior, ca. 1925, bronze-clad, 5½", rarity 5*, $175.00.

Plate 1648. Weizmann Bust, 1949, Ari Arts, 6", marked © 1949 AriArts, rarity 5*, $150.00.

Plate 1649. Wisdom, ca. 1928, Armor Bronze, bronze-clad, 8", Wisdom, A Johnson (sculptor), shopmark, rarity 5, polychrome, $450.00; monochrome, $300.00.

Plate 1650. Wisdom Well (Littco), ca. 1929, Littco, iron, 5½", rarity 4, $75.00.

Plate 1651. Wizened Scholar, ca. 1925, Marion Bronze, bronze-clad, 6", rarity 5*, $300.00.

Plate 1652. Workers, ca. 1920, Gorham, bronze, 13", marked EE Codman (sculptor), Gorham Co, rarity 5*, $9,000.00.

Plate 1653. World, ca. 1920, Galvano Bronze, bronze-clad, 6¼", marked P Beneduce (sculptor), rarity 5, $275.00.

Plate 1654. Wrestlers, iron, 5¼", rarity 4, $100.00.

242

Plate 1655. Wrestlers (Solid Bronze), ca. 1924, bronze, 5½", marked Solid Bronze, rarity 5, $150.00.

Plate 1656. Ye Philosopher, ca. 1924, Armor Bronze, bronze-clad, 6½", marked S Morani (sculptor), rarity 5, $195.00.

Marine Life

Plate 1657. Angelfish, ca. 1930, attr JB Hirsch, gray metal on polished stone base, 6", rarity 3, $120.00.

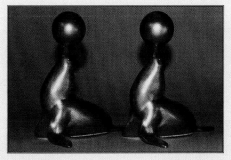

Plate 1658. Barclay Seals, ca. 1935, McClelland Barclay, gray metal, 6", marked McClelland Barclay, rarity 4, $150.00.

Plate 1659. Bass, ca. 1950, Bruce Fox, aluminum, 7", shopmark, rarity 5, $175.00.

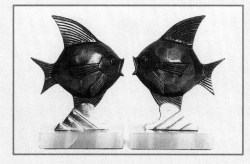

Plate 1660. Deco Fish, bronze on onyx base, 7", rarity 5, $400.00.

Plate 1661. Deco Marlin, ca. 1935, chrome and bronze, 3¼", rarity 5, $225.00.

Plate 1662. Deco Seal, ca. 1930, chrome and bronze, 6¼", rarity 5, $225.00.

Plate 1663. Dolphins, iron, 6", marked Dolphins shopmark Corp. Connecticut foundry logo, rarity 5, $150.00.

Plate 1667. Glass Angelfish, ca. 1940, American Glass Co., glass, 8¼", rarity 4, $135.00.

Plate 1664. Fantail, ca. 1925, gray metal on marble base, 6", rarity 5, $195.00. *Made in France.*

Plate 1668. Goldfish, 1992, Rookwood, pottery, 4½", shopmark, rarity 4, $85.00.

Plate 1665. Fish, gray metal, 6½", rarity 5, $80.00.

Plate 1669. Kissing Fish, Littco, iron, 6", rarity 3, $95.00.

Plate 1666. Fish School, ca. 1932, K & O, gray metal, 4½", shopmark, rarity 5, polychrome, $195.00; monochrome, $155.00.

Plate 1670. Mermaid, ca. 1930, gray metal, 6", rarity 5, $250.00.

Plate 1671. Mermaid (JB Hirsch), ca. 1925, attr JB Hirsch, gray metal on marble base, 5", rarity 5*, $275.00.

Plate 1675. Pouting Fantail, ca. 1925 (French), gray metal on marble base, 6", rarity 5*, $195.00.

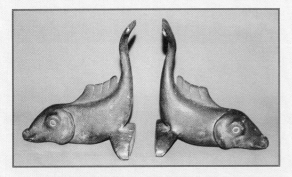

Plate 1672. Porpoise, ca. 1925, bronze, 6", rarity 5*, $300.00.

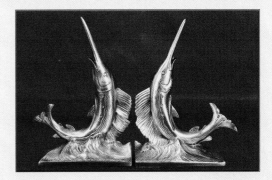

Plate 1676. Sailfish, ca. 1965, PM Craftsman, gray metal, 8", shopmark, rarity 3, $65.00.

Plate 1673. Porpoise (Frankart), ca. 1930, Frankart, gray metal, 5", marked Frankart Pat Applied For, rarity 5, $125.00.

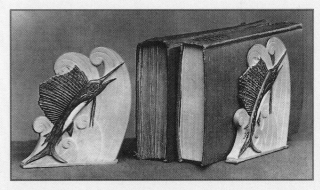

Plate 1677. Sailfish (Gorham), ca. 1920, Gorham, bronze, 5", marked Gorham Co, rarity 5*, $250.00.

Plate 1674. No Halo, ca. 1940, glass, 6½", rarity 4, $125.00.

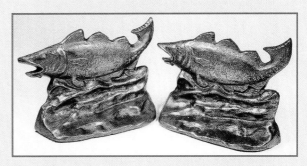

Plate 1678. Salmon, ca. 1920, iron, 4½", Cape Cod, rarity 5*, $195.00.

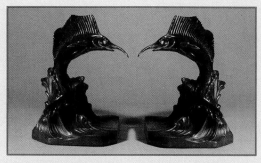

Plate 1679. Sailfish and Wave, ca. 1928, Jennings Brothers, gray metal, 5", shopmark, #1258, rarity 4, $110.00.

Plate 1680. Seahorse, ca. 1920, Gorham, bronze, 5½", marked M Y Murray (sculptor), Gorham Co, rarity 5*, $700.00.

Plate 1681. Seahorse (August), ca. 1950, Wendell August, aluminum, 5½", shopmark, rarity 5, $150.00.

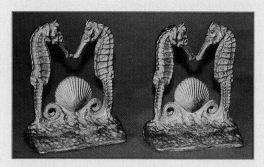

Plate 1682. Seahorse Couple, ca. 1935, bronze, 6", rarity 5*, $95.00.

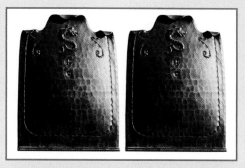

Plate 1683. Seahorse Emblem, ca. 1915, Hayden Manufacturing Co, bronze, shopmark (flexed arm with hammer), Made By Hand, rarity 5*, $275.00. Photo courtesy of Judith Sapinski.

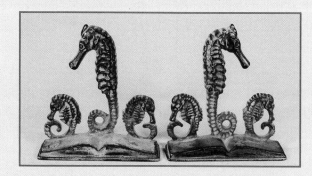

Plate 1684. Seahorse Family, ca. 1925, iron, 5¾", rarity 3, $75.00.

Plate 1685. Seals, gray metal on marble base, 5", marked H. Moreau, rarity 5, $500.00.

Plate 1686. Seashell, ca. 1935, Revere, spring-coiled steel and resin, 5", shopmark, rarity 3, $45.00.

Plate 1687. Shell and Seahorses, 1932, McClelland Barclay, bronze, 5¼", marked McClelland Barclay © 1932, rarity 5, $275.00.

Plate 1688. Sleek Seals, ca. 1930, Ronson, gray metal, 8", company tag #144661, rarity 5, $225.00. Photo courtesy of Richard Weinstein.

Plate 1689. Sunbathing Seal, ca. 1930, Ronson, gray metal, 4", rarity 5, $125.00. Photo courtest of Dave Udstuen.

Plate 1690. Trout, ca. 1934, gray metal, 6½", rarity 4, $125.00.

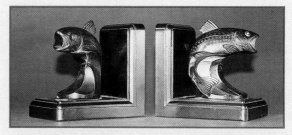

Plate 1691. Trout (PM Craftsman), ca. 1965, PM Craftsman, gray metal, 4", marked PMC, rarity 3, $50.00.

Plate 1692. Two Fish, ca. 1925, Hubley, iron, 5¼", rarity 5, $150.00. Photo courtesy of Agris Kelbrants.

Plate 1693. Whale, ca. 1965, PM Craftsman, gray metal, 7½", company label, rarity 3, $50.00.

Medical

Plate 1694. Nashville Surgical Supply Co., ca. 1930, B & B, Bakelite, 4¾", marked B & B Remembrance St. Paul Patent #2284849, rarity 4, $50.00.

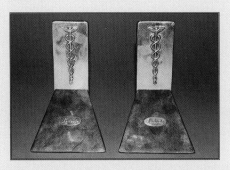

Plate 1695. Lederle Caduceus, ca. 1995, Lederle, brass, 6", marked Lederle, rarity 4, $25.00.

Military

Plate 1696. Asian Warriors, ca. 1930, JB Hirsch, gray metal with celluloid face on polished stone base, 7¼", rarity 5, $225.00. *Modeled after a piece by Bruno Zach.*

Plate 1697. Crusaders, ca. 1926, Hubley, iron, 5½", marked #300, rarity 3, $75.00. Photo courtesy of Jay Mendlovitz.

Plate 1698. General Grant, ca. 1925, iron, 7¼", rarity 5*, $100.00.

Plate 1699. General McArthur, 1942, 6½", marked RS (sculptor, Rose Santoro), rarity 5*, $125.00.

Plate 1700. Centurion, ca. 1925, JB Hirsch, gray metal with celluloid face on polished stone base, 6¾", rarity 5, $300.00.

Plate 1701. Courtly Knight, ca. 1925, iron, 4", rarity 5, $75.00. Photo courtesy of Agris Kelbrants.

Plate 1702. English Knights, ca. 1935, bronze, 9½", rarity 5*, $200.00.

Plate 1703. Heroic Iwo Jima, ca. 1930, gray metal, 6½", rarity 5, $95.00. Photo courtesy of Agris Kelbrants.

Plate 1707. Knight on Horse, 1930, Creation Company, gray metal, 6¼", marked C Co, rarity 5, $125.00.

Plate 1704. Iwo Jima, ca. 1935, bronze, 8", rarity 5, $150.00.

Plate 1708. Knights, ca. 1956, Marion Bronze, iron, 8", marked MB, rarity 5, $235.00.

Plate 1705. Knight in Armor, ca. 1930, Schwartz & Bro, iron, 7", marked S Robert Schwartz and Bro, C-45, rarity 4, $175.00.

Plate 1709. Knights (Armor Bronze), ca. 1926, Armor Bronze, bronze-clad, 7¼", shopmark, rarity 5, $195.00.

Plate 1706. Knights in Armor, ca. 1920, brass, 9¾", rarity 5*, $650.00.

Plate 1710. Knights (K & O), ca. 1928, K & O, gray metal, 6", shopmark, rarity 4, $175.00.

Plate 1711. Knights on Horses, ca. 1925, attr Pompeian Bronze, bronze-clad, 6¼", rarity 5, $195.00.

Plate 1715. Minute Man (JB), ca. 1930, Jennings Brothers, gray metal, 9", JB 1755, rarity 5, $195.00.

Plate 1712. Knights William and Edward, ca. 1925, gray metal, 18", marked William the Conqueror, Edward the Black Prince, rarity 5*, $250.00. Photo courtesy of Mary Collins.

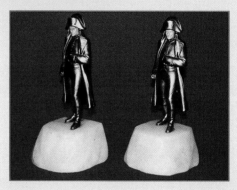

Plate 1716. Napoleon, ca. 1925, attr JB Hirsch, gray metal with celluloid face on marble base, 8", rarity 5, $250.00. *See page 21 for details.*

Plate 1713. Military Family, ca. 1918, Kathodian Bronze Works, bronze-clad, 6½", marked KBW, rarity 5*, $300.00.

Plate 1717. Peace Goodwill, 1934, gray metal, 6", marked designed by an ex-soldier © 1934 RS Gephardt, rarity 5, $125.00.

Plate 1714. Minute Man (JB), ca. 1930, Jennings Brothers, brass, 9", marked JB1755, rarity 5, $195.00.

Plate 1718. Quest, ca. 1925, gray metal, 4¾", rarity 4, $75.00.

Plate 1719. Raising the Flag, ca. 1925, iron, 8", rarity 5, $175.00.

Plate 1723. St George and the Dragon (Just), ca. 1930 (Denmark), gray metal, 4", marked Just, 1626, rarity 5, $95.00.

Plate 1720. Revolutionary Soldier, ca. 1985, iron, 8", rarity 3, $50.00.

Plate 1724. Tank, ca. 1925, Judd, iron, 4", marked 9922, rarity 5, $175.00.

Plate 1721. Roman Horseman, ca. 1928, Littco, iron, 6", rarity 3, $50.00.

Plate 1725. Yankee Soldiers, ca. 1980, iron, 7½", rarity 2, $35.00.

Miscellaneous

Plate 1722. Soldier with Saber, ca. 1931, JB Hirsch, gray metal figure, celluloid face and knee on marble base, 8¼", rarity 5, $275.00.

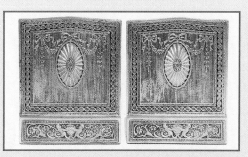

Plate 1726. Adam, ca. 1920, Tiffany, bronze, 6", marked Tiffany #1853, rarity 5*, $1,800.00.

Plate 1727. Alaskan Inhabitants, 1978, Washington Mint, Inc, marbelloid, 6½", marked John Wills (sculptor), rarity 4, $50.00.

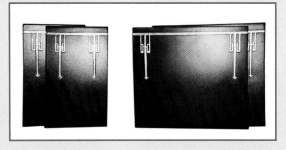

Plate 1728. Arrow, ca. 1914, Heintz Art Metals, silver on bronze, 5", shopmark, rarity 5, $275.00.

Plate 1729. Arts and Crafts, 1920, copper, 4¾", shopmark Carl Sorenson, rarity 4, $175.00.

Plate 1730. AYW, ca. 1920, iron, 5¾", rarity 5*, $110.00.

Plate 1731. Baby Shoes, 1940, gray metal, 5½", marked 1940, rarity 3, $75.00.

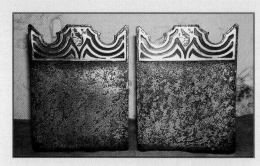

Plate 1732. Bird Crest, ca. 1914, Heintz Art Metals, Silver on bronze, 5", shopmark, rarity 5, $275.00. Photo courtesy of David Surgan.

Plate 1733. Bookend Candleholder, ca. 1930, Jennings Brothers, gray metal, 6", marked JB," rarity 5, $115.00.

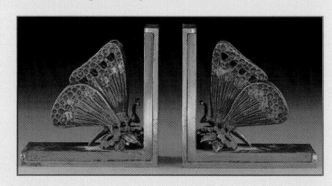

Plate 1734. Brandt's Butterflies, ca. 1929, Edgar Brandt, iron, marked "E. Brandt," rarity 5*, $24,000.00. Photo courtesy © 2004 Artists Rights Society (ARS) New York/ADAGP Paris.

Plate 1735. Candelabra, ca. 1914, Heintz Art Metals, silver on bronze, 5", shopmark, rarity 5, $275.00. Photo courtesy of David Surgan.

Plate 1736. Celebration, ca. 1930, Jennings Brothers, gray metal, 6", marked JB, rarity 4, $90.00. Photo courtesy of Agris Kelbrants.

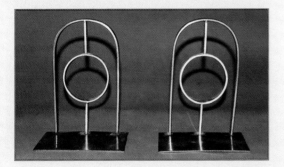

Plate 1737. Circle in Arch, ca. 1931, Flemish Brass, brass, 6", shopmark, rarity 5, $110.00.

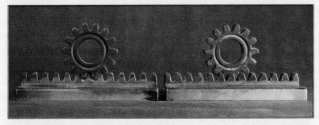

Plate 1738. Cogwheel, ca. 1965, San Diego Machinists, brass, 3½", rarity 5, $150.00.

Plate 1739. Colonial Trio, ca. 1925, bronze, 5", rarity 5, $95.00. *A bronze version of this pair has been seen with the name "The Offer," embossed along the bottom front.*

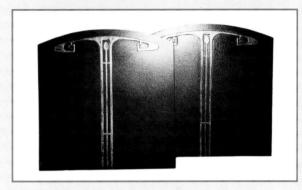

Plate 1740. Cross Bow, ca. 1914, Heintz Art Metals, silver on bronze, 5", shopmark, rarity 5, $275.00. Photo courtesy of David Surgan.

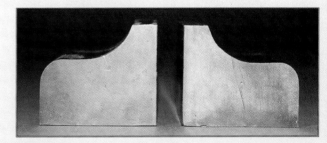

Plate 1741. Cubic Symmetry, ca. 1935, bronze, 3", rarity 5*, $110.00.

Plate 1742. Decorative Scroll, ca. 1925, Judd, gray metal on iron base, 5", rarity 5, $225.00.

Plate 1743. Drag-onfly, ca. 1914, Heintz Art Metals, silver on bronze, 5", shopmark, rar-ity 5, $375.00. Photo courtesy of David Surgan.

Plate 1747. Ermine, ca. 1900, wood (hand-carved), 6¾", rarity 5*, $450.00.

Plate 1744. Egyptian, ca. 1920, Tiffany, bronze, 5¾", marked Tiffany Studios, New York, #1138, rarity 5, $1,200.00.

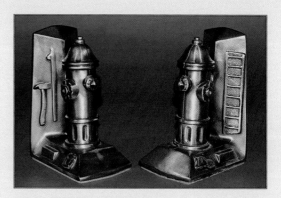

Plate 1748. Fire Hydrant, ca. 1975, gray metal, 8", rarity 4, $50.00.

Plate 1745. Emblem, ca. 1925, Marion Bronze, bronze-clad, 4", shopmark, rarity 5, $110.00. Photo courtesy of Jim Rule.

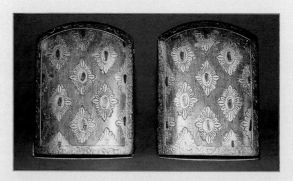

Plate 1749. Florentine, ca. 1985, wood, 5¾", rar-ity 1, $10.00.

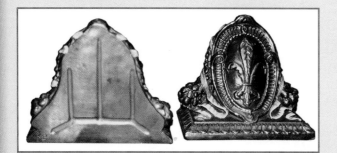

Plate 1746. Emblem, ca. 1925, 4", shopmark, rarity 5, $110.00. Photo courtesy of Jim Rule.

Plate 1750. Four H, ca. 1930, brass, 5", rarity 5, $75.00.

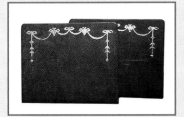

Plate 1751. Garlands, ca. 1914, Heintz Art Metals, silver on bronze, 5", shopmark, rarity 5, $275.00. Photo courtesy of David Surgan.

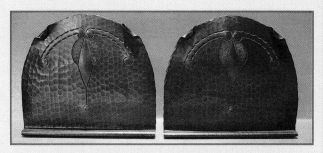

Plate 1755. Hammered Arch Design, ca. 1914, copper, 5½", shopmark, rarity 4, $175.00. Photo courtesy of Sue Benoliel.

Plate 1752. Geometric, ca. 1935, brass and copper, 5½", rarity 5, $195.00.

Plate 1756. Hands, ca. 1940, gray metal, 8½", rarity 5, $75.00. Photo courtesty of Mary Colins.

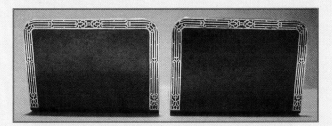

Plate 1753. Geometric (Silvercrest), ca. 1930, Silvercrest, silver on bronze, 4¼", marked Silvercrest, rarity 5, $275.00. Photo courtesy of Sue Benoliel.

Plate 1757. Herald, ca. 1930, Silvercrest, silver on bronze, 4½", marked Silver Crest, rarity 4, $125.00.

Plate 1754. Globe, ca. 1950, Marion Bronze, bronze, 8", shopmark, rarity 5, $150.00.

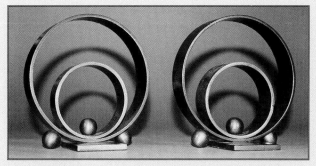

Plate 1758. Hoops and Balls, ca. 1936, Chase, brass and copper, 5¼", shopmark, rarity 5, $250.00. *Designed by Walter Von Nessen.*

255

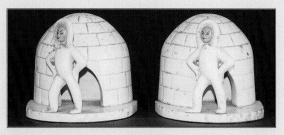

Plate 1759. Igloo, 1949, Kentucky Tavern, aluminum, 5", marked GDCO (Glenmore Distilleries Company), Kentucky Tavern, rarity 5, $295.00.

Plate 1760. Key and Ring, ca. 1935, brass, 8", rarity 4, $85.00.

Plate 1761. Lizard, ca. 1920, Gorham, bronze, 10", marked C W Ancell (sculptor), Gorham Co, rarity 5*, $2,000.00.

Plate 1762. Looney Tunes, 1994, Disney, chalk, 9½", rarity 4, $85.00.

Plate 1763. Love, ca. 1925, Arthur Metal Product Company, 5¼", marked Solid Bronze, Arthur Metal Product Company, Los Angeles, Cal., bronze, rarity 5; iron, rarity 4, $65.00. Photo courtesy of Agris Kelbrants.

Plate 1764. Mayo Tunnel, ca. 1940, Mine Equipment Co, iron, 5", marked Mayo, rarity 4, $75.00.

Plate 1765. Moon (Chase), 1940, Chase, brass and Bakelite, 4⅝", shopmark, rarity 5, $195.00.

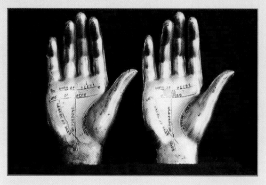

Plate 1766. Palmistry, ca. 1940, gray metal, 6½", marked © Ted Arnold Ltd, rarity 5*, $100.00. Photo courtesy of Agris Kelbrants.

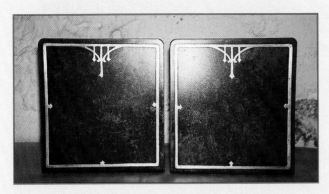

Plate 1767. Perimeter, ca. 1914, Heintz Art Metals, silver on bronze, 5", shopmark, rarity 5, $275.00. Photo courtesy of David Surgan.

Plate 1768. Pig, ca. 1930, bronze, 8½", rarity 5*, $110.00. Photo courtesty of George Korpontinos.

Plate 1769. Poised Butterfly, ca. 1985, PM Craftsman, gray metal, 5½", company paper tag, rarity 3, $35.00. Photo courtesy of Phil Klabel.

Plate 1770. Pontiac, 1983, Bruce Fox, aluminum, 6", marked Bruce Fox (designer), company paper tag, rarity 5, $65.00.

Plate 1771. Quill, Fostoria, glass, 9", rarity 5, $300.00.

Plate 1772. Rhinoceros, ca. 1920, Gorham, bronze, 6½", marked Gorham, A V Hyatt (sculptor), rarity 5*, $2,500.00.

Plate 1773. Scroll, ca. 1930, gray metal, 5¼", rarity 5, $95.00. Photo courtesy of Agris Kelbrants.

Plate 1774. Scroll (PMC), ca. 1960, PM Craftsman, gray metal, 5", shopmark, rarity 3, $35.00. Photo courtesy of Agris Kelbrants.

Plate 1775. Simplicity, ca. 1938, Polar Manufacturing Co., leather, 5", company paper tag, rarity 2, $35.00.

Plate 1776. Spiral, ca. 1920, Tiffany, bronze, 6", marked Tiffany, rarity 5, $675.00.

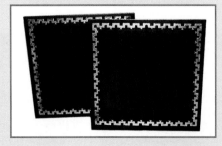

Plate 1777. Square Wave, ca. 1914, Heintz Art Metals, silver on bronze, 5", shopmark, rarity 5, $275.00. Photo courtesy of David Surgan.

Plate 1778. Stained Glass, ca. 1925, Bradley and Hubbard, iron, 5½", shopmark, rarity 5, $225.00. *Shopmark is imprinted underneath the back plate, which must be detached to view; original glass has been replaced.*

Plate 1779. Student, ca. 1920, Tiffany, bronze, 6", marked Tiffany Studios New York, rarity 5, $1,200.00. Photo courtesy of John Asfor.

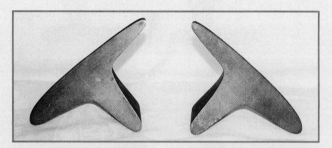

Plate 1780. T Form, ca. 1950, bronze, 4", marked Aubock (sculptor) Austria, rarity 5, $195.00.

Plate 1781. Train, ca. 1924, gray metal, 5¼", rarity 4, $95.00. *Material and style looks like Frankart, but is not marked.*

Plate 1782. Triangle and Ring, ca. 1925, Roycroft, copper, 5", shopmark, rarity 4, $195.00. Photo courtesy of Sue Benoliel.

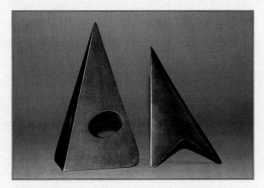

Plate 1783. Triangular, ca. 1950, bronze, 6", marked Aubock (sculptor) Austria, rarity 5, $195.00.

Plate 1784. Truck, ca. 1925, iron, 5½", rarity 5, $195.00.

Plate 1785. Turtle, ca. 1935, Brass, 8", marked Emilio Mardff (sculptor), rarity 5, $450.00.

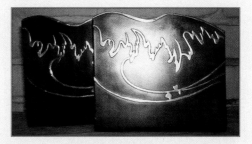

Plate 1786. Waves, ca. 1914, Heintz Art Metals, silver on bronze, 5", shopmark, rarity 5, $325.00. Photo courtesy of David Surgan.

Plate 1787. Whatever-It-Is, ca. 1930, gray metal on marble base, 6", rarity 5*, $90.00.

Plate 1788. White Floral, ca. 1929, Harlich and Co, leather, 5¾", marked Harlich & Co, Chicago, rarity 3, $45.00.

Monkeys

Plate 1789. Lincoln Imp, ca. 1926, bronze, 6", marked Lincoln Imp England, rarity 5, $175.00.

Plate 1790. Lincoln Imp (petite), ca. 1926, bronze, 4¼", marked Lincoln Imp England, rarity 5, $110.00.

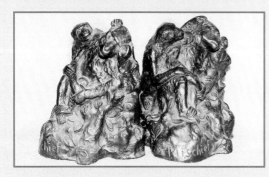

Plate 1791. Mischief, 1915, Armor Bronze, bronze-clad, 6½", marked J. A. Meliodon 1915, rarity 5, $275.00. Photo courtesy of Joseph Ferrier.

Plate 1792. Monkey Scholars, ca. 1925, Marion Bronze, bronze-clad, 6½", rarity 5, $350.00.

Plate 1793. Monkey Jester, ca. 1922, Marion Bronze, bronze-clad, 6½", rarity 5*, $350.00.

Plate 1794. Monkeys, ca. 1925, bronze on marble base, 6½", marked H Laurent (sculptor) Marce Guillemard #151, rarity 5*, $1,500.00. *Made in France.*

Plate 1795. Monkeys in Book, ca. 1930, Jennings Brothers, gray metal, 4½", marked JB 2462, rarity 5, $150.00.

Plate 1796. No Evil X 3 (B&H), ca. 1928, Bradley and Hubbard, iron, 5½", shopmark, rarity 5, $195.00.

Musical

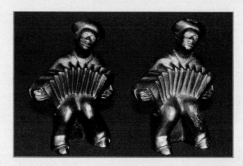

Plate 1797. Accordion Player, ca. 1925, Hubley, iron, 6", rarity 5, $150.00.

Plate 1798. Angelic Harpist, ca. 1928, JB Hirsch, gray metal figure, celluloid face and hands, marble on stone base, 6½", rarity 5, $295.00.

Plate 1799. Bagpiper, ca. 1925, (attr Austria), gray metal on marble base, 7¾", rarity 5*, $575.00.

Plate 1800. Banjo Lady, ca. 1930, Nuart Creations, gray metal, 5", marked Nuart Creations, NYC, rarity 4, $125.00.

Plate 1801. Beethoven, 1932, JB Hirsch, gray metal figure with celluloid face and keyboard, on marble or polished stone base, 4½", marked JBH 1932, rarity 4, $250.00.

Plate 1802. Beethoven (Judd), ca. 1926, Judd, iron base, gray metal figure, 6", rarity 4, $125.00.

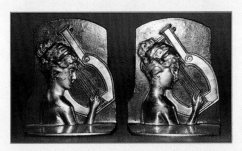

Plate 1803. Celeste, ca. 1925, Ronson, gray metal, 5", company paper tag, polychrome, rarity 5; monochrome, rarity 4; polychrome, $150.00; monochrome, $120.00.

Plate 1804. Cellist, ca. 1932, JB Hirsch, gray metal figure, celluloid face, on marble base, 6¾", marked Ruhl (sculptor) JB Hirsch 1932, rarity 4, $225.00.

Plate 1805. Cellist (JBH), ca. 1940, JB Hirsch, chalk on polished stone base, 6", marked JBH 1932, rarity 5, $95.00. *It appears that chalk figures were made from the same molds as the originals, probably during WWII because of metal shortages.*

261

Plate 1806. Cellist (Pompeian Bronze), ca. 1927, Pompeian Bronze, bronze-clad, 6¼", marked Pompeian Bronze Company ©, rarity 4, $175.00.

Plate 1807. Chopin, ca. 1925, Bradley and Hubbard, iron, 6", shopmark, rarity 5, $175.00.

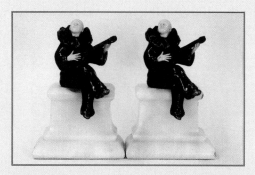

Plate 1808. Clown Minstrel, ca. 1925, attr JB Hirsch, gray metal figure, celluloid head and hands, on marble base, 7½", rarity 5, $275.00.

Plate 1809. Clown Minstrel and Dog, ca. 1932, K & O, gray metal, 7", shopmark, rarity 5, $175.00.

Plate 1810. Clown Minstrel on Burro, ca. 1932, K & O, gray metal, 6½", Made in USA, shopmark, rarity 5, $175.00.

Plate 1811. Drum, ca. 1965, Marion Bronze, bronze-clad, 7½", rarity 5, $125.00.

Plate 1812. Entertainer, ca. 1926, Pompeian Bronze, bronze-clad, 9½", marked Pompeian Bronze Company ©, rarity 5*, $375.00.

Plate 1813. Flautist, ca. 1925, bronze-clad, 9¾", rarity 5, $250.00.

Plate 1814. Horn and Violin, ca. 1920, Tiffany, bronze, 7", marked Tiffany, rarity 5, $800.00.

Plate 1815. Glass Lyre, 1943, Fostoria Glass, glass, 7", rarity 4, $150.00.

Plate 1816. Harpist, ca. 1932, JB Hirsch, polished stone base, gray metal figure, celluloid head, 6½", rarity 5, $275.00.

Plate 1817. Kings Minstrel, ca. 1925, JB Hirsch, gray metal figure, celluloid face, on marble base, 7¾", rarity 5, $475.00.

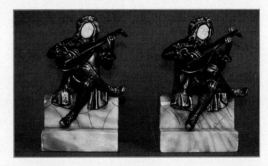

Plate 1818. Kings Minstrel, different version.

Plate 1819. Ladies and Lyre, ca. 1925, Hubley, iron, 5½", marked Hubley #328, rarity 5, $135.00.

Plate 1820. Lady Jester, ca. 1929, X-1, gray metal, 7¼", marked #66, polychrome, rarity 5; monochrome, rarity 4, polychrome, $375.00; monochrome, $225.00.

Plate 1821. Lady Jester, different finish.

Plate 1822. Lost Hope, ca. 1925, bronze, 4½", rarity 5, $195.00. Photo courtesy of Jim Phillips.

Plate 1823. Lost Hope (Bronzmet), ca. 1925, BronzMet, iron, 4½", marked Bronzmet, rarity 4, $95.00.

Plate 1824. Lost Hope (Galvano), ca. 1925, attr Galvano Bronze, bronze-clad, 6⅞", rarity 5, $175.00.

Plate 1825. Lost Hope (K & O), ca. 1932, K & O, gray metal, 6¼", shopmark, polychrome, rarity 5; monochrome, rarity 4; polychrome, $175.00; monochrome, $125.00.

Plate 1826. Lyre, ca. 1965, PM Craftsman, gray metal, 6", marked PMC, rarity 2, $35.00.

Plate 1827. Musical Couple, ca. 1925, gray metal figures, celluloid face and hands, marble base, 5½", marked Germany (inscribed under marble base), rarity 5*, $495.00.

Plate 1828. Musical Couple on Log, ca. 1925, gray metal on onyx base, 5½", rarity 5, $175.00.

Plate 1829. Mythologic Musicians (Carlier), ca. 1925, gray metal, 7", marked Carlier (sculptor), foundry mark, rarity 5, $1,250.00. *Made in France.*

Plate 1830. Pierrot and Pierrette Serenade, ca. 1930, bronze on marble base, 7½", rarity 5*, $675.00.

Plate 1831. Pierrot Plays, ca. 1925, gray metal, 5", rarity 5, $175.00.

Plate 1832. Pierrot Plays (ABH), ca. 1945, ABH, gray metal with celluloid face on marble base, 6½", marked ABH Made in Japan, rarity 5, $150.00.

Plate 1833. Pierrot Plays (APT), ca. 1925, APT, gray metal, 5", marked APT NY, rarity 4, $150.00.

Plate 1834. Pierrot Plays on Log, ca. 1945, gray metal with celluloid face on marble base, 5¾", rarity 5, $225.00.

Plate 1835. Pierrot Plays on Log (K & O), ca. 1932, gray metal, 4¾", rarity 4, $135.00.

Plate 1836. Roman Cellist, 1921, Pompeian Bronze, bronze-clad, 6½", rarity 4, polychrome, $175.00; monochrome, $150.00. *Copyright #63561 issued to Peter Maneredi, of Italy, domiciled in the U.S. August 31, 1921.*

Plate 1837. Roman Cellist, color variation.

Plate 1838. Romantic Serenade, ca. 1930, leather, 5", rarity 5, $65.00.

Plate 1839. Serenade Tonight, ca. 1929, iron, 4¼", rarity 5*, $295.00.

Plate 1840. Serenade Tonight (Hubley), ca. 1925, iron, 5½", marked #233, polychrome, rarity 5; monochrome, rarity 4; polychrome, $195.00; monochrome, $125.00.

Plate 1841. Violins, ca. 1925, Marion Bronze, bronze-clad, 7", rarity 5, $125.00.

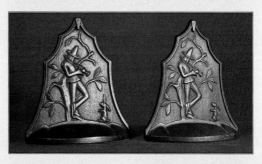

Plate 1842. Wanderer, 1930, Connecticut Foundry, iron, 5¾", marked The Wanderer, 1930, shopmark, rarity 4, $125.00.

Mythological

Plate 1843. Andromeda, ca. 1910, gray metal, 6½", marked Alliot (sculptor), Andromede, par A. Alliot, rarity 5*, $275.00. *Made in France.*

Plate 1844. Angel, ca. 1920, Gorham, bronze, 7", marked Sulamith Sokolsky (sculptor), Gorham Co, rarity 5*, $2,500.00.

Plate 1845. Aurora, ca. 1925, bronze, 4¾", rarity 5*, $225.00.

Plate 1849. Cherub Pan and Goat (Carlier), ca. 1924 , gray metal, 8", marked Carlier (sculptor), rarity 5*, $750.00. *Made in France.*

Plate 1846. Centaur, ca. 1920, gray metal, 8¾", marked Pat App #528, rarity 4, $175.00.

Plate 1850. Cherub Pan with Rabbit, ca. 1940, gray metal, 6¼", marked Louise Wilder (sculptor) © 1940, rarity 5*, $200.00.

Plate 1847. Cherub and Goddess, 1927, bronze, 5⅝", marked S Moselsio (sculptor) © Real bronze, rarity 5, $195.00.

Plate 1851. Cupid and Psyche, ca. 1928, X-1, gray metal, 4½", rarity 5*, $135.00.

Plate 1848. Cherub Pan and Goat, ca. 1930, gray metal on marble base, 8", rarity 5, $300.00. *Made in France.*

Plate 1852. Cupid and Psyche (CF), 1928, Connecticut Foundry, iron, 5¾", marked Cupid and Psyche 1928 shopmark, rarity 4, $125.00.

Plate 1853. Dartmoor Pixie, ca. 1950, bronze, 5¾", marked 699770 England, rarity 4, $160.00.

Plate 1857. God and Goddess, ca. 1925, Bradley and Hubbard, iron, 6", shopmark, rarity 5, $195.00. Photo courtesy of Agris Kelbrants.

Plate 1854. Dragon, 1949, Imperial Cathay Crystal, glass, 5", rarity 5, $400.00. *These have been sold as bookends, but are actually candleholders.* Photo courtesy of Michael Horseman.

Plate 1858. Grand Pegasus, ca. 1925, gray metal on polished stone base, 7¾", rarity 5, $275.00.

Plate 1855. Elf, ca. 1935, bronze, 3⅞", rarity 5, $165.00.

Plate 1859. Hermes, ca. 1925, attr Armor Bronze, bronze-clad, 7", marked CT, rarity 5, $295.00. Photo courtesy of Jim Phillips.

Plate 1856. Faun and Mermaid, ca. 1920, Gorham, bronze, 5½", Gorham Co, rarity 5*, $2,500.00.

Plate 1860. Icon, ca. 1930, 6", Chile, rarity 4, $50.00. *This pair was also produced without the inscription "Chile" by the White Pine Mine, Ontonagon County, Michigan.*

Plate 1861. Leda and the Swan, ca. 1925, iron, 4", rarity 4, $100.00.

Plate 1862. Mermaid and Scallop Shell, ca. 1920, Gorham, bronze, 5¾", marked N Thompson (sculptor), Gorham Co, rarity 5*, $1,200.00.

Plate 1863. Musical Pan, ca. 1920, Gorham, bronze, 6¼", marked B Putnam, rarity 5*, $1,200.00.

Plate 1864. No Evil X 4, ca. 1925, Bradley and Hubbard, iron, 6", shopmark, rarity 5, $225.00.

Plate 1865. Nymph and Boyish Pan, ca. 1920, Gorham, bronze, 7½", marked MacMurray (sculptor), Gorham Co, rarity 5*, $2,500.00.

Plate 1866. Pan, ca. 1925, bronze, 7¾", marked Marcel Debut (sculptor), France, rarity 5*, $2,500.00. *See page 22 for details.*

Plate 1867. Pan (McClelland Barclay), ca. 1925, McClelland Barclay, gray metal, 7", marked McClelland Barclay, rarity 5, $175.00.

Plate 1868. Pan (Gorham), ca. 1920, Gorham, bronze, 6¾", marked E Freeman (sculptor), Gorham Co., rarity 5*, $1,500.00.

Plate 1869. Pan and Nymph (Fugere), ca. 1930, brass on marble base, 6", marked France; Fugere (sculptor signature) on marble base, rarity 5*, $395.00.

Plate 1873. Pegasus (DAL), 1925, Decorators Art League, iron, 4¼", marked DAL 1925, rarity 3, $65.00. *See page 22 for details.*

Plate 1870. Pan and Nymph (RBW), ca. 1915, Roman Bronze Works, bronze, 6½", marked Urich (sculptor); Roman Bronze Works, N.Y., rarity 5*, $1,500.00.

Plate 1874. Pegasus (Le Verrier), ca. 1925, Le Verrier, bronze, 7", marked Le Verrier Paris, rarity 5, 1925, $1,100.00; current production, $500.00.

Plate 1871. Pan and Nymph (Silvestre), ca. 1925, bronze, 7", marked Silvestre, rarity 5, $750.00. *Made in France.*

Plate 1875. Pegasus and Goddess, ca. 1920, Albany Foundry, iron, 4½", marked Albany Foundry Co #154, rarity 4, $120.00.

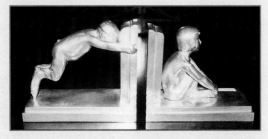

Plate 1872. Pan and Nymph (Silvestre) petite, ca. 1925, Susse Freres, bronze, 4", marked Silvestre, rarity 5, $295.00. *Made in France.*

Plate 1876. Pegasus on Pedestal, ca. 1925, bronze, 6½", rarity 5, $350.00.

Plate 1877. Pegasus Skyward, ca. 1925, gray metal, 7", marked W.W. (Wheeler Williams, sculptor), ©, rarity 5, $395.00.

Plate 1878. Prancing Pegasus, ca. 1928, Judd, iron, 6", marked J co, rarity 5, $125.00.

Plate 1879. Pushing Pan, 1914, Gorham, bronze, 8¼", marked E James (sculptor), Gorham Co. rarity 5*, $2,200.00.

Plate 1880. Satyr and Bacchante, ca. 1920, bronze on polished stone, 6", rarity 5*, $1,800.00.

Plate 1881. Satyr and Bacchante, ca. 1930, (McClelland Barclay), gray metal, 6¾", marked McClelland Barclay, rarity 5, $275.00.

Plate 1882. Venus, ca. 1925, iron, 6", rarity 4, $75.00.

Plate 1883. Winged Victory, 1931, bronze, 6½", 1931, rarity 5*, $300.00.

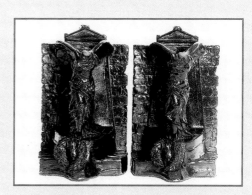

Plate 1884. Winged Victory (Armor Bronze), 1922, attr Armor Bronze, bronze-clad, 9½", marked J A Meliodon (sculptor), rarity 5, $495.00.

271

Plate 1885. Winged Victory (CF), 1930, Connecticut Foundry, iron, 6½", Victory Copr 1930 shopmark, rarity 5, $125.00.

Plate 1886. Winged Victory (KBW), ca. 1918, Kathodian Bronze Works, bronze-clad, 7", marked KBW, rarity 5, $250.00.

Plate 1887. Winged Victory (PMC), ca. 1960, PM Craftsman, gray metal, 7", rarity 4, $75.00.

Plate 1888. Zodiac, ca. 1918, Tiffany, bronze, 5¾", marked Tiffany Studious, New York #1019, polychrome, rarity 5; monochrome, rarity 4; polychrome, $750.00; monochrome, $400.00. Photo courtesy of Sue Benoliel.

Plate 1889. Zodiac, polychrome

Native Americans

Plate 1890. Adorned Indian, ca. 1923, Ronson, gray metal, 5¾", marked AMW, Newark, NJ, rarity 5*, $500.00.

Plate 1891. American Indian, ca. 1925, Ronson, iron, 5¼", marked LV Aronson 1925, rarity 5, $125.00.

Plate 1892. Appeal to the Great Spirit, ca. 1926, gray metal, 7¼", rarity 4, $250.00.

Plate 1893. Appeal to the Great Spirit (BFM), ca. 1925, BFM, iron, 5¾", marked logo B.F.M., rarity 4, $150.00.

Plate 1897. Appeal to the Great Spirit (Littco), ca. 1928, Littco, iron, 5¾", company paper tag, rarity 5, $225.00.

Plate 1894. Appeal to the Great Spirit (CED), ca. 1926, gray metal, 7¼", marked CED (initials of sculptor, Cyrus Edwin Dallin), rarity 5, $295.00.

Plate 1898. Awaiting the Prey (JB), ca. 1928, Jennings Brothers, gray metal, 6", shopmark, rarity 4, $165.00. Photo courtesy of Agris Kelbrants.

Plate 1895. Appeal to the Great Spirit (CF), 1929, Connecticut Foundry, iron, 5¾", shopmark, Appeal to the Great Spirit 1929, rarity 4, $85.00.

Plate 1899. Awaiting the Prey (K & O), ca. 1935, K & O, gray metal, 6¾", shopmark, polychrome, rarity 5; monochrome, rarity 4, polychrome, $235.00; monochrome, $165.00.

Plate 1896. Appeal to the Great Spirit (CT), ca. 1925, CT, iron, 6½", shopmark, rarity 5, $95.00.

Plate 1900. Birchbark Trip, ca. 1930, Ronson, gray metal, 5½", rarity 5, $225.00.

273

Plate 1901. Braided Indian, ca. 1915, Griffoul, bronze, 6½", marked Griffoul, rarity 5, $295.00.

Plate 1905. Cochise, ca. 1930, iron, 4½", rarity 5, $125.00.

Plate 1902. Chief, ca. 1935, Dodge, gray metal, 7⅛", Dodge, Inc. shopmark, rarity 5*, $300.00. Photo courtesy of Agris Kelbrants.

Plate 1906. Daughter of the Sioux, ca. 1925, attr Pompeian Bronze, bronze-clad, 5½", marked Paul Herzel (sculptor), A Daughter of the Sioux, rarity 5, $225.00.

Plate 1903. Chief Erotica, ca. 1920, bronze, 5⅜", rarity 5, $175.00. *Although not always obvious at first glance, the structure of the profile is made through the confluence of lines of erotic figures.*

Plate 1907. Doleful Indian, ca. 1920, bronze, 8¼", rarity 5*, $350.00.

Plate 1904. Cleared Path, ca. 1928, bronze, 6¾", marked A. Dloumy, rarity 4, $175.00. Photo courtesy of Sue Benoliel.

Plate 1908. End of the Trail, ca. 1925, bronze-clad, 8", rarity 4, $200.00.

Plate 1909. End of the Trail (Solid Bronze), ca. 1928, Solid Bronze, bronze, 4", marked Solid Bronze, rarity 4, $125.00.

Plate 1913. End of the Trail (Gifthouse), 1927, Gifthouse Inc, iron, 5¼", marked © 1927 Gifthouse Inc, NYC, rarity 4, $100.00.

Plate 1910. End of the Trail (Ronson), ca. 1930, Ronson, gray metal, 6", company tag #11478, polychrome, rarity 4; monochrome, rarity 3; polychrome, $110.00; monochrome, $95.00.

Plate 1914. End of the Trail (McClelland Casket), ca. 1930, McClelland Casket, gray metal, 6¾", marked McClelland Casket Hardware Co., rarity 5*, $100.00. *One might wonder when the casket company makes an item called "End of the Trail" (insight thanks to Brenda Diaz).*

Plate 1911. End of the Trail (BronzMet), ca. 1925, iron, 5", marked BronzMet, rarity 4, $110.00.

Plate 1915. End of the Train (LV Aronson), 1925, Ronson, gray metal, 4¼", marked LV Aronson 1925, rarity 4, $95.00.

Plate 1912. End of the Trail (Galvano), ca. 1928, Galvano, bronze-clad, 8", marked Galvano Bronze P. Mori & Son, rarity 5, $275.00.

Plate 1916. Feather, silver plate over bronze, 7½", rarity 5, $450.00.

275

Plate 1917. Full Headdress, ca. 1928, Judd, iron, 5", rarity 4, $225.00.

Plate 1921. Hunter and Dog, ca. 1930, Judd, bronze, 5⅜", marked Bronze 9698, rarity 5, $150.00.

Plate 1918. Hiawatha, ca. 1925, Bradley and Hubbard, bronze, 6¼", shopmark, rarity 5, $225.00.

Plate 1922. Illini Indian, ca. 1925, bronze, 5½", rarity 4, $195.00.

Plate 1919. Horseback Hunter, ca. 1925, iron, 4", marked #38, polychrome, rarity 5*; monochrome, rarity 4; polychrome, $95.00; monochrome, $65.00.

Photo courtesy of Agris Kelbrants.

Plate 1923. In Pursuit, 1924, Ronson, gray metal, 4", marked LV Aronson, 1924, rarity 4, $100.00. Photo courtesy of Richard Weinstein.

Plate 1920. Horseback Hunter, polychrome.
Photo courtesy of Blythe Curry.

Plate 1924. Indian, ca. 1925, bronze, 5½", rarity 5, $250.00.

Plate 1925. Indian (Armor Bronze), ca. 1925, Armor Bronze, bronze-clad, 8", A. Meliodon (sculptor), shopmark, ©, rarity 5*, polychrome, $650.00; monochrome, $475.00.

Plate 1926. Indian (KBW), ca. 1923, Kathodian Bronze Works, bronze-clad, 8", marked KBW, rarity 5*, $350.00.

Plate 1927. Indian (Ronson), 1924, Ronson, gray metal, 7", marked LV Aronson 1924, rarity 5, $125.00. *This bookend was also copied in iron by another manufacturer, with the same imprint.*

Plate 1928. Indian (Hubley), ca. 1925, Hubley, iron, 5", rarity 4, polychrome, $100.00; monochrome, $65.00.

Plate 1929. Indian Archer, ca. 1922, gray metal, 7¾", rarity 5, $475.00.

Plate 1930. Indian Archer (WB), ca. 1925, Weidlich Brothers, gray metal, 5½", shopmark, rarity 4, $110.00.

Plate 1931. Indian Brave, ca. 1926, Judd, iron, 5", rarity 4, $195.00. *Also comes in expandable.*

Plate 1932. Indian Chief, ca. 1926, iron, 5", rarity 4, $75.00.

Plate 1933. Indian Couple, ca. 1920, Attr Armor Bronze, bronze-clad, 7", rarity 5, $395.00. Photo courtesy of George Haule.

Plate 1934. Indian Family, ca. 1929, bronze, 5", rarity 4, $195.00. Photo courtesy of Jocelyn Serbe.

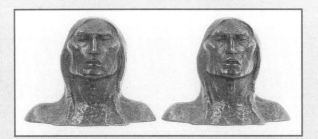

Plate 1935. Indian Head, bronze, 5⅜", marked West (sculptor) 1915, rarity 4, $195.00.

Plate 1936. Indian Lancer, ca. 1930, hollow-cast bronze on marble base, 8½", rarity 5*, $495.00.

Plate 1937. Indian Lancer (JB), ca. 1926, Jennings Brothers, gray metal, 5", shopmark, #1996, rarity 5, $250.00.

Plate 1938. Indian Lookout, 1924, Ronson, gray metal, 4½", marked LV Aronson 1924, rarity 5, $150.00.

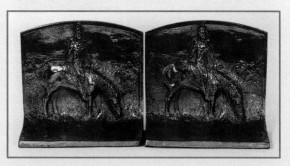

Plate 1939. Indian Lookout (Sander), ca. 1920, bronze, 5¼", marked A A Sander (sculptor), Real Solid Bronze, rarity 5, $300.00.

Plate 1940. Indian Maiden's Bowl, ca. 1930, bronze-clad, 5", rarity 5, $125.00. Photo courtesy of Kay Ross.

Plate 1941. Indian on Bucking Horse, ca. 1927, bronze-clad, 7¾", rarity 5, $400.00.

Plate 1942. Indian Patriarch, ca. 1925, iron, 4⅛", rarity 4, $85.00

Plate 1943. Indian Potter, ca. 1925, Littco, iron, 4½", rarity 4, $135.00. *Also seen in polychrome, bronze and copper flashed.*

Plate 1944. Indian Profile, ca. 1925, iron, 4⅞", rarity 4, $125.00.

Plate 1945. Indian Rider, ca. 1930, K & O, gray metal, 6¾", marked K & O Label, rarity 5*, $175.00.

Plate 1946. Indian Scout, 1927, Jennings Brothers, gray metal, 7½", marked JB 1927, rarity 4, $195.00.

Plate 1947. Indian Scout (Armor Bronze), ca. 1920, Armor Bronze, bronze-clad, 9½", RUHL (sculptor), shopmark, rarity 5, polychrome, $600.00; monochrome, $450.00. Photo courtesy of Billie Trepanier.

Plate 1948. Indian Spear Fishing, ca. 1925, Jennings Brothers, gray metal, 8½", marked JB 2245, rarity 5, $350.00.

279

Plate 1949. Indian War Dancers, ca. 1920, Pompeian Bronze, bronze-clad, 8", marked Paul Herzel, Pompeian Bronze Label, rarity 5*, $795.00. Courtesy of Billie Trepanier.

Plate 1950. Indian Warrior, ca. 1925, Hubley, iron, 6", rarity 4, $150.00.

Plate 1951. Indian with Dog, ca. 1925, iron, 5¾", rarity 4, $80.00.

Plate 1952. Indian with Spear, ca. 1926, Jennings Brothers, gray metal, 9½", shopmark 1699, rarity 5, $325.00.

Plate 1953. Indians, ca. 1925, BronzMet, iron, 4¼", marked BronzMet Logo, rarity 4, $125.00.

Plate 1954. Kneeling Indian, ca. 1925, Pompeian Bronze, bronze-clad, 7¾", shopmark, rarity 5, polychrome, $325.00; monochrome, $225.00.

Plate 1955. Last Trail (CF) 1928 petite, 1928, Connecticut Foundry, iron, 3½", The Last Trail © shopmark, rarity 2, $45.00. *Although the proper name of this sculpture is "End of the Trail," the manufacturer took the liberty of renaming it and marking it "The Last Trail" (and the two following).*

Plate 1956. Last Trail (CF) 1930, 1930, Connecticut Foundry, iron, 6", The Last Trail Copr 1930, shopmark, rarity 4, $75.00.

Plate 1957. Last Trail (CF) 1928, 1928, Connecticut Foundry, iron, 5", shopmark, "The Last Trail," rarity 3, $75.00.

Plate 1958. Medicine Man, ca. 1920, Armor Bronze, bronze-clad, 8½", marked J B Lambert (Jack Lincoln Lambert, sculptor), rarity 5, polychrome, $700.00; monochrome, $400.00. Photo courtesy of Billie Trepanier.

Plate 1959. Medicine Man, monochrome version.

Plate 1960. One Feather, ca. 1928, Z-R, iron, 6¼", shopmark #44, rarity 4, $125.00.

Plate 1961. One Feather with Braid, ca. 1925, attr Hubley, bronze, 6", marked Gregory Allen (sculptor), rarity 5, $175.00. Photo courtesy of Agris Kelbrants.

Plate 1962. Peace pipe, ca. 1930, K & O, iron, 6", shopmark, rarity 5, $125.00. Photo courtesy of Mike Kelln.

Plate 1963. Ready for War, ca. 1932, attr Pompeian Bronze, gray metal, 9½", rarity 5, $275.00.

Plate 1964. Red Cloud, 1911, Griffoul, bronze, 7", marked 1911, sculptor signature (appears to be GIF), Griffoul, rarity 5, $295.00.

281

Plate 1965. Red Man, ca. 1924, iron, rarity 4, $50.00. Photo courtesy of Jack McCreadie.

Plate 1966. Sachem (bronze), 1929, various, bronze, 6", rarity 4, $125.00. *This was one of the most popular Native American bookends ever issued. It was marketed by at least a dozen different manufacturers.*

Plate 1967. Sachem (JB), Jennings Brothers, gray metal, 6½", marked JB2081, rarity 5, $225.00.

Plate 1968. Sachem (iron), ca. 1929, various, iron, 6¼", rarity 3, $75.00.

Plate 1969. Scout, 1924, Solid Bronze, bronze, 4⅛", marked Solid Bronze 1924, rarity 4, $150.00.

Plate 1970. Search the Plain, ca. 1925, Ronson, gray metal, 6½", company tag #16505, rarity 5, $225.00.

Plate 1971. Searching Indian, ca. 1925, Armor Bronze, bronze-clad, 7¼", J Ruhl (sculptor), shopmark ©, rarity 4, $225.00.

Plate 1972. Sitting Bull, ca. 1924, bronze, 6¾", rarity 5, $350.00. Photo courtesy of John Asfor.

Plate 1973. Standing Indian Brave, ca. 1920, Pompeian Bronze, bronze, 12½", marked P. Manfredi (sculptor), rarity 5*, $650.00. Photo courtesy of Billie Trepanier.

Plate 1974. Standing Indian with Spear, ca. 1925, bronze-clad, 8", rarity 5*, $395.00.

Plate 1975. Trail's End, ca. 1925 , iron, 5¾", rarity 3, $95.00.

Plate 1976. Tribal Elder, ca. 1925, iron or bronze, 5", bronze, rarity 4; iron, rarity 3, bronze, $175.00; iron, $95.00.

Plate 1977. Young Indian Chief, ca. 1925, bronze, 6", rarity 4, $175.00.

Nature

Plate 1978. Arch and Vines, 1924, Ronson, gray metal, 5", shopmark, rarity 5, $110.00. *This same figure has been seen in monochrome black, and with an full-figural elephant in the foreground.* Photo courtesy of Dave Udstuen.

Plate 1979. Arrowleaf, ca. 1914, Heintz Art Metal, silver on bronze, 5", shopmark, rarity 5, $375.00. Photo courtesy of David Surgan.

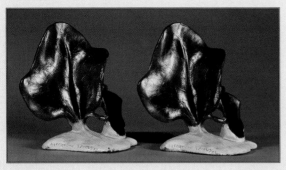

Plate 1980. Autumn Leaves, ca. 1930, McClelland Barclay, gray metal, 5¾", marked signature on base, rarity 5, $275.00.

Plate 1981. Avalanche Lilly, ca. 1914, Heintz Art Metal, silver on bronze, 5", shopmark, rarity 5, $275.00. Photo courtesy of David Surgan.

Plate 1982. Bamboo, ca. 1914, Heintz Art Metal, bronze with silver overlay, 5", shopmark, rarity 5, $275.00. Photo courtesy of David Surgan.

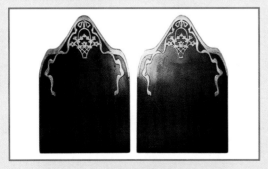

Plate 1983. Basket of Flowers, ca. 1914, Heintz Art Metal, bronze with silver overlay, 5¼", shopmark, rarity 4, $275.00. Photo courtesy of David Surgan.

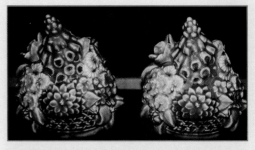

Plate 1984. Basket of Flowers (Rookwood), 1927, Rookwood, pottery, 6", marked XXVII, #2237, polychrome, rarity 5; monochrome, rarity 4; polychrome, $450.00; monochrome, $350.00. Photo courtesy of George Houle.

Plate 1985. Bear and Beehive, ca. 1940 (attr England), pewter, 8", $100.00.

Plate 1986. Bouquet, 1920, Ronson, gray metal, 6", marked LVA 1920, rarity 5, $135.00.

Plate 1987. Bouquet and Urn, ca. 1920, iron, 5", marked Jersey 10, rarity 5, $95.00.
Photo courtesy of Agris Kelbrants.

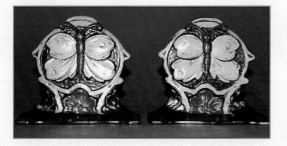

Plate 1988. Butterfly, ca. 1925, iron, 5½", rarity 4, $85.00.

Plate 1989. Cactus, ca. 1947, Dodge, gray metal, 7", shopmark, rarity 5, $150.00.

Plate 1990. California Pepper, ca. 1914, Heintz Art Metal, bronze with silver overlay, 5", shopmark, rarity 5, $275.00. Photo courtesy of David Surgan.

Plate 1991. Cathedral, ca. 1975, Virginia Metal Crafters, brass, 6", rarity 3, $50.00.

Plate 1992. Cattail, ca. 1914, Heintz Art Metal, bronze with silver overlay, 5", shopmark, rarity 5, $275.00. Photo courtesy of David Surgan.

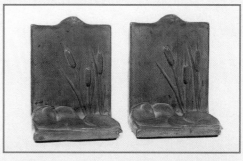

Plate 1993. Cattails (McClelland Barclay), ca. 1930, McClelland Barclay, gray metal, 4¾", marked "McClelland Barclay, rarity 4, $135.00.

Plate 1994. Colorado Pine, ca. 1930, bronze, 7", marked Colorado, rarity 5*, $195.00.

Plate 1995. Conventional Scroll Design, ca. 1925, Ronson, gray metal, 4¼", company paper tag #10512, rarity 4, $65.00. Photo courtesy of Richard Weinstein.

Plate 1996. Date Palm, ca. 1914, Heintz Art Metal, bronze with silver overlay, shopmark, rarity 5, $275.00. Photo courtesy of David Surgan.

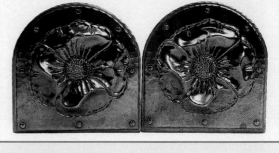

Plate 2000. Flower, ca. 1925, Roycroft, copper, 5¼", shopmark, rarity 5, $350.00.

Plate 1997. Dogwood, ca. 1965, PM Craftsman, gray metal, 5¼", marked PMC 57D, rarity 3, $40.00.

Plate 2001. Flower Basket, ca. 1925, Hubley, iron, 5¾", rarity 4, $150.00. Photo courtesy of Sue Benoliel.

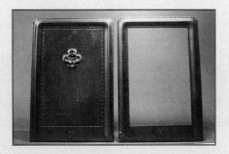

Plate 1998. Embossed Flower, ca. 1920, Roycroft, copper, 8½", shopmark, rarity 4, $225.00. Photo courtesy of Sue Benoliel.

Plate 2002. Flower Basket (Fleuron), ca. 1930, Fleuron, Durez Resin, 4¼", marked Fleuron, North Tonawanda, rarity 5*, $125.00.

Plate 1999. Floral Garlands, ca. 1925, Judd, iron, 5", marked 9862, rarity 5*, $225.00. Photo courtesy of Agris Kelbrants.

Plate 2003. Flowered Mantle, ca. 1914, Heintz Art Metal, Bronze with silver overlay, 5¼", shopmark, rarity 5, $275.00. Photo courtesy of David Surgan.

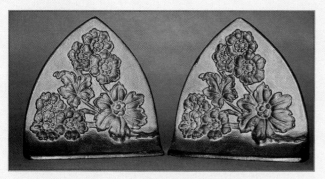

Plate 2004. Flowers, 1922, Albany Foundry, iron, 9", marked Albany Foundry 1922, rarity 5, $195.00.

Plate 2008. Foxglove, ca. 1940, Roseville, pottery, 5", shopmark, rarity 5, $325.00.

Plate 2005. Flowers (B&H), ca. 1925, Bradley and Hubbard, iron, 5¾", shopmark, rarity 5, $125.00.

Plate 2009. Frog and Water Lilly, ca. 1925, iron, 4", rarity 5*, $275.00. Photo courtesy of Agris Kelbrants.

Plate 2006. Forest Cabin, ca. 1922, Albany Foundry, iron, 6½", marked Albany Foundry, rarity 4, $85.00.

Plate 2010. Fronds, ca. 1925, Albany Foundry, iron, 4½", marked #48, rarity 5, $85.00. Photo courtesy of Agris Kelbrants.

Plate 2007. Four Flowers, ca. 1950, pottery, 6", rarity 5*, $25.00. *No recognized shopmark is on this pair; it may have been "home-made."*

Plate 2011. Fruit, 1919, Rookwood, pottery, 5", marked XIX, #2186, rarity 5, $750.00.

287

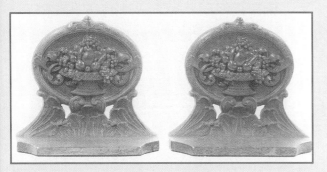

Plate 2012. Fruit Basket, ca. 1925, Judd, iron, 5⅝", marked J Co 9860, rarity 5, $160.00.

Plate 2013. Green Floral, ca. 1914, Heintz Art Metal, silver on bronze, 5", shopmark, rarity 5, $275.00.

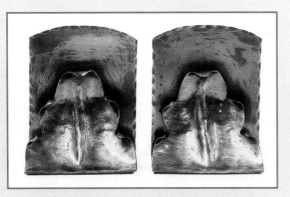

Plate 2014. Leaf, ca. 1935, Craftsman, Inc, copper, 4½", marked Craftsman, Inc Hand Made #206, rarity 3, $75.00.

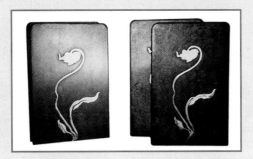

Plate 2015. Lilly, ca. 1915, Heintz Art Metal, silver on bronze, 5", shopmark, rarity 5, $275.00. Photo courtesy of David Surgan.

Plate 2016. Lilly Pad, ca. 1945, Dodge, gray metal, 4½", company paper tag, rarity 3, $50.00.

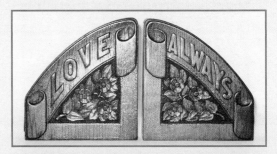

Plate 2017. Love Always, ca. 1935, wood, 7", marked A four-leaf clover, rarity 5*, $75.00.
Photo courtesy of John Gustav Delly.

Plate 2018. Magnolia, ca. 1940, Roseville, pottery, 5", shopmark, rarity 3, $250.00.

Plate 2019. Maple Leaf, ca. 1965, PM Craftsman, gray metal, 6", marked PMC 57D, rarity 3, $40.00.

Plate 2020. Mariposa, ca. 1914, Heintz Art Metal, silver on bronze, 5", shopmark, rarity 5, $275.00. Photo courtesy of David Surgan.

Plate 2021. Mixed Bouquet, ca. 1925, Albany Foundry, iron, 5¾", shopmark, rarity 5, $150.00. Photo courtesy of Sue Benoliel.

Plate 2022. Oak Leaf, ca. 1965, PM Craftsman, gray metal, 6½", shopmark, rarity 3, $45.00.

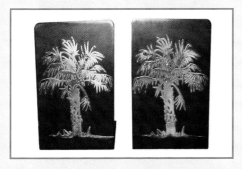

Plate 2023. Palm, ca. 1914, Heintz Art Metal, silver on bronze, 5", shopmark, rarity 5, $325.00. Photo courtesy of David Surgan.

Plate 2024. Pine Cone, ca. 1914, Heintz Art Metal, bronze with silver overlay, 5", shopmark, rarity 5, $275.00. Photo courtesy of David Surgan.

Plate 2025. Pine Cone (Roseville), ca. 1940, pottery, 5", shopmark, rarity 5, $350.00.

Plate 2026. Pine Needles, ca. 1914, Heintz Art Metal, bronze and silver overlay, 5", shopmark, rarity 5, $275.00. Photo courtesy of David Surgan.

Plate 2027. Poppy, ca. 1914, Heintz Art Metal, bronze and silver overlay, 5", shopmark, rarity 5, $275.00. Photo courtesy of David Surgan.

Plate 2028. Primrose, ca. 1930, Syracuse Ornamental, syrocowood, 6", rarity 5, $75.00.

Plate 2029. Rocks and Flowers, ca. 1930, K & O, gray metal, 3", shopmark, rarity 5, $45.00. Photo courtesy of Agris Kelbrants.

Plate 2030. Roses, ca. 1930, leather, 5", rarity 4, $40.00.

Plate 2031. Royal Fruit Bowl, ca. 1920, iron, 8½", rarity 4, $135.00.

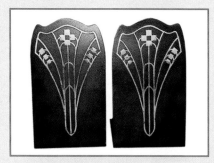

Plate 2032. Sconce, ca. 1914, Heintz Art Metals, silver on bronze, 5", shopmark, rarity 5, $325.00.

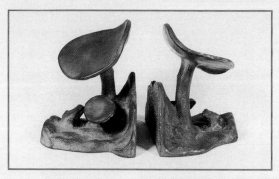

Plate 2033. Toadstool and Frog, ca. 1922, McClelland Barclay, gray metal, 4¼", rarity 5, $195.00. *Other finishes seen include green/bronze.*

Plate 2034. Tri-berry, ca. 1935, Craftsman, Inc, Copper, 5", marked #269, rarity 4, $50.00.

Plate 2035. Vines, ca. 1930, brass, 5", rarity 5, $150.00. *This is an expandable book rack.*

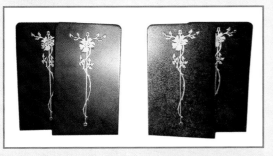

Plate 2036. Violet, ca. 1914, Heintz Art Metal, silver on bronze, 5", shopmark, rarity 5, $275.00. Photo courtesy of David Surgan.

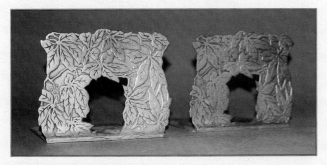

Plate 2037. Virginia Creeper, ca. 1910, Marshall Field, bronze, 4¾", "Virginia Creeper," shopmark, rarity 5*, $225.00.

Plate 2038. Water Lilies (Rookwood), 1939, Rookwood, pottery, 3¾", marked XXXIX, #2836, rarity 4, $375.00.

Plate 2039. Water Lilly Roseville, ca. 1940, Roseville, pottery, 5", shopmark, rarity 4, $250.00.

Plate 2040. Wheat, ca. 1930, Jennings Brothers, gray metal, 6", marked JB company paper tag, rarity 5, $150.00.

Plate 2041. Wild Flower, ca. 1914, Heintz Art Metal, silver on bronze, 5", shopmark, rarity 5, $325.00. Photo courtesy of David Surgan.

Plate 2042. Wind in the Willows, ca. 1930, iron, 6½", marked #12515, rarity 5, $175.00.

Plate 2043. Winter Berry, ca. 1914, Heintz Art Metal, silver on bronze, 5", shopmark, rarity 5, $325.00. Photo courtesy of David Surgan.

Plate 2044. Zinnias, ca. 1925, iron, 5, rarity 4, $75.00.

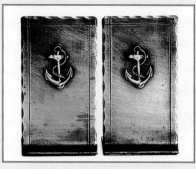

Plate 2048. Anchor (Craftsman), ca. 1930, Craftsman, brass, 4¼", shopmark, 209, rarity 5, $95.00.

Plate 2045. Zion Park, ca. 1968, sandstone on wood, 8", marked Zion Park, rarity 5, $75.00.

Plate 2049. Anchor (Dodge), ca. 1947, Dodge, gray metal, 5¾", company paper tag, rarity 3, $45.00.

Nautical

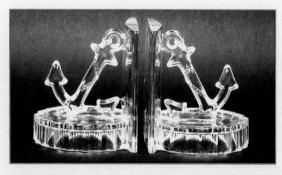

Plate 2046. Anchor, ca. 1940, glass, 4½", rarity 5, $100.00.

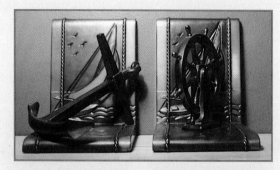

Plate 2050. Anchor and Pilot Wheel, ca. 1934, Ronson, gray metal, 4¾", company paper tag #167363, rarity 5, $110.00. Photo courtesy of Agris Kelbrants.

Plate 2047. Anchor (Chase), ca. 1935, Chase, brass, 6¼", shopmark, rarity 3, $75.00.

Plate 2051. Anchor Lady, ca. 1928, JB Hirsch, Inc., gray metal figure, celluloid face and hands on marble base, 8½", rarity 5, $300.00.

Plate 2052. Anchor on Rope, ca. 1930, gray metal, 5¼", rarity 4, $75.00. Photo courtesy of Agris Kelbrants.

Plate 2053. At the Helm, ca. 1930, Ronson, gray metal, 6", company paper tag, rarity 4, $150.00.

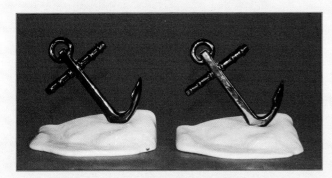

Plate 2054. Blue Sand Anchor, ca. 1920, porcelainized iron, 6", rarity 5, $150.00.

Plate 2055. Bronze Anchor, ca. 1930, bronze, 5, rarity 5*, $750.00.

Plate 2056. Cape Cod Fisherman, 1928, Connecticut Foundry, iron, 5¾", shop-mark, Connecticut Foundry © 1928, poly-chrome, rarity 5*; monochrome, rarity 4; polychrome, $175.00; monochrome, $50.00. *Polychrome Connecticut Foundry pieces are very rare.*

Plate 2057. Cape Cod Fisherman, mono-chrome versions.

Plate 2058. Captain, ca. 1925, iron, 5", rarity 4, $125.00.

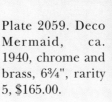

Plate 2059. Deco Mermaid, ca. 1940, chrome and brass, 6¾", rarity 5, $165.00.

Plate 2060. Fisherman, ca. 1930, gray metal figure on marble base, 10½", rarity 5*, $400.00.

Plate 2064. Let er Blow, ca. 1925, bronze-clad, 7", marked Let er Blow, rarity 5*, $225.00. Photo courtesy of Louis and Janet Dianni.

Plate 2061. Fisherman Bust, ca. 1960, PM Craftsman, gray metal, 5½", marked 603hc Patent Appld For, rarity 3, $75.00.

Plate 2065. Lighthouse and Seagull, ca. 1928, Graham Bronze, bronze, 6", rarity 5, $175.00.

Plate 2062. Fisherman with Net, ca. 1928, Littco, iron, 6¾", rarity 4, $150.00.

Plate 2066. Lighting the Way, ca. 1925, JB Hirsch, Inc., gray metal figure, celluloid face, on polished stone base, 8", rarity 5, $235.00.

Plate 2063. Harbor Scene, ca. 1925, Bradley and Hubbard, iron, 5½", shopmark, rarity 5, polychrome, $195.00; monochrome, $165.00. Photo courtesy of Agris Kelbrants.

Plate 2067. Lighting the Way Anchored, ca. 1925, JB Hirsch, Inc., gray metal figure, celluloid face, on polished stone base, 8", rarity 5, $250.00. *The only difference between this and "Lighting the Way" is the presence of the added anchor, which is a bit less common.*

Plate 2068. Men at Sea, ca. 1925, iron, 5", rarity 3, $50.00.

Plate 2069. Neptune, ca. 1920, gray metal, 7¼", rarity 5*, $250.00.

Plate 2070. New Bedford Whaler, ca. 1925, Jennings Brothers, gray metal, 7", marked JB 3139, rarity 4, $250.00. *Back of bookend reads "In Honor of the Whaleman Whose Skill Hardihood and Daring Brought Fame and Fortune to New Bedford and Made its Name Known in Every Seaport of the Globe." Designed by Bela Lyon Pratt, stands now in front of the New Bedford Library.*

Plate 2071. New Bedford Whaler (PMC), ca. 1960, PM Craftsman, gray metal, 7", company paper tag, marked PMC, rarity 4, $95.00.

Plate 2072. Pilot Wheel, ca. 1930, Ronson, gray metal, 4¾", company paper tag #16572, rarity 4, $110.00. Photo courtesy of Richard Weinstein.

Plate 2073. Pilot Wheel (Chase), ca. 1940, Chase, brass base, walnut, and bakelite, 6⅜", shopmark, rarity 4, $150.00.

Plate 2074. Pilot Wheel and Anchor, ca. 1927, gray metal, 7½", rarity 5, $300.00.

Plate 2075. Pilot Wheel on Books, ca. 1930, gray metal, 5¾", marked 142696, rarity 5*, $110.00. Photo courtesy of Agris Kelbrants.

Plate 2078. They That Go Down to the Sea (Lamp), ca. 1930, Jennings Brothers, gray metal, 16", marked JB 2353 © Leonard Craske (sculptor), rarity 5, $125.00.

Plate 2076. Steady at the Wheel, ca. 1975, iron, 5½", company paper tag, rarity 4, $75.00. *A single example of a pair of this same metal with the company tag "Japan" has been seen, but it was configured as the horse Pegasus.*

Plate 2079. They That Go Down to the Sea, different finish.

Plate 2080. USS Vulcan, ca. 1965, attr San Diego Naval Machinists, bronze, 5¾", marked USS Vulcan AR-5 Presented to CWO4 Russell W. Golding From R-2 Division, rarity 5*, $125.00. *See page 25 for details.*

Plate 2077. They That Go Down to the Sea, ca. 1930, Jennings Brothers, gray metal, 8½", marked JB 2353 © Leonard Craske (sculptor), rarity 4, $150.00. *Paper tag reads: "They That Go Down to the Sea in Ships, Copy of statue at Gloucester, Mass, Designed and copyrighted by Leonard Craske, Manufactured by The Jennings Bros Mfg Co, Bridgeport, Conn." This same bookend pair is also currently produced in monochrome finish by PM Craftsman.*

Plate 2081. Village Lighthouse, ca. 1925, bronze, 4½", rarity 5, $165.00. Photo courtesy of Agris Kelbrants.

Plate 2082. Weather-beaten Mariner, ca. 1930, Ronson, gray metal, 5¼", marked Ronson, polychrome, rarity 5; monochrome, rarity 4; polychrome, $195.00; monochrome, $150.00.

Plate 2086. Freedom Parade, ca. 1925, Verona, iron, marked g, Verona #695, rarity 4, $95.00.

Patriotic

Plate 2083. Betsy Ross, ca. 1925, iron, 6", rarity 4, $75.00.

Plate 2087. Human-itas, 1998, Virginia Metal Crafters, brass, 7¾", marked The Doors to the Library of Congress, rarity 3, $50.00.

Plate 2084. Drum and Fife, ca. 1925, Hubley, iron, 6¼", rarity 4, $75.00.

Plate 2088. Let Freedom Ring, ca. 1925, CT, iron, 5", shopmark, rarity 4, $65.00. *Scene depicts signing of the Declaration of Independence.*

Plate 2085. E Pluribus Unum, ca. 1930, bronze, 6", rarity 4, $75.00.

Plate 2089. Liberty Bell, ca. 1925, iron, 4¾", rarity 3, $40.00.

Plate 2090. Liberty Bell (Armor Bronze), 1917, Armor Bronze, bronze-clad, 6¾", shopmark, © 1917, rarity 5*, $295.00.

Plate 2094. Minute Man and Liberty Bell, ca. 1925, iron, 5⅝", rarity 5, $165.00. Photo courtesy of Agris Kelbrants.

Plate 2091. Liberty Bell (MB), ca. 1960, Marion Bronze, bronze-clad, 7", shopmark, rarity 5, $125.00. Photo courtesy of Julie December.

Plate 2095. New Colossus' Face, ca. 1930, bronze, 6", rarity 5*, $175.00. Photo courtesy of Annette Schabowski.

Plate 2092. Liberty Bell (Verona), ca. 1928, Verona, iron, 4¾", marked Verona #695, rarity 4, $50.00.

Plate 2096. Statute Of Liberty, ca. 1930, Harlich, leather, 5¾", marked Harlich & Co, Chicago, rarity 5, $35.00. *See page 24 for details.*

Rabbits, Rodents, and Squirrels

Plate 2093. Liberty Bell Sesquicentennial, 1926, iron, 6¼", rarity 5*, $175.00.

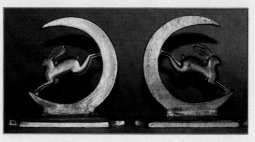

Plate 2097. Moon Rabbit, ca. 1935, brass, 5", rarity 5*, $150.00.

Plate 2098. Mouse and Cheese, ca. 1925, gray metal figure, Bakelite cheese, 4", marked H Moreau (sculptor), rarity 5, $495.00. *Made in France.*

Plate 2099. Munching Squirrel, ca. 1930, gray metal on marble base, 5", marked Frecourt (sculptor), rarity 5*, $175.00. *Made in France.*

Plate 2100. Rabbit, ca. 1925, gray metal, 8", rarity 5*, $125.00.

Plate 2101. Rabbit (Pompeian Bronze), ca. 1920, Pompeian Bronze, bronze-clad, 5", marked Pompeian Bronze Co #137, rarity 5*, $350.00. Photo courtesy of Billie Trepanier.

Plate 2102. Squirrel (Fontinelle), ca. 1920, bronze (silver plated), 7", marked L Fontinelle (sculptor), France, rarity 5*, $1,600.00.

Plate 2103. Squirrel (Pompeian Bronze), ca. 1920, Pompeian Bronze, bronze-clad, 5½", marked Paul Herzel (sculptor), rarity 5*, $195.00. Photo courtesy of Billie Trepanier.

Religious

Plate 2104. Angelus Call to Prayer, ca. 1925, gray metal, 4⅝", rarity 5, $50.00.

Plate 2105. Angelus Call to Prayer (CF), 1928, Connecticut Foundry, iron, 5½", marked Angelus Call to Prayer, rarity 3, $55.00.

Plate 2106. Angelus Call to Prayer (Hubley), ca. 1925, Hubley, iron, 5½", rarity 3, polychrome, $100.00; monochrome, $50.00.

Plate 2107. Angelus Call to Prayer, monochrome.

Plate 2108. Angelus Call to Prayer (K & O), ca. 1925, K & O, gray metal, 5", shopmark, rarity 5, $125.00.

Plate 2109. Angelus Call to Prayer (K & O) (squared), ca. 1925, K & O, gray metal, 5", shopmark, rarity 5, $125.00. *Note squared off corners, compared to other arched background.*

Plate 2110. Friar, ca. 1928, Littco, iron, 5", company paper tag, rarity 4, $85.00.

Plate 2111. Go Ye Into All the World, 1939, Mitchell Art Company, gray metal, 4", marked 1939, Mitchell Art Company, LA, Cal, rarity 5, $175.00.

Plate 2112. Good Book, ca. 1924, Armor Bronze, bronze-clad, 6¾", shopmark, rarity 5*, $250.00.

Plate 2113. In His Service (IHS), ca. 1925, K J Killoran, iron, 4¾", marked KJ Killoran, Boston, MA, rarity 5, $75.00.

Plate 2114. Holy Mother and Child, 1924, Snead Ironworks, iron, 4¾", marked 1924 (© #73078 registered to Olga Popoff Muller, December 1, 1924), rarity 4, $95.00.

Plate 2115. Holy Mother and Child (DAL), ca. 1925, Decorators Art League, iron, 4⅝", marked DAL, rarity 4, $75.00.

Plate 2116. I Am the Way (Cross), ca. 1925, Cross Publishing Company, iron, 5¼", marked CBF 1, Cross Publ Co, Elizabeth NJ, Made in USA, rarity 5*, $95.00. Photo courtesy of Agris Kelbrants.

Plate 2117. Joan of Arc (Hubley), ca. 1925, Hubley, iron, 5¼", rarity 4, $95.00.

Plate 2118. Joan of Arc (Profile), ca. 1925, iron, 6", rarity 5, $150.00. Photo courtesy of Agris Kelbrants.

Plate 2119. Library Monk (Marion Bronze), ca. 1950, Marion Bronze, bronze-clad, 6¼", rarity 5, $95.00.

Plate 2120. Library Monk (Ronson), 1920, Ronson, gray metal, 6½", marked LV Aronson 1922, rarity 4, $165.00.

Plate 2121. Library Monk (Ronson) petite, 1922, Ronson, gray metal, 4¼", marked LV Aronson 1922, rarity 4, $75.00.

301

Plate 2122. Madonna and Child, ca. 1925, Verona, iron, 6¾", marked Verona, rarity 5, $175.00.

Plate 2126. Monk (Marion Bronze), ca. 1956, Marion Bronze, bronze-clad, 7¼", marked MB, rarity 5, $200.00.

Plate 2123. Menorah, ca. 1935, iron, 5", marked IOBB (International Organization of Bnai Brith), rarity 5, $75.00.

Plate 2127. Monk (PB), ca. 1925, Pompeian Bronze, bronze-clad, 7¼", marked Pompeian Bronze, NY, rarity 5, $250.00.

Plate 2124. Monk (Armor Bronze), ca. 1925, Armor Bronze, bronze-clad, 7½", marked Armor Bronze ©, rarity 4, $225.00.

Plate 2128. Monk and Quill, 1914, Gorham, bronze, 6½", marked F B Soper (sculptor), Gorham Co, rarity 5*, $900.00.

Plate 2125. Monk (K & O), ca. 1926, K & O, gray metal, 7¼", shopmark, rarity 4, $175.00.

Plate 2129. Monk in Library, ca. 1965, Marion Bronze, bronze-clad, 6¾", rarity 4, $75.00.

Plate 2130. Monk in Library (BronzMet), 1924, Bronzmet, iron, 3¾", shopmark G D 20; Pat Jul 22, 1924, rarity 4, $45.00. Photo courtesy of Agris Kelbrants.

Plate 2131. Monk in Library (Ronson), 1920, Ronson, gray metal, 6½", marked LV Aronson 1920, rarity 4, $95.00.

Plate 2132. Monk Studying, ca. 1925, Bradley and Hubbard, iron, 6¾", shopmark, rarity 5, $195.00. Photo courtesy of Agris Kelbrants.

Plate 2133. Monk with Book, ca. 1925, Judd, gray metal, 7¾", rarity 5, $325.00.

Plate 2134. Moses, ca. 1985, Gold-scheider, Alabaster, marked G. Rug-geri, rarity 5*, $75.00. Photo courtesy of John Gustav Delly.

Plate 2135. Nazarene, ca. 1930, aluminum, 6½", rarity 5, $135.00. Photo courtesy of Agris Kelbrants.

Plate 2136. Peace and Hope, ca. 1970, gray metal, 6", Israel, rarity 4, $50.00.

Plate 2137. Praying Monks, 1911, Roman Bronze Works, bronze, 11¾", marked Louis Potter 1911 Roman Bronze Works NY, rarity 5, $2,500.00.

303

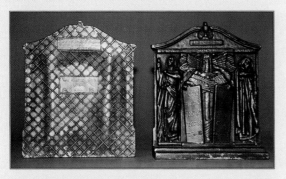

Plate 2138. Prophets, 1925, New Century Club, gray metal, 6½", marked Century Club Boston 1900–1925, rarity 5, bronze, $175.00; gray metal; $125.00.

Plate 2142. Ten Commandments, 1922, Ronson, gray metal, 3¾", marked LV Aronson 1922, rarity 5, $175.00.

Roosevelt

Plate 2139. Scribe (Snead), ca. 1925 , Snead & Co, iron, 4¼", marked Snead & Co., Jersey City, NJ, Patent Pending, rarity 4, $50.00.
Photo courtesy of Agris Kelbrants.

Plate 2143. FDR Bust, 1933, Ronson, gray metal, 3", marked Franklin D. Roosevelt, JS 1933 AMW, rarity 5, $135.00.

Plate 2140. St. Francis, 1945, Rookwood, pottery, 7¼", marked XLV #6883, rarity 5, $500.00. *Designer: Zanetta.*

Plate 2141. Studious Monk, ca. 1925, Galvano Bronze, bronzeclad, 6½", rarity 5, $150.00. Photo courtesy of Agris Kelbrants.

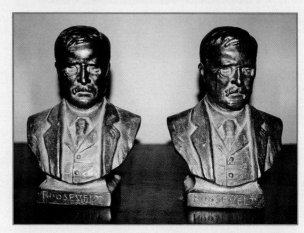

Plate 2144. Roosevelt (Handel), ca. 1920, Handel, bronze, 5", company paper tag, rarity 5*, $250.00.

Plate 2145. Roosevelt Bust (Gift House), 1926, Gift House, Inc, iron, 6⅝", marked © 1926 Gift House, Inc NYC, rarity 5, $175.00.

Plate 2146. Roosevelt Medallion, 1921, Ronson, gray metal, 4¾", marked LV Aronson 1921 Made in USA, rarity 5, $110.00.

Plate 2147. Roosevelt Profile (Fraser), 1925, bronze, 5⅜", marked James Fraser, rarity 5, $125.00. *James Fraser did do some Roosevelt portraiture, but this particular portrait is attributed to Gregory Allen. It is uncertain whether this might represent a mis-signed reproduction*

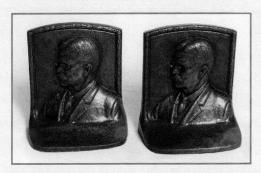

Plate 2148. Roosevelt Profile (Judd), 1925, Judd, bronze, 5⅜", marked Gregory S Allen (sculptor), rarity 5, $225.00.

Plate 2149. Roosevelt: Nothing to Fear but Fear, ca. 1946, 6¼", rarity 5*, $95.00.

Plate 2150. Teddy Roosevelt, ca. 1930, Jennings Brothers, gray metal, 5", shopmark, rarity 5, $195.00.

Plate 2151. Teddy Roosevelt Bust, ca. 1925, 6½", rarity 4, $115.00. Photo courtesy of Agris Kelbrants.

Shakespeare

Plate 2152. Shakespeare, ca. 1925, Pompeian Bronze, bronze-clad, 5", marked Pompeian Bronze ©, rarity 4, $150.00.

305

Plate 2153. Shakespeare (Nuart), ca. 1930, Nuart, gray metal, 5¾", rarity 5, $150.00.

Plate 2157. Shakespeare Shrine (B & H), ca. 1925, Bradley and Hubbard, iron base, gray metal figure, 5½", shopmark, rarity 4, $150.00.

Plate 2154. Shakespeare Bust, ca. 1925, bronze-clad, 5", rarity 4, $100.00.

Plate 2158. Shakespeare's Books, ca. 1925, Judd, iron, 4½", marked 9878 Judd Manufacturing Co, rarity 5, $195.00.

Plate 2155. Shakespeare Quote, ca. 1925, Bradley and Hubbard, iron, 6", shopmark, rarity 5, $150.00. Photo courtesy of Sue Benoliel.

Plate 2159. Shakespeare's Books and Cherub, ca. 1925, Judd, iron, 5½", marked Judd Manufacturing 9766, rarity 5, $225.00.

Plate 2156. Shakespeare Shrine, ca. 1925, K & O, gray metal, 6⅛", shopmark, rarity 5, $175.00.

Plate 2160. Shakespeare's Library, ca. 1925, Bradley and Hubbard, iron, 6⅛", shopmark, rarity 4, $150.00.

Plate 2161. Shakespeare Seated, ca. 1926, Armor Bronze, bronze-clad, 7", GS Allen (sculptor), shopmark, polychrome, rarity 5; monochrome, rarity 4; polychrome, $225.00; monochrome, $175.00.

Plate 2165. Blue Waters, ca. 1932, attr Pompeian Bronze, bronze-clad, 7", rarity 5, $175.00. Photo courtesy of Jim Rule.

Ships

Plate 2162. Adrift (gray metal), ca. 1925, gray metal, 5", rarity 4, $85.00.

Plate 2166. Constitution, ca. 1925, iron, 5", marked Old Ironsides, Constitution, rarity 5, $85.00.

Plate 2163. Adrift (iron), ca. 1925, iron, 4⅞", rarity 3, $65.00.

Plate 2167. Crest of the Wave, ca. 1925, iron, 4½", rarity 4, $50.00. Photo courtesy of Agris Kelbrants.

Plate 2164. Billowing Sails, ca. 1925, Hubley, iron or bronze, 5¼", marked 615 (iron), bronze, rarity 4; iron, rarity 3, bronze, $45.00; iron, $30.00. Photo courtesy of Agris Kelbrants.

Plate 2168. Designed for Speed, ca. 1922, iron, 5½", rarity 4, $75.00.

Plate 2169. Dragon Sail, ca. 1925, Augsburg, iron, 5½", marked Augsburg, rarity 5, $275.00. Photo courtesy of Agris Kelbrants.

Plate 2173. Full-rigger, 1940, Ronson, gray metal, 5¼", marked 1940 AMW Inc, Newark NJ, USA, rarity 5, $135.00. Photo courtesy of Richard Weinstein.

Plate 2170. English Galleon, 1928, Connecticut Foundry, iron, 5⅝", English Galleon Copr 1928 shopmark, rarity 4, $100.00.

Plate 2174. Full Sail, ca. 1925, iron, 5¾", rarity 4, $50.00.

Plate 2171. Frigate, ca. 1925, iron, 6", rarity 5, $100.00. Photo courtesy of Agris Kelbrants.

Plate 2175. Galleon, ca. 1925, iron, 5½", marked #944 rarity 2, $45.00. Photo courtesy of Agris Kelbrants.

Plate 2172. Frigate Constitution, ca. 1920, Gorham, bronze, 5¾", marked Hugo Carlborg (sculptor), rarity 5, $425.00.

Plate 2176. Galleon (Occupied Japan), ca. 1946, gray metal, 6¾", marked Made in Occupied Japan, CPO, rarity 4, $75.00.

Plate 2177. Galleon at Sea, ca. 1925, bronze-clad, 7½", rarity 5, $160.00.

Plate 2178. Galleon Voyage, ca. 1925, bronze, 4¾", marked Galleon in the Time of Elizabeth 1558–1603, rarity 5, $90.00.

Plate 2179. Galleon Voyage (Ronson), ca. 1925, gray metal, 5", company paper tag, rarity 4, $90.00. Photo courtesy of Richard Weinstein.

Plate 2180. High Seas Adventurer, ca. 1925, iron, 7¼", rarity 5, $100.00.

Plate 2181. Invincible Armada, ca. 1926, Armor Bronze, bronze-clad, 7", Invincible Armada 1588 shopmark, polychrome, rarity 5; monochrome, rarity 4; polychrome, $160.00; monochrome, $100.00.

Plate 2182. Invincible Armada, polychrome version.

Plate 2183. Many Sails, ca. 1925, iron, 6", rarity 5, $85.00. Photo courtesy of Agris Kelbrants.

Plate 2184. Mayflower, ca. 1932, Jennings Brothers, gray metal, 4⅝", marked JB 2333 Patent Appld For, rarity 4, $90.00.

Plate 2185. Noah's Ark, ca. 1930, iron, 4¾", rarity 4, $125.00. Photo courtesy of Agris Kelbrants.

Plate 2186. Ocean Voyage, ca. 1927, Bradley and Hubbard, iron, 5½", shopmark, rarity 3, $70.00.

Plate 2187. Old Ironsides, ca. 1927, iron or bronze, 5½", marked Old Ironsides, bronze, rarity 4; iron, rarity 3, bronze, $65.00; iron, $45.00.

Plate 2188. Old Ironsides (CF), 1929, Connecticut Foundry, iron, 5¾", marked Old Ironsides, Copr 1929, rarity 5, $110.00.

Plate 2189. Old Ironsides at Sea, ca. 1925, iron, 5¼", marked Old Ironsides, rarity 5, $75.00. Photo courtesy of Agris Kelbrants.

Plate 2190. Pilgrims Landing, ca. 1925, Bradley and Hubbard, iron, 5½", shopmark, polychrome, rarity 5; monochrome, rarity 4; polychrome, $165.00; monochrome, $110.00.

Plate 2191. Pirate Galleon, 1928, Connecticut Foundry, iron, 4½", Pirate Galleon 1928 shopmark, rarity 4, $40.00.

Plate 2192. Placid Waters, ca. 1925, iron, 5¼", rarity 4, $60.00.

Plate 2193. Ride the Waves, ca. 1925, AM Greenblatt, brass, 5½", marked AM Greenblatt Studios, rarity 5, $110.00.

Plate 2197. Sailing Home, ca. 1925, iron, 5½", rarity 5, $75.00. Photo courtesy of Agris Kelbrants.

Plate 2194. Sailboat, ca. 1929, Littco, iron, 7½", polychrome, rarity 5; monochrome, rarity 4; polychrome, $195.00; monochrome, $125.00.

Plate 2198. Sailing Ship, ca. 1925, bronze, 6", rarity 4, $60.00.

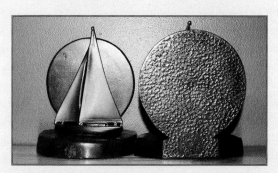

Plate 2195. Sailboat (Nuart), ca. 1932, Nuart, gray metal, 6½", shopmark, rarity 4, $110.00.

Plate 2199. Sailing Under the Maltese Cross, ca. 1925, iron, rarity 4, $50.00.

Plate 2196. Sailboats, ca. 1960, PM Craftsman, gray metal, 5¼", marked PMC 64B, rarity 4, $35.00.

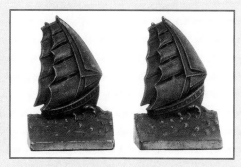

Plate 2200. Sailing Ship (B & H), ca. 1925, Bradley and Hubbard, iron, 5½", shopmark, rarity 4, $90.00.

311

Plate 2201. Schooner, ca. 1925, iron, 6", rarity 3, $50.00. Photo courtesy of Agris Kelbrants.

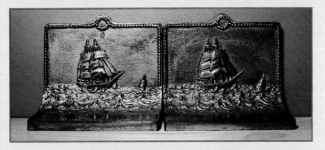

Plate 2202. Schooner (B&H), ca. 1925, Bradley and Hubbard, bronze, 4½", shopmark, rarity 5, $125.00. Photo courtesy of Agris Kelbrants.

Plate 2203. Sea Journey, ca. 1925, iron, 4", rarity 2, $20.00.

Plate 2204. Sea Worthy, ca. 1925, bronze, 6", rarity 5, $110.00.

Plate 2205. Ship, ca. 1925, iron, 6", polychrome, rarity 4; monochrome, rarity 2, polychrome, $110.00; monochrome, $65.00.

Plate 2206. Ship, polychrome version.

Plate 2207. Ship (B & H), ca. 1925, Bradley and Hubbard, iron, 6¼", shopmark, rarity 4, $125.00.

Plate 2208. Ship (Hubley), ca. 1925, Hubley, iron, 7", rarity 4, $110.00.

Plate 2209. Ship (Littco), ca. 1925, Littco, iron, 4", rarity 1, $15.00.

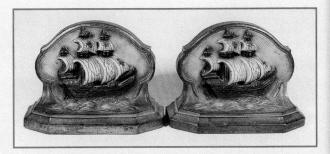

Plate 2213. Ship (X-1), ca. 1925, X-1, gray metal, 4½", marked 513, polychrome, rarity 5; monochrome, rarity 4; polychrome, $125.00; monochrome, $175.00.

Plate 2210. Ship (New Martinsville), ca. 1940, New Martinsville Glass, glass, 5½", rarity 5, $175.00.

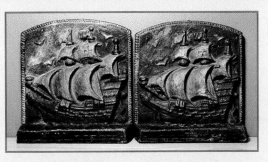

Plate 2214. Ship and Gulls, ca. 1925, iron, 4¾", rarity 5, $75.00. **Photo courtesy of Agris Kelbrants.**

Plate 2211. Ship (Rookwood), 1934, Rookwood, pottery, 5", marked XXXIV #2694," rarity 5, $450.00.

Plate 2215. Ship and Mariner, ca. 1925, Bradley and Hubbard, iron, 5¼", shopmark, rarity 4, $100.00.

Plate 2212. Ship (Snead), 1925, Snead, iron, 3¾", marked Snead and Co, Jersey City, NJ Patent Pending, rarity 2, $35.00.

Plate 2216. Ship at Sunrise, ca. 1925, Littco, iron, 5½", polychrome, rarity 4; monochrome, rarity 3; polychrome, $75.00; monochrome, $65.00.

313

Plate 2217. Ship of Dreams, ca. 1925, Victory Manufacturing Co., iron, 6¾", marked Victory MFG Co, Pennsylvania Forge Co, May Your Ship of Dreams Arrive with the New Year, rarity 5, $90.00.

Plate 2218. Ship with Anchor, ca. 1925, iron, 4¼", rarity 2, $25.00.

Plate 2219. Ship President, ca. 1925, Judd, iron, 5½", marked President, J Co, rarity 5, polychrome, $165.00; monochrome, $135.00.

Plate 2220. Ship President, polychrome version.

Plate 2221. Smooth Waters, ca. 1925, iron, 5¾", rarity 4, $75.00. Photo courtesy of Agris Kelbrants.

Plate 2222. Spanish Galleon, 1928, iron, 6", marked Spanish Galleon © 1928, rarity 3, $50.00.

Plate 2223. Speedboat, ca. 1934, Jennings Brothers, gray metal, 3½", marked JB, rarity 5, $275.00.

Plate 2224. Stormy Waters, ca. 1920, gray metal, 5¾", rarity 5, $125.00. Photo courtesy of Agris Kelbrants.

Plate 2225. Tall Ship, ca. 1925, iron, 6", rarity 4, $50.00. Photo courtesy of Agris Kelbrants.

Plate 2226. Treasure Ship, 1927, Armor Bronze, bronze-clad, 7½", marked Vanderdeken, rarity 5, $135.00.

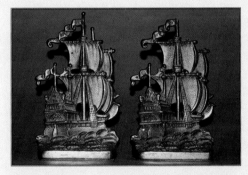

Plate 2227. Two Flags, 1928, Seville Studios, iron, 9", marked Seville Studios, 1928, rarity 4, $90.00.

Plate 2228. Viking, ca. 1925, attr Hubley, iron or bronze, 5¾", bronze, rarity 5; iron, rarity 4; bronze, $140.00; iron, $95.00.

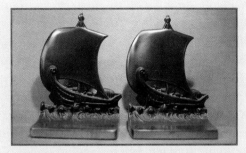

Plate 2229. Viking Ship, ca. 1928, Bradley and Hubbard, iron or bronze, 6", shopmark, bronze, rarity 5; iron, rarity 4; bronze, $150.00; iron, $90.00.

Plate 2230. Viking Vessel, ca. 1925, gray metal, 6", polychrome, rarity 5; monochrome, rarity 4; polychrome, $120.00; monochrome, $65.00.

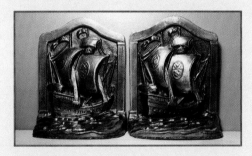

Plate 2231. Voyager, ca. 1925, unknown, bronze-clad, 6", rarity 5, $125.00. Photo courtesy of Agris Kelbrants.

Plate 2232. Warship, ca. 1927, iron, 4", rarity 2, $30.00.

315

Plate 2233. Wide Sails, ca. 1925, bronze, 6", rarity 5, $175.00. Photo courtesy of Agris Kelbrants.

Plate 2237. Chariot Rounding the Bend, ca. 1930, iron, 6½", marked #695, rarity 4, $125.00.

Plate 2234. Wind in the Sails, ca. 1925, Solid Bronze, bronze, 6¼", marked Solid Bronze, rarity 5, $120.00.

Plate 2238. Charioteer, ca. 1924, attr JB Hirsch, gray metal on polished stone base, 5", rarity 5, $275.00.

Plate 2235. Yankee Clipper, 1928, Connecticut Foundry, iron, 4¼", marked Yankee Clipper © 1928 Connecticut Foundry, rarity 5, $90.00.

Plate 2239. Charioteer (Armor Bronze), ca. 1925, Armor Bronze, bronze-clad, 5¼", marked Cross, rarity 5*, $175.00.

Sports

Plate 2236. Carroll Park, 1930, iron, 6", marked Carroll Park 1930, rarity 5, $175.00.

Plate 2240. Charioteer (Hoyt), 1930, Hoyt Metal Company, bronze, 4½", marked A souvenir marking the opening of our New Brass Foundry Hoyt Metal Co of Canada LTD, June 23, 1930, GF Allen, LP Francis, VP Bingham, rarity 5, $125.00.

Plate 2241. Discus Thrower, ca. 1928, Littco, iron, 7", rarity 3, $150.00.

Plate 2242. Discus Thrower (JB), ca. 1930, Jennings Brothers, gray metal, 7", marked JB1924, rarity 5, $195.00.

Plate 2243. Discus Thrower (Pompeian Bronze), ca. 1930, Pompeian Bronze, bronze-clad, 8½", marked Disc Thrower PB Co, rarity 5*, $295.00.

Plate 2244. Fisherman, ca. 1925, gray metal, 5½", rarity 4, $80.00.

Plate 2245. Football Player, ca. 1925, Hubley, iron, 5½", rarity 4, $175.00.

Plate 2246. Fox Chase, ca. 1925, Hubley, iron, 5", rarity 5, $150.00. Photo courtesy of Agris Kelbrants.

Plate 2247. Glory, ca. 1930, Pompeian Bronze, bronze-clad, 4¾", marked Glory Pompeian Bronze Company, rarity 5, $195.00.

Plate 2248. Golf Player, ca. 1920, Gorham, bronze, 6", marked T B Starr (sculptor), Gorham Co, rarity 5*, $750.00.

317

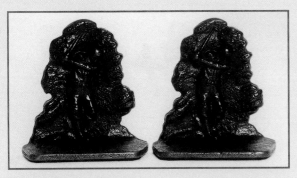

Plate 2249. Golfer (ACW), ca. 1920, ACW, iron, 4¼", marked ACW Co, rarity 4, $75.00.

Plate 2250. Golfer (Dodge), ca. 1941, Dodge, gray metal, 5", company paper tag, rarity 5, $100.00.

Plate 2251. Golfer (JB), ca. 1930, Jennings Brothers, gray metal, 13", shopmark, rarity 5*, $450.00.

Plate 2252. Golfer (Ronson), 1923, Ronson, gray metal, 4½", marked LV Aronson 1923, rarity 5, $350.00.

Plate 2253. Grand Old Man, ca. 1925, Western Foundry, iron, 6", marked Grand Old Man, rarity 5, $125.00. *Grand Old Man is Amos Alonzo Stagg, football coach at University of Chicago. See page 18 for details.*

Plate 2254. His and Hers Jumpers, ca. 1932, attr Jennings Brothers, gray metal, 5¾", rarity 5*, $225.00.

Plate 2255. Horse Tamer, ca. 1928, Littco, iron, 4¾", marked Horse Tamer, rarity 3, $75.00.

Plate 2256. Horserace, ca. 1934, Nuart, gray metal, 4¼", shopmark, rarity 5, $275.00.

Plate 2257. Hunter and Dog, ca. 1925, Hubley, iron, 6¼", marked 423, rarity 5, polychrome, $195.00; monochrome, $175.00. Photo courtesy of Sue Benoliel.

Plate 2258. Hunter and Dog, polychrome version.

Plate 2259. Jockey, ca. 1932, K & O Company, gray metal, 4½", shopmark, polychrome, rarity 5; monochrome, rarity 4, polychrome, $175.00; monochrome, $115.00. Photo courtesy of Richard G. Thompson.

Plate 2260. Jockey at Fence, ca. 1947, Kentucky Tavern Creations, aluminum, 6½", marked A Kentucky Tavern Creation; GDCO (stands for Glenmore Distilleries Company), rarity 5, $175.00.

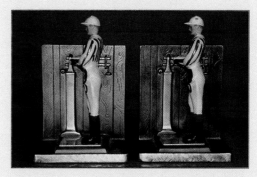

Plate 2261. Jockey with Saddle, ca. 1947, Kentucky Tavern Creations, aluminum, 7½", marked A Kentucky Tavern Creation; GDCO (stands for Glenmore Distilleries Company), rarity 5, $175.00.

Plate 2262. Jumper (JB), ca. 1930, Jennings Brothers, gray metal, 4½", marked JB, rarity 5, $150.00. *Original pair has metal, not "horsehair" tail.*

Plate 2263. Jumper and Hound, ca. 1925, gray metal on marble base, 6", rarity 5*, $450.00. *Made in Austria.*

Plate 2264. Jumpers, ca. 1930, attr K & O, gray metal, 6", rarity 5, $175.00.

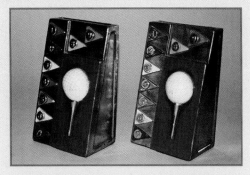

Plate 2265. Just 9 Holes, ca. 1950, Marion Bronze, bronze-clad, 6½", shopmark, rarity 5*, $175.00.

Plate 2269. Perfect Swing, ca. 1930, Ronson, gray metal, 6½", rarity 5, $225.00.

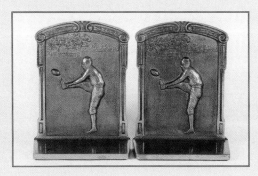

Plate 2266. Kicker, ca. 1925, Judd, bronze, 6", marked AD 9979, rarity 5*, $225.00.

Plate 2270. Photo Finish, ca. 1928, Jennings Brothers, gray metal, 4½", marked JB 809, rarity 5, $350.00.

Plate 2267. Knute, ca. 1926, bronze, 6¼", rarity 5, $195.00. Photo courtesy of Agris Kelbrants.

Plate 2271. Polo, ca. 1925, iron, 4½", rarity 5, $100.00.

Plate 2268. Man-O-War, ca. 1924, Z-R, iron, 6", marked Z-R, rarity 5, $125.00.

Plate 2272. Polo (B & H), ca. 1925, Bradley and Hubbard, iron, 5⅝", shopmark, rarity 5, $250.00.

Plate 2273. Polo (Griffoul), 1914, Griffoul, bronze, 7", marked Griffoul; 1914, Laura Gardin Fraser (sculptor), rarity 5*, $3,000.00. Photo courtesy of Gerald Schultz.

Plate 2274. Polo (Hubley), ca. 1925, Hubley, iron, 6", rarity 5, $125.00. Photo courtesy of Billie Trepanier.

Plate 2275. Polo (Littco), ca. 1925, Littco, iron, 5½", rarity 4, $110.00. *This pair has been repainted; original color: green background, bronze figure.*

Plate 2276. Profanity, 1928, Connecticut Foundry, iron, 6", 1928, shopmark, rarity 5, polychrome, $275.00; monochrome, $175.00.

Plate 2277. Profanity, polychrome version.

Plate 2278. Race Horse, ca. 1925, Jennings Brothers, gray metal, 7¼", marked Pat Pending, rarity 5*, $250.00. Photo courtesy of Billie Trepanier.

Plate 2279. Riding Couple, ca. 1925, gray metal, 4½", rarity 5, $185.00. *Made in Austria.*

Plate 2280. Rock of Notre Dame, ca. 1925, bronze, 6", rarity 5, $225.00.

321

Plate 2281. Rose Jockey, ca. 1932, JB Hirsch, Inc., gray metal figure on polished stone base, 5", rarity 5, $135.00.

Plate 2285. Soccer , ca. 1935, gray metal, 7", rarity 5*, $250.00. *Made in France.* Photo courtesy of Marilyn Barfoot.

Plate 2282. Ski Girl, ca. 1925, iron, 4", marked Ski Girl, rarity 5, $75.00.

Plate 2286. Swimmer, ca. 1946, attr Dodge, gray metal, 5¾", rarity 4, $75.00.

Plate 2283. Ski Jump, ca. 1928, Weidlich Brothers, gray metal, 7½", shopmark, rarity 5*, $275.00.

Plate 2287. Tackle, ca. 1925, CT, iron, 5½", marked CT ©, rarity 4, $110.00.

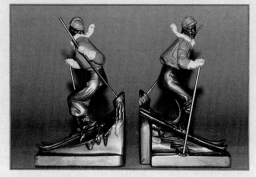

Plate 2284. Ski Queen, ca. 1932, K & O, gray metal, 6½", shopmark, rarity 5, $175.00.

Plate 2288. Teeing Off, ca. 1930, bronze, 5¼", rarity 5, $225.00.

Washington

Plate 2289. Ten Pins, ca. 1925, Marion Bronze, bronze-clad, 7", rarity 5, $180.00.

Plate 2293. George Washington, ca. 1926, Judd, iron, 5½", marked #9679, rarity 4, $95.00.

Plate 2290. Tennis Player, ca. 1920, Gorham, bronze, 5¾", marked T B Starr (sculptor), Gorham Co, rarity 5*, $750.00.

Plate 2294. Liberty Justice Equality, ca. 1950, gray metal, 7", rarity 4, $65.00. Photo courtesy of Agris Kelbrants.

Plate 2291. Thoroughbred, ca. 1925, Galvano Bronze, bronze-clad, 6½", marked The Thoroughbred, rarity 5, polychrome, $225.00; monochrome, $150.00. Photo courtesy of Mary Collins.

Plate 2295. President General, ca. 1925, Hubley, bronze or iron, 5¼", marked artist signed Allen to right of horse's forefoot, bronze, rarity 4; iron, rarity 3, bronze, $150.00; iron, $75.00.

Plate 2292. Whipper-in, ca. 1925, Hubley, iron, 4¾", rarity 4, $75.00.

Plate 2296. Washington, ca. 1925, iron, 6⅛", marked Washington, rarity 4, $65.00.

Plate 2297. Washington and Lincoln, ca. 1925, K&O, gray metal, 4", shopmark, rarity 5, $75.00. Photo courtesy of Agris Kelbrants.

Plate 2298. Washington Bust, ca. 1920, iron, rarity 4, $75.00.

Plate 2299. Washington Bust (JB Hirsch), ca. 1925, JB Hirsch, gray metal figure, celluloid head, on polished stone base, 5½", marked J Ruhl (sculptor), rarity 5, $150.00.

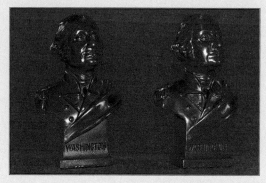

Plate 2300. Washington Bust (Ronson), 1932, Ronson, gray metal, 5½", marked Art Metal Works, 1932, rarity 4, $95.00.

Plate 2301. Washington Bust on Pedestal, ca. 1930, gray metal, 4½", rarity 5, $45.00. Photo courtesy of Agris Kelbrants.

Plate 2302. Washington Cameo, 1929, Connecticut Foundry, iron, 4¼", shopmark, rarity 5*, $85.00. Photo courtesy of Agris Kelbrants.

Plate 2303. Washington Crossing the Delaware, ca. 1932, K&O, gray metal, 6¾", shopmark, polychrome, rarity 4; bronze, rarity 4; polychrome, $195.00; bronze, $125.00.

Plate 2304. Washington Crossing the Delaware (CT), ca. 1925, CT, iron, 5¼", marked © CT, rarity 4, $95.00.

Western

Plate 2309. Bronco , 1946, Russwood, bronze, 7¾", Russwood, rarity 5*, $300.00.

Plate 2305. Washington Crossing the Delaware (Frankart), ca. 1935, Frankart, gray metal, 7", shopmark, rarity 5, $195.00.

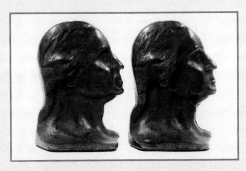

Plate 2306. Washington Head, ca. 1925, iron, 4½", marked Thore Bicentennial, rarity 5, $100.00.

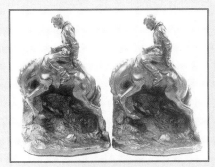

Plate 2310. Bronco Cowboy, ca. 1918, Kathodian Bronze Works, bronze-clad, 8", KBW ArtBronz, rarity 5, $395.00.

Plate 2307. Washington Profile, ca. 1925, iron, 4¼", rarity 5, $50.00.
Photo courtesy of Agris Kelbrants.

Plate 2311. Bronco Rider, ca. 1929, AC, bronze, 5½", marked © AC, 136, 5" on reverse, rarity 5, $100.00. Photo courtesy of Phil Klabel.

Plate 2308. Washington: Public Opinion Should be Enlightened, 1915, Griffoul, bronze, 5½", marked GH (sculptor) 1915 G Washington, rarity 5, $295.00.

Plate 2312. Bronco Rider (Dodge), ca. 1947, Dodge, gray metal, 5", rarity 4, $75.00.

Plate 2313. Bronco Rider (Gift House), 1927, Gift House, Inc, iron, 6", D43L 1927 Gift House Inc, NYC shopmark, rarity 4, $175.00.

Plate 2314. Bronco Rider (Gorham), ca. 1920, Gorham, bronze, 8", marked C Perry (sculptor), Gorham Co, rarity 5*, $1,200.00.

Plate 2315. Bucking Bronco, ca. 1925, iron, 6", rarity 5, $175.00. Photo courtesy of Agris Kelbrants.

Plate 2316. Bucking Horse, ca. 1925, Pompeian Bronze, bronze-clad, 11", marked Paul Herzel (sculptor), rarity 5, $850.00. Photo courtesy of Billie Trepanier.

Plate 2317. Buffalo Skull, ca1915, Gorham, bronze, 6¾", marked H Moller (sculptor), Gorham Co, rarity 5*, $1,750.00.

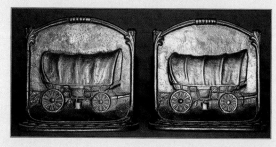

Plate 2318. Covered Wagon, ca. 1926, W H Howell, iron, 4½", marked WH Howell, #14, rarity 4, $65.00.

Plate 2319. Cowboy, ca. 1945, attr Dodge, gray metal, 9", marked Gladys Brown, rarity 5, $250.00.

Plate 2320. Cowboy and Broncho, 1930, Connecticut Foundry, iron, 6", Cowboy and Broncho, 1930 #923, shopmark, rarity 5, $150.00.

Plate 2321. Cowboy on Rearing Horse, ca. 1925, Pompeian Bronze, bronze-clad, 7½", marked Pompeian Bronze, rarity 5, $650.00. Photo courtesy of Billie Trepanier.

Plate 2322. Cowboy Respite, 1931, Andersen-Starr, gray metal, 7", marked © 1931 No.239 Andersen-Starr, rarity 5, $200.00.

Plate 2323. Cowboy Serenade, ca. 1930, K & O Company, gray metal, 6", shop-mark, polychrome, rarity 5; mono-chrome, rarity 4, polychrome; $275.00; monochrome, $175.00. Photo courtesy of Mike Kelln.

Plate 2324. Desert Rider, ca. 1929, gray metal, 5¼", rarity 5, $150.00.

Plate 2325. Go West, ca. 1925, W H Howell, iron, 3¾", marked W H Howell, rarity 5, $75.00. Photo courtesy of Agris Kelbrants.

Plate 2326. Hagenauer-oid, ca. 1945, gray metal, 4¼", marked Made in Japan, Y, rarity 5, $35.00.

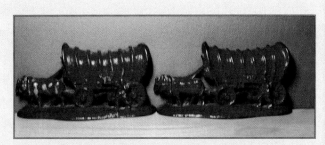

Plate 2327. Ox Wagon, 1931, iron, 3", marked 1849, rarity 4, $65.00. Photo courtesy of Agris Kelbrants.

Plate 2328. Pony Express, ca. 1930, Jennings Brothers, gray metal, 6½", marked HAMN (sculptor Herman A MacNeil), The Pony Express), rarity 5*, $475.00. *See page 23 for details.*

Plate 2329. Range Riders, ca. 1920, bronze on marble base, 7", marked Riedel (sculptor), Made in Austria, rarity 5*, $3,500.00.

Plate 2330. Ride 'em Cowboy, ca. 1932, Pompeian Bronze, bronze-clad, 6", marked Paul Herzel (sculptor), Pompeian Bronze, rarity 5, polychrome, $275.00; monochrome, $175.00. Photo courtesy of Sue Benoliel.

Plate 2331. Remington Rye, ca. 1929, Roman Bronze Works, bronze and brass, 6½", marked artist signature, Roman Bronze Works, Inc., New York, rarity 5, $195.00.

Plate 2332. Ridin' High, ca. 1925, Pompeian Bronze, bronze-clad, 6", marked Paul Herzel (sculptor), rarity 5, $275.00.

Plate 2333. Rodeo, 1946, Russwood, bronze, 6", marked 1946, Solid Bronze, Russwood, ©, rarity 5, $175.00.

Plate 2334. Roper, ca. 1925, Pompeian Bronze, bronze-clad, 5½", marked Paul Herzel (sculptor), rarity 5, $225.00.

Plate 2335. Roundup, ca. 1945, gray metal, 5", marked Til Goodan, rarity 5, $250.00.

Plate 2336. Roundup (Solid Bronze), ca. 1927, Solid Bronze, bronze, 4¾", marked Solid Bronze, rarity 5, $125.00. Photo courtesy of Agris Kelbrants.

Plate 2337. Siesta Cactus, ca. 1930, attr Dodge, gray metal, 6¾", rarity 5, $225.00. Photo courtesy of Agris Kelbrants.

Plate 2340. Wagons West, ca. 1925, LVL, iron, 3½", marked LVL, rarity 4, $75.00.

Plate 2338. Trecking West, ca. 1930, Cincinnati Artists, bronze, 6", marked Cincinnati Artists, rarity 5, $195.00.

Plate 2341. Westward Ho, ca. 1925, Syracuse Ornamental, syrocowood, 5", rarity 3, $50.00.

Plate 2339. Village Blacksmith, ca. 1930, bronze, 5½", rarity 4, $95.00.

Plate 2342. Wagon Train, ca. 1947, Dodge, gray metal, 4", marked Dodge, rarity 4, $70.00.

Shopmarks

Plate 2343. Armor Bronze, "Armor Bronze, National Metalizing Company, New York City."

Plate 2344. Wendell August Forge, "Wendell August Forge."

Plate 2345. Bradley and Hubbard (Type 1), "Bradley and Hubbard Mfg Co."

Plate 2346. Bradley and Hubbard (Type 2), "Bradley and Hubbard Mfg Co, Meriden, Conn."

Plate 2347. BrookArt Bronze Company, "BrookArt Bronze Company, Brooklyn NY."

Plate 2348. Bruce Fox, "Bruce Fox, Incorporated, New Albany, Indiana."

Plate 2349. Burwood Products Company, "Genuine Burwood, Burwood Products Company, Traverse City, Michigan, USA"

Plate 2350. Carence Crafters.

Plate 2351. Collection Francaise, "Collection Francaise Made in USA."

Plate 2352. Connecticut Foundry, The "c" inside a triangle in a circle is the company shopmark, and often misconstrued to be a © symbol.

Plate 2353. Crescent Art Novelties.

Plate 2354. Dodge, "Created and Made by Dodge, Los Angeles, Newark, Miami."

Plate 2355. Flemish Copper Company, "Flemish Copper B Co."

Plate 2356. "Gotham Art Bronze, Inc," "Galvano Bronze, Gotham Art Bronze, Inc."

Plate 2357. Handel Lamps, "Handel Lamps."

Plate 2358. Harlich, "Made by Harlich MFG Co., Chicago."

Plate 2359. J. B. Hirsch.

Plate 2360. Hummel, "M J Hummel."

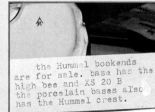

Plate 2361. Hummel (porcelain), V mark typically seen on porcelain.

Plate 2362. Jennings Brothers, "JB Artware of Distinction, Jennings Bros Mfg Co."

Plate 2363. Judd, This label does not indicate the name "Judd," however it is typical of their labels, and includes the usual company four digit product number.

Plate 2364. Judd (Bell Emblem).

Plate 2365. K & O, "MFGS of K & O Co Art Goods."

Plate 2366. Kentucky Tavern, "Kentucky Tavern Industries, Glenmore Distilleries Company."

Plate 2367. La France Bronze Arts.

Plate 2369. Littco

Plate 2370. Marion Bronze, "Manufactured by Marion Bronze, Metuchen, New Jersey."

Plate 2371. Old Mission Copper, "Old Mission Copper, San Francisco."

Plate 2372. Ronson (Type 1), Ronson.

Plate 2368. Littco, "Littco Products, Design of the Item Owned by Littlestown HDWE & FDRY Co."

Plate 2373. Ronson (Type 2), "Art and Utility Everlasting Ronson All Metal Art Wares."

Plate 2374. Ronson (Type 3), "Fashioned by Ronson."

Plate 2375. Russwood, "Solid Cast Bronze, by Russwood."

Plate 2376. Schreiber Cintio, "Bronze by Schreiber Cintio."

Plate 2377. Strikalite, "A Product of Strikalite Ltd, New York."

Plate 2378. Syracuse Ornamental Corporation, "SyrocoWood Patent Pending Made in USA , Syracuse NY."

Plate 2379. "SC Tarrant Company, Inc," "Galvano Bronze, The S C Tarrant Company Inc, New York."

Plate 2380. Thorens, Thorens Movement, "Tales of Hoffman La Paloma Made in Switzerland."

Plate 2381. Weidlich Brothers, "WB."

Plate 2382. Wilkinson Ltd, "Bizarre, Clarice Cliff, Wilkinson LTD, England, Newport Potteries, England."

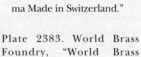

Plate 2383. World Brass Foundry, "World Brass Foundry Co 1930."

Index

All numbers are plate numbers.